Iphigene

My Life and *The New York Times*

Iphigene

My Life and *The New York Times*

The Memoirs of Iphigene Ochs Sulzberger

as written by
Susan W. Dryfoos

Foreword by Barbara W. Tuchman
Introduction to the New Edition by
Harrison E. Salisbury

Times BOOKS

My grandmother and I wish to gratefully acknowledge the skill and friendship of manuscript editors Elizabeth J. Macklin and Anthony Austin, photography editor Sam Falk, and researcher Linda Amster. Special gratitude also to Margaret Harrison and Douglas Mazonowicz for their devotion and encouragement.

Susan W. Dryfoos

Introduction to the New Edition

When Adolph S. Ochs died in 1935 he left two remarkable legacies: his daughter, Iphigene, and his newspaper, the *New York Times*. There was no way for him to know that the affairs of his brilliant and sparkling daughter and the fine newspaper he had created would be entwined for close to one hundred years.

You cannot think of Iphigene Ochs Sulzberger without thinking of the *New York Times*. And it is impossible to imagine the *Times* without Iphigene Sulzberger.

Iphigene was born September 19, 1892. Four years later, shy one month, Adolph Ochs assumed ownership of the faltering *New York Times*, and on August 19, 1896, he published his declaration of intent:

"It will be my earnest aim that the *New York Times* give the news, all the news, in concise and attractive form, in language that is parliamentary in good society, and give it as early, if not earlier, than it can be learned through any reliable medium; to give the news impartially, without fear or favor, regardless of party, sect, or interest involved; to make the columns of the *New York Times* a forum for the consideration of all questions of public importance, and to that end to invite intelligent discussion from all shades of opinion."

Writing in her memoir an incredible eighty-three years later, Iphigene Sulzberger noted, a bit wryly, that the public of the day, bemused by the fire and brimstone of William Randolph Hearst, Joseph Pulitzer and James Gordon Bennett, was a bit skeptical. Only time would convince them that Adolph Simon Ochs meant what he said.

At this writing Iphigene Sulzberger is approaching her ninety-fifth birthday, and Mr. Ochs' *Times* is ninety-one. Both to an extraordinary degree retain the character of their early years. The *New York Times*, as its modern founder clearly anticipated, has evolved to reflect the transformation of America and the world, and Iphigene Sulzberger, ever alert, interested in that world, her family and the *Times*, has changed as well. What has not changed is the Ochs endowment, true and vibrant, in both.

Iphigene's book can be read on many planes: as the reflections of a woman of a humane and inquiring personality; of a daughter, wife, mother, grandmother and great-grandmother of singular perception and responsibility; of a citizen of her country and the world; and of a woman who learned the profession of news at the knee of her father and never forgot it.

To say that Iphigene has been one of the quietly wise women of her times is to scratch only the surface of a complex life. To enumerate her extensive family association with the *Times* is to catalogue the human relationship. Her father purchased the *New York Times* in 1896 and gave that distinguished but failing newspaper a new charter. His goal was to create the finest newspaper in New York, the best paper in the United States and the greatest of the world. Today, more than a half century after his death, the *Times* has grown in the manner he wished it to, and in fact, under the gentle but clear eye of his daughter, has fulfilled Mr. Ochs's aspirations in a manner in which not even he could have conceived.

Iphigene Sulzberger has never been listed on the masthead of the *Times* (nor in *Who's Who!*). In fact, to this day she has regarded it as her father's paper. She would sniff at the idea that she in any way has served as a vestal to keep burning the lamp of her father's spirit. Yet the thread of continuity is there through all her roles: daughter of the publisher; wife of the publisher (Arthur Hayes Sulzberger); mother-in-law of the publisher (Orvil Dryfoos); mother of the publisher (Arthur Ochs "Punch" Sulzberger); grandmother of the likely publisher-to-be (Arthur Ochs Sulzberger, Jr.).

Iphigene Sulzberger's memoir, written by her granddaughter, Susan Dryfoos, with sensitivity and love, is not a matriarch's tale of a family dynasty, although the Ochs-Sulzberger tribe is a dynasty and a matriarchy. It is a cavalcade of the American dream, of Jewish emigrants from the Germany of 1840 driven to seek a new home and life in America, and it is a dazzling tale of business and professional success.

And the teller of this tale, still an impish girl in her nineties, reveals herself as a woman of wit, charm and serious purpose who can describe both a walk in Central Park with her father in the 1890's and a meeting with Richard Nixon in the 1960's with the clarity of a drypoint etching.

Iphigene's memory is astoundingly acute. She still remembers meeting, on a train taking her from Germany to Holland at the outbreak of World War I, a lovely young German who was about to volunteer for the Army. She never saw nor heard from him again. Years later she read Remarque's *All Quiet on the Western Front*. It affected her deeply, and one night shortly afterwards, she awakened in tears, certain Remarque's hero was her young German. "What is the matter?" her husband, Arthur, exclaimed. "He's dead, he's dead," she cried, sharing her fears with her husband.

Iphigene was deeply affected by World War I. When at Barnard, she became, she thought, a socialist, a supporter of liberal causes (they would have been called leftist by the conservative editorial page of the *Times*). She tried to persuade her father to hire her hero, Walter Lippmann. Her father, in whose eyes Lippmann was a "radical," dutifully agreed to talk with Lippmann, but the young man turned up his nose at the paper.

The memoirs provide indelible snapshots of New York and

America over nearly one hundred years: the day Adolph Ochs brought his wife and daughter to live in a second-rate theatrical hotel in New York in 1896; life in a classic brownstone on the Upper West Side; and summer at Abenia, a great estate on Lake George, "a perfectly hideous old Victorian house," Iphigene recalls, jammed with heavy 1870's mahogany and countless guests and relatives.

Iphigene was the little girl who noticed that the king was wearing no clothes. When William Howard Taft came to lunch at the Ochs house at 308 West Seventy-fifth Street she was impressed by "his enormous size" and affability but (unlike Amy Carter) was not invited to the luncheon table. She consoled herself: "After all," she remembers, "I did get a new dress for the occasion." When President Theodore Roosevelt sent her his photograph she sent him a thank-you note with "love and kisses." She was nine. She describes a brief flirtation with a young and handsome Guglielmo Marconi, inventor of the wireless. They went to Coney Island with some friends, did the Shoot-the-Chute and drank an ice cream soda from two straws.

Once Iphigene, her husband and her father lunched at the White House with President and Mrs. Coolidge. Very dull. When friends asked Iphigene about it she found herself saying that when they came to take the White House elevator she started to enter but Coolidge stopped her. Presidents went first, he said. She argued that women did. He had an etiquette book brought to him and read a passage saying Presidents indeed had precedence. So Iphigene let him enter ahead of her.

There wasn't a word of truth in the story. Like a naughty girl she had made it all up. For years the story haunted her—suppose Coolidge found out!

This is the irrepressible spirit of Iphigene, which today delights her friends and her family, especially her brood of grandchildren and great-grandchildren. Like her father, she was born with a quick tongue. It has its tang.

It would be a mistake to think that Iphigene Sulzberger is all spice. She looks on the world with wise and temperate eyes. The things she cannot abide are cant and evil and injustice. Tolerance lies at the center of her character. She believes in perfectability, but she does not expect people to attain perfection. At least not easily.

Nowhere is this more evident than in her views on religion. She is a Jew and believes in her faith, but it is a tolerant faith. Her family is ecumenical. It embraces many creeds and ethnic origins. Her mother's father, Isaac M. Wise, was the famous rabbi who led the Reform Judaism movement in the United States. A refugee from Bohemia, he founded the Hebrew Union College in Cincinnati and the Union of American Hebrew Congregations.

Rabbi Wise was an enlightened liberal and believed in the faith of Judaism but not in what he regarded as archaic customs. He opposed men wearing hats in temple, and he brought women down from the balcony to the main floor, almost causing a riot. His liberal view was carried on by his daughter, Iphigene's mother, who did not observe dietary laws. She did not eat kosher foods. "My soul is not in my stomach," she said, "so it doesn't make any difference what I put there so long as it is digestible."

This temperament was much akin to his granddaughter's. She, too, warred against dogma into her nineties, often engaging rabbis and priests on a favorite topic: What made them believe they possessed a monopoly of God?

Rabbi Wise had maintained close relations with the Roman Catholic archbishop of Cincinnati and sent two of his daughters, one of them Iphigene's mother, to a convent school. Two of Iphigene's Ochs aunts attended that school as well.

The Ochses and Sulzbergers remained firm in their Jewish faith but independent in their views. Adolph Ochs was not a supporter of Zionism. Mr. Ochs opposed the creation of a Jewish state. So did Iphigene and her husband, initially. After the horrors of the Holocaust, however, they modified their views.

Iphigene was not a woman to accept ideas on faith. She had been taught by her father to examine propositions carefully and objectively. She was influenced by her professors at Barnard, especially William Sheppard, James Harvey Robinson and Vladimir Simkhovitch. It was her exposure to these critical observers of history that sharpened her already quick eye and caused her to challenge the enlightened but conservative views of her father. Out of her youthful and sometimes passionate confrontations with her father emerged her own personality, with its blend of independent thought, keen observation and moderation in expression. She was still capable of jumping up and down, as she did at the Democratic National Convention in 1924 (she was a supporter of Al Smith), and shouting at the top of her lungs, "Oil, Oil, Oil!" against McAdoo in an echo of the Teapot Dome scandal, but she respected her father's patient, cautionary advice: Are you sure of your facts? On what do you base your position?

In the midst of what must have been fairly tempestuous scenes, Adolph Ochs invariably directed his daughter's attention to Benjamin Franklin's autobiography—the story of a life strikingly similar to his own. In Mr. Ochs's copy of the work appeared a passage in which Franklin explained that "I made it a rule to forbear all . . . positive assertion of my own." He forbade himself to use such words as "certainly" and "undoubtedly," substituting "I conceive," "I apprehend" or "it appears to me at present."

It is impossible to believe that the irrepressible Iphigene always adhered to this rule, but she tried, and as she recorded, when she began to dream, as she did while working at the Henry Street Settlement House, of leading a charge against the capitalist exploiters, Franklin's words held her back. In the end, she recalled, Benjamin Franklin won out over the words of Karl Marx and other social revolutionaries.

Iphigene Sulzberger does not look out on the world with the benign repose which some may suppose comes with years. She supports, as always, the personal principles on which her own life is founded. She does not shout from the housetops, but if a president, a governor or a mayor commits an act of incivility or cruelty she responds in the Benjamin Franklin mode. If, as sometimes happens, the *Times* commits what she regards as a blunder, or fails to meet her expectations, she dictates a quiet letter to the editor, signing one of the many noms de plume she has employed over the years. Sometimes the letters are published, sometimes not. That is, she believes, the prerogative of the editor, but at least she has said what she believes needs to be said.

Both Iphigene and Mr. Ochs' *Times* are in their nineties now.

They have, I think, aged well. Each has benefited by the other, and we, as a people, as friends or as mere observers, have benefited most of all. In her memoirs Iphigene for the first time gives us an insight into how this has come about.

Harrison E. Salisbury
Taconic, Connecticut

Foreword

Although the elite, meaning the best capacities in any society, has become a disparaged concept in our addled days, it is not a disparageable thing. It exists whether we like it or not, and Iphigene Ochs Sulzberger is the best argument in its favor that I know. She is high class in every way a woman can function—in devotion to family, in strong social conscience, in elegance of person and winning ways that gain her ends, in alert intelligence and irreverent humor, in energy and unfailing curiosity, in friendship and a welcoming home. In short, she has taken and used the best of the civilizing process and this has produced a thoroughly delightful and thoroughly admirable person. The two do not always coexist.

How shall we account for this phenomenon? Ease of circumstances and, as time went on, an existence of privilege, prominence and power can certainly enhance life wonderfully and, insofar as they make life agreeable, can help to mold agreeable character. They can also, if the material is not right, make the possessor selfish, arrogant and lazy.

Iphigene had the advantage of good genes: from her father, the memorable Adolph Ochs who, at a rock-bottom stage in family fortunes, started at age eleven as a newspaper delivery boy, rising at three A.M. and walking four miles on the job. At twenty he bought the debt-ridden *Chattanooga Times* with a bank loan of three hundred dollars, and subsequently the moribund *New York Times*, with results the world knows. Her maternal grandfather was the mettlesome Rabbi Isaac M. Wise of Cincinnati, founder of Reform Judaism. Her mother, whose married life for the first fifteen years was lived in the home of her parents-in-law surrounded by relatives, compensated for the housekeeping that was done for her and for the loss of two babies in infancy by staying in bed until noon reading books. She wrote little book reviews for her husband's paper and after the move to New York focused her interest on the city's cultural opportunities, taking Iphigene with her wherever she went—to museums, theaters, shops, opera, concerts, lectures.

As the adored only child, Iphigene in her mother's eyes "could do no wrong," and in her father's as well she was the center of attention. He took her along on his Sunday walks in Central Park, made up stories for her, discussed the week's events, worried over her studies, took her on visits to notables, and proudly watched her lay the cornerstone of the new *Times* building at age ten. Contrary to custom which prescribed concealment until eighteen, she came downstairs to dinner parties as an early beauty in her mid-teens, barely rescued on one occasion from an amorous Guglielmo Marconi. She toured Europe in the summers with her parents, whose "curiosity was boundless" and "energy unlimited."

Given stimulating parents, this concentration of love and attention on one child is, I imagine, an important factor in explaining Iphigene. It established a foundation of self-confidence which in turn became the source—if I may use a term that is now almost obsolete—of loving-kindness to others. The person who fears no rebuff is the most giving. Turner Catledge, former managing editor of the *Times*, caught the essence when he wrote that she is "a woman you instinctively love and want to please."

Expelled at twelve from Dr. Sachs' School for "impertinence," which meant talking back to the formidable Head (who intimidated my mother at the same school), Iphigene in maturity developed the tact and kindness of the self-assured. Entertaining a congenial Wendell Willkie, who seemed to her always fated to lose, she cheated at gin rummy to let him win. Confronted by Lester Markel, the notoriously uncivil Sunday editor, with the question, "Why don't you like me?" Iphigene, who probably did not feel highly compatible, managed to convince him that she liked him indeed and "after that we always had a very friendly relationship." This was her way of making prickly and difficult egos soften, not to gratify her exercise of charm but to make rough places at the paper more manageable.

Rough places were encountered, too, in the course of thirty years' active service on the Parks Council of New York City, for a while as its president. In another sphere of public service, I recommend her campaign to have a two-year course in American history taught in the nation's schools as a wonderful lesson in advocacy and persistence, if not success.

Appointed by her father to the *Times* Board of Directors when still in her twenties, Iphigene has been, since his death in 1935, one of the three trustees, along with her husband and then her son, of the Ochs Estate, which owns the controlling interest in the *Times*. As such, she has had the longest connection of anyone with the paper. Through her, the continuity of family control from father to husband to son-in-law to son has been maintained for over sixty years and, through her, will be passed on to the next generation—her grandchildren. Four (out of thirteen) are now working at the paper.

The grandchildren now in their twenties and thirties are probably the most important element in their grandmother's life. One or more is often present among the weekend guests at her Connecticut home, and the share of a granddaughter in the authorship of this memoir is what made it a true reflection after many false starts with other editors. Through Iphigene's steady companionship and interest in their lives, her influence makes itself felt and will endure at the paper after the source is gone.

The Sulzbergers' position as publishers of America's leading newspaper has opened doors everywhere for Iphigene, from the Kremlin to the White House, where she has been a guest of every incumbency from the Coolidges to the Kennedys. It has acquainted her with heads of state from Hirohito to the Shah and with most of the movers and shakers of her time from Al Smith to Churchill.

Let us not suppose, however, that life with the *Times* is necessarily a consistent pleasure or smooth enjoyment of the perquisites of power. It has its power struggles, quarrels and crises, errors, compromises and harsh choices. It caused Adolph Ochs two nervous breakdowns and almost universal execration during World War I because of a favorable reaction to a peace overture by Austria. Whether or not professional stress was responsible, Arthur Hays Sulzberger was a victim of several strokes and an invalid after his retirement in deteriorating health for his last eleven years, which Iphigene calls "the most difficult years of our lives." The tensions and anxieties of the devastating 114-day strike in 1962–63 overstrained the already weak heart of her son-in-law Orvil Dryfoos and caused his death two months after the strike had ended. Fortunately resilient, Punch Sulzberger has surmounted the fury over publication of the Pentagon Papers and the rending battle with the *Times* Washington bureau, and survives.

Problems have not been made easier by the fact of the family being Jewish. This is not something Iphigene refers to in its negative aspects, although these have been present and operative as in one case revealed by Harrison Salisbury in his recent book, *Without Fear or Favor*. President Roosevelt, angry at the *Times'* attack on his court-packing proposal, denounced a legal maneuver by the Ochs Trust to avoid loss of family control through inheritance taxes, referring to it in private conversation as "a dirty Jewish trick." Inevitably conveyed to Arthur Sulzberger and preserved in a memorandum in his private file, this ugly little item does not appear in Iphigene's account, but it reveals that even in the man who brought Frankfurter and Morgenthau onto the Court and Cabinet and chose Sam Rosenman and Ben Cohen as close advisers an attitude lies beneath the skin of American life that leaves its mark.

The sanguine in heart are not subdued or dismayed. A natural happiness and sense of fun have lightened life for Iphigene. There are stories in her book that will make the reader laugh aloud, especially one (page 121) about her argument with Calvin Coolidge as to which of them should enter the White House elevator first, the lady or the President. Her report caused such a flutter in listeners that she eventually had to admit she had made the story up in an imaginative moment. A tale with a similar twist that is not in the book is of travelling with another lady and meeting rude treatment and poor food in a restaurant in Madrid recommended by the hotel's concierge. The next evening Iphigene asked him again, saying she wanted the best and that the headwaiter must be told that she was a distinguished visitor. "Tell him," she said, "tell him . . . oh, tell him I am the Mother of the Gracchi." This inventive identity, made up on the spur, had an uncalled-for success—bows, fine service, the best table. It has the Iphigene touch.

If I may recall another private memory, it is of seeing Iphigene rise in the middle of a luncheon at the Cosmopolitan Club to rescue a ladybug from an indoor plant and let it fly out the window.

Except once, to ensure by her trustee's vote that her husband would succeed her father as publisher, Iphigene does not intervene in the management or policy of the paper. As a supporter of the Loyalists in the Spanish Civil War when the paper was nervously neutral, of Adlai Stevenson against the paper's choice of Eisenhower, of statehood for Israel when her husband and the paper remained anti-Zionist, she may disapprove or disagree with editorial policy, but she exerts no pressures, pulls no private wires. One suspects here a conscious and private "grand refusal," for she certainly had the character and strength of mind and opportunity to play a more active role had she wanted to. After her children were grown and married, she worked full time at the paper for some years to extend its coverage of women's affairs and its circulation in schools and colleges; but otherwise she has kept deliberately aloof. Her presence is a moral weight in the background. She is keeper of the conscience that Adolph Ochs expressed in his founding commitment: "to consider all questions of public importance" and "to give the news impartially without fear or favor."

Although the subject of this book was born nine years before Queen Victoria died, one does not think of her as old. She does not look it or act it nor, I suspect, think it. At seventy-six, after her husband's death, she made a conscious decision to reopen and restore an active life. At eighty-one, she traveled to China, unfazed by a tour from Kweilin in the south to dinner with Chou En-lai in the Great Hall of the People in Peking. At eighty-eight last April, she visited London to greet her eighth and newest great-grandchild.

Iphigene does not need this introduction. It could have been said in one line: She is an example of the best.

Barbara W. Tuchman

Preface

Set forth here are some of the highlights of my lifetime: stories about people and the events they shaped as I saw them and remembered them and as they were described to me by friends and acquaintances; stories of myself—the amusing moments, the difficult times, the things that mattered and moved my life.

I speak from memory, since I have never kept a journal and am not the type to save letters. Fortunately, my memory is good, but a memory is apt to play tricks on one. Therefore, what I relate undoubtedly has errors and should not be thought of as a historical record. It is, rather, my memory's record.

I feel somewhat embarrassed about this book's "going public." It had a private printing and was not meant for general circulation, but so many of my friends encouraged me to permit publication, and my granddaughter was eager to make her professional debut. I hope this will encourage her to continue writing, for I, as a proud grandmother, think she shows real talent.

Many people who touched my life and made a deep impression on me are not mentioned here. Some of these are people of the world my father made. Though the days of the family newspaper have long gone, the editors who are now responsible for running the New York Times *and the* Chattanooga

Times—*and the able staffs of both papers—are like family to me, as in the past they were to Papa and Arthur.*

My narrative pretty well ends in my eighty-first year with my trip to China. With the exception of a trip to Vienna in 1980, my other travels have been comparatively uneventful. Vienna was very different from when I had visited there with my parents in 1908. Then we had stood on the street corner and saw Franz Josef reviewing his troops. This time I had tea with some of the Hapsburgs in their castle down the Danube. Their empire is of the past, and they seemed to have come down in the world as I have gone up, and so we met.

As an old woman looking back over the years, I am full of hope because I realize that on the whole man has made progress. Naturally, the progress has not been steadily forward but rather up and down. In politics I am a liberal not a conservative, for I remember Professor James Harvey Robinson used to tell his class that progress is a vehicle being painfully dragged up a hill and exclaiming, "Who ever heard of a vehicle going uphill that needed to have brakes applied!"

Being optimistic, dear reader, I commend to you the advice of Thomas Jefferson: "Always expect the best; you are no oftener wrong than when you expect the worst."

Iphigene Ochs Sulzberger

Iphigene

My Life and *The New York Times*

1

One story I often heard during my childhood was of a clash of loyalties within the family at the time of the Civil War.

My grandfather Julius Ochs abhorred slavery. He had seen the inhumane treatment of the Negroes while crisscrossing the South on business in the early 1850's. So that his children might know his feelings about slavery, he kept a diary. "I saw attractive mulatto girls placed on the auction stand and subjected to a critical physical examination by lustful men. . . . I saw the poor wretches in droves, direct from Africa. . . . Beatings and lashings with ugly thongs were frequent occurrences. These sights sickened me. Once I saw a poor wretch so horribly beaten that tears of pity gushed from my eyes."

Revolted by this "villainous relic of barbarism," as he later put it in his memoirs, he moved north to Cincinnati when the Civil War broke out in 1861, and enlisted in the Army. He was immediately appointed captain.

His wife, Bertha, was also passionate on the slavery issue, but she took the opposite side. She was a die-hard Confederate, a true daughter of the Old South.

Grandmother was born in Landau, Bavaria, in the Palatinate, and went to school in Heidelberg. During the 1848 revolution, one of her classmates was publicly executed. To show their sympathy, Bertha and another girl stained their handkerchiefs with the student's blood. It was a dangerous thing to do, and her parents were informed that they had better get Bertha out of the country. She was shipped to America, to an uncle. His name was Mayer Levy, but he had dropped the Levy and was known as Mayer. Mr. Mayer lived in Natchez, Mississippi, in the heart of the slave country. It was there that my grandmother came by her narrow-mindedness about Negroes. She, who had protested the crushing of freedom in Germany, could not see the similarity in what the Southerners were doing to the Negroes.

In the war, my grandfather's unit was charged with preventing the rebels from smuggling arms and ammunition across the Ohio River into Kentucky. While he did this, my grandmother, it turned out, would cross the Ohio River bridge from Cincinnati to the Kentucky side, smuggling drugs to the Confederates! I don't know how many times she made the trip, but she would hide the drugs in the baby carriage and take the baby (I think it was my Uncle George) for a stroll across the bridge. Her small consignments may have been nothing more than quinine, but one day she was caught by Union guards and an order was issued for her arrest.

That must have been an embarrassing situation for Grandfather, but because of his position as a commissioned officer loyally and dutifully serving the Union cause, he was able somehow to get the warrant nullified.

My grandparents, by then, had been married for six years. I'm not sure how they managed to reconcile their differences on the war, but they must have worked something out, for they remained devoted to each other without modifying their beliefs. Nearly twenty-five years after the war, when my grandfather died and was buried in Chattanooga, a unit of the Grand Army of the Republic officiated at the funeral and the Union flag was draped over his coffin, in accordance with his wishes. My grandmother was a charter member of the Chattanooga chapter of the Daughters of the Confederacy, and when she died twenty years after him, at the age of seventy-five, members of her chapter attended the funeral and a Confederate flag was placed in her coffin, at her request. My grandparents are buried side by side in the Mizpah Cemetery in Chattanooga.

Bertha Levy met Julius Ochs in 1851, in Natchez, while shopping in a store he owned. I imagine he had a full, dark beard then, as he did when later photographed in his army uniform, and must have been good-looking. Bertha was trim and stylish enough, though no great beauty. Their acquaintance at that time was brief, for Julius soon moved his business to another town.

Two years later yellow fever struck the South, and about 25,000 people died in the Mississippi Valley. One day, while reading a list of victims in the paper, Julius came across the name of Bertha Levy of Natchez. Yet a year later he saw her again at a party in Nashville. She told him she had been very ill, all but dead. In a final effort the doctors had packed her in ice, and the treatment had saved her life.

It wasn't long after the second meeting that Julius, who was then twenty-nine, and Bertha, who was twenty-two, were married. They were married for thirty-three years and had seven children. The first child, Louis, died at the age of two and a half, of scarlet fever. The second child, born on March 12, 1858, was named Adolph Simon Ochs. He was my father. His younger sister was Nannie; then came George, Milton, Ada and Mattie.

Julius Ochs died four years before I was born, and Bertha, whose name is my middle name, died when I was sixteen; what I know of them comes mostly from stories that were handed down in the family or from my grandfather's quite touching manuscript. In order not to repeat what he wrote—he told of his life in considerable detail—I shall mention only that he was a well-educated man. He spoke seven languages, played the guitar and composed a couple of light operas. He was not, however, a great success in business. In the early days he was a salesman and small shopkeeper; on one occasion, he taught French at a girls' school. He later accepted a job from his son at the *Chattanooga Times*. This must have been difficult to do without a loss of self-esteem. But, then, he must have been a man of enormous character, and although he could not always provide for his wife and children as well as he wished, he always kept the respect and admiration of his family and friends. He wasn't a go-getter; rather, he was gentle and introspective and, I understand, quite lovable. In Knoxville, Tennessee, where he settled when the war ended, he became a justice of the peace and unofficial rabbi of the small Jewish community.

My father didn't have the carefree years of childhood. He felt his responsibilities as the eldest, and, at the age of eleven, decided to supplement the family income by going to work as a delivery boy for the local newspaper, the *Knoxville Chronicle*. It was a tiring job, getting up at 3 a.m. and walking as many as four miles in the morning chill. Those were lean years for the Ochs family and Julius couldn't refuse the small change that Adolph and, later, his younger brothers brought home as carriers, but he accepted their help with a heavy heart. I think it was my Uncle Milton who told me that Julius felt such remorse that he'd accompany his boys down to the *Chronicle* every morning and help them fold and sort their newspapers before they started off.

When my father was thirteen years old he went to Providence, Rhode Island, to work in a grocery store owned by his uncle Gustave Rodenberg, but he was most unhappy there. The one enjoyable time he had was on July Fourth, when the grocery store was closed and he was given permission to set up a lemonade stand outside. He made, I believe, twelve dollars, which was a real fortune in those days.

Back in Knoxville, he went to work in a drugstore, with the thought of becoming an apothecary. But the work didn't appeal to him, and one day in the fall of 1872 he walked into the editor's office at the *Chronicle* and got himself a full-time job. He was hired as a chore boy and printer's devil.

It must have been quite a moment for him when the editor,

Captain William Rule (almost everybody had a military title in those days), agreed to take him on. My father was only fourteen, and undersized at that, and he was entering a man's world. The story goes that his first chore was to shine the captain's chimney lamp. He polished and scrubbed the lamp, then the floor. Then he cleaned the press rollers and refilled type cases. By the time he left for home, the *Chronicle* office was transformed from musty disorder to respectable neatness.

Papa used to tell me that he would never have become a newspaperman if it hadn't been for his fear of ghosts. When he left work each night at midnight, his walk home would take him by the cemetery. It would be the very hour when ghosts were said to walk. He said he wasn't about to take any chances; he didn't mind waiting a couple of hours to have company on the way home. He'd wait until 2 a.m. for the composing-room foreman, who lived a few houses away from him. It was during those hours of waiting that he observed and listened, and learned a great deal of the printer's trade.

After three years at the *Chronicle*, my father went to work as a printer and part-time reporter for the Louisville *Courier-Journal*. There, in 1875, one of his assignments was to cover the funeral of Andrew Johnson. But he was homesick and returned to Knoxville to work as a printer on the *Tribune*. The paper's business manager, Franc M. Paul, and its editor, Colonel John MacGowan, persuaded him to join them in starting a newspaper in Chattanooga. He was then nineteen years old.

Chattanooga, the scene of some of the bloodiest and most decisive battles of the Civil War, was still a frontier town. There were no sidewalks and the streets were awash in mud. It was common to see men carrying pistols for protection. In this atmosphere the *Chattanooga Dispatch* was launched in 1877; my father was its business solicitor. The newspaper lived up to only one meaning of its name: It disappeared after just a few months. My father found himself in a town that seemed to have no future, in a business that seemed to have no security. For this wasn't the only paper to go broke—in that period of Reconstruction, papers were dying in the South almost as soon as they were born.

At least my father had managed to keep the paper's ancient

handpress, and that turned out to be important. Chattanooga at that time had no city directory, and he set about compiling and printing one himself. Though the old handpress collapsed halfway through the job and had to be replaced by another one, he turned out a 126-page *Chattanooga City Directory and Business Gazetteer*. I have a bound copy in my library.

The project was a great success. My father made enough money to pay back the debt incurred when the *Dispatch* went bust. In the process, he established for himself a reputation for earnestness and honesty. Also, in the course of compiling the directory, he came to know every major businessman and politician in town. And in the spring of 1878, less than a year after his arrival in Chattanooga, he found the opportunity he had probably dreamed of ever since he had worked as a chore boy for Captain William Rule.

The *Chattanooga Times* was a newspaper in dire straits. Its owner, S. A. Cunningham, was in despair. The paper had only 250 subscribers, and not all of them paid their bills. The building that housed the paper was old and run-down; the one handpress wheezed with age. Debts piled up. The paper couldn't afford to keep up with the latest technology. Then it had to give up the telegraph news. In fact, about the only thing the *Chattanooga Times* had was a name.

My father wanted to buy it, and asked Colonel MacGowan, his partner in the *Dispatch* fiasco, to be editor-in-chief. Mr. Mac-Gowan didn't hesitate. A lawyer and a scholar and accustomed to giving commands, Mr. MacGowan at forty-seven was willing to work for the twenty-year-old Adolph Ochs for a starting salary of $1.50 a day. Four journeyman printers and one reporter, Will Kennedy, all a good deal older than my father, threw in their lot. Despite his youth, my father must have been a very persuasive man.

Assured of a staff, Papa approached the First National Bank of Chattanooga for a loan of $300. Theodore G. Montague, the bank's cashier, asked, "Do you have any collateral?" My father admitted he didn't.

"Well, have you anyone you think would sign your note?"

My father replied, "I don't know anybody in town who knows me as well as you do."

The banker signed the note himself, and lent him the money.

With $250 of the $300, my father bought a half interest in the *Chattanooga Times*. My grandfather had come from Knoxville to sign the transfer papers, since his son was one year short of the legal age of twenty-one.

On July 2, 1878, with a staff of eight, the new publisher went to work. His operating capital was exactly $37.50. Of this he spent $25 for the New York Associated Press Service, which provided news from other parts of the country. For the first few months he paid his staff with money orders redeemable in advertisers' stores. I remember asking Papa if the paper made any money in the beginning. He said it must have, because that's what he lived on. His mother, brothers and sisters were still living in Knoxville, and every night he would mail them two dollars, which paid a good part of their bills.

He must have worked exceedingly long hours, with little sleep, to revive that paper. It owed up to $1,500. Its type was so worn that it had to be replaced within the first year. He was borrowing money with his left hand to pay off debts with his right.

As though he didn't have enough to handle, a yellow-fever epidemic struck the Tennessee Valley. All the readers and advertisers fled. The *Times* was reduced from four pages to one. It almost went under. But somehow it held on.

Difficult as those years were, a note of levity appears in an editorial written by my father on March 12, 1879. The day marked his twenty-first birthday, and the editorial congratulated his readers on now reading a newspaper published by a man and not a boy.

It was four years before my father was able to purchase the remaining half interest in the *Times*. He bought it for $5,500, more than twenty times as much as he had paid for the original half interest. This was a price fixed by arbitrators. The paper had done well under his stewardship. He had started something dramatically different from the journalism of his day.

Newspapers in those times depended on gimmickry; they survived by currying favor with special-interest groups; a standard tactic was to slander one's competitors. My father didn't practice that sort of journalism. He concentrated solely on the news, particularly civic affairs, and he took the personal slant out of reporting. He strove to report on the day's happenings accurately and soberly, and directed his paper toward the intelligent reader who wanted the facts. In his initial declaration of policy he wrote: "We shall give the people a chance to support that which they have been asking for, a paper primarily devoted to the material, educational, and moral growth of our progressive city and its surrounding territory."

It was evidently what people wanted, for they did give him their support. My father had succeeded in his lofty ambition—to publish a paper independent of political, social or religious pressures. It was an arduous philosophy, and though it would later become the foundation of what might be considered the world's finest newspaper, he would be forced to fight over and over again for his beliefs.

2

In Cincinnati, three hundred miles to the north, another newspaper was started at about this time by a man in his fifties. My father and his parents were very interested in this publication. The man was Rabbi Isaac M. Wise, and the paper, called the *American Israelite*, espoused a new religious movement known as Reform Judaism. The Ochs family thought it was the wave of the future.

Rabbi Wise was probably the country's leading rabbi. In time he was to organize the Union of American Hebrew Congregations and the Central Conference of American Rabbis, and in his own town would found the Hebrew Union College, the first Jewish theological seminary in the United States. He had come by his liberal ideas early in life, and had promoted them against considerable opposition.

As a young rabbi in Bohemia, then a part of the Austro-Hungarian Empire, he got into trouble with the Government. A law of the time sought to keep the Jewish population down by limiting marriages among Jews to a fixed number; there could be no new marriage unless a Jewish married couple had died. Isaac Wise announced that he would marry any Jewish couple who came to him, and he did exactly that.

The authorities told him to leave the country or prepare to go to jail, and the rabbi, with his wife and daughter, went off to America. His first pulpit was, I think, in Albany. There he proposed that the men in his congregation take off their hats and that the women come down from the balcony. The reaction to these ideas was so violent that he had to escape by the back door.

Rabbi Wise, as may be surmised, didn't see much sense in many of the Orthodox traditions. He never served kosher food. "My soul is not in my stomach," he used to say—as Mother told me—"so it doesn't make any difference what I put there, so long as it is digestible." He had many followers, and his new approach to Judaism might well have overcome the old in this country had it not been for the great influx of Jews from Eastern Europe. Those immigrants were practically medieval in their religious practices. But, then, they had been isolated from the rest of the world and cruelly persecuted, and it was their devotion to their ancient precepts that had given them the strength to persevere. It was natural for them to be afraid of abandoning their old ways, even in the New World.

Isaac Wise settled in Cincinnati, where he raised twelve children. Eight were by his first wife, Theresa Bloch, who died of a brain tumor—Emily, Leo, Julius, Isadore, Ida, Helen, Iphigenia and Harry. His children by his second wife, Selma Bondy, were Elsa (who died at the age of twenty-two), Jonah and Regina (twins born when Isaac was sixty-three) and Isaac, Jr. Iphigenia, the seventh child, was my mother.

For a rabbi's daughters, my mother and her sister Helen received an unusual kind of education: They went to a convent school run by the Sisters of Notre Dame. The private academy for young ladies the two eldest Wise girls had attended had closed, and their father found the convent school a good alternative.

The Roman Catholic Archbishop of Cincinnati once asked

him, "Aren't you worried, Rabbi, that if you send your daughters to us, we might convert them?"

"Bishop," my grandfather retorted, "if you can convert those girls after my teachings, you're most welcome to have them."

It seems that some of the convent teachings did rub off on Helen. She eloped with James Molony, causing great scandal in Cincinnati's Jewish community. Molony was certainly not Jewish, but neither was he a Catholic, as his name suggests. His father had left Ireland to escape family pressure on him to enter the Catholic priesthood. In the United States he had married a Presbyterian of *Mayflower* lineage, and their son was raised a Presbyterian.

Despite the usual problems inherent in marrying outside one's own faith, Aunt Helen and Uncle Jim got along happily. There was no friction about the children's upbringing; Jim was perfectly content to have them brought up Jewish. While adhering to the Jewish religion, Aunt Helen always maintained ties with her old convent school, and even served for a time as president of its alumnae association. Her daughter, Iphigene, married Gilbert Bettman, and their children were raised as Jews.

My mother always said the convent gave her a good grounding in literature, poetry and writing. (The nuns also tried to teach her sewing, but unfortunately they got nowhere on that.) She was so enthusiastic about the school that her two sisters-in-law—my father's sisters Ada and Mattie—decided to enroll. Mattie so adored it that the family was afraid she might become a nun. They need not have worried: She practiced her Judaism with deep devotion, never missing a service. Even when she was ill or too old to attend temple, she read the prayers at home.

The second-eldest child of Rabbi Wise, Leo, had a bent for journalism and went to work for his father as editor of the *American Israelite*. In 1882, while purchasing some newsprint, Leo met a fellow journalist named Adolph Ochs. They struck up a friendship, and Leo invited the young man home for dinner.

As the story was told to me, the young Mr. Ochs arrived at the Wise household and was shown into the parlor by a maid. He was seated, waiting for Leo, when a young lady entered the room. She was a small, slender woman, only about five feet tall, with big, beautiful dark eyes, an abundance of dark hair and a rather high-bridged nose. (I remember one time when we were in France, visiting the Bourbon tombs, Mama kept pointing out the bas-relief portraits and busts and exclaiming, "Aha! See, all the profiles are like mine!")

My father was not very tall—five feet seven and a half, I think. That was above average in those days, and no one who knew him ever thought of him as a little man. He had a great presence about him. Even at that early age his appearance was striking. He had grown a bushy black mustache to make himself look older (my mother got him to shave it off as soon as she could), and had curly black hair. In later years he was an extraordinarily impressive looking man, with a remarkable head.

I remember one time we were in Karlsbad, when my father was about fifty, and he came back from the baths very amused and pleased. The Czar of Bulgaria had been there. Seeing my father sitting wrapped in a towel, he sent word to him that he looked like a Roman senator. My father sent back word that the Czar looked like an emperor.

As early as his twenties, my father must have had something of this imposing quality about him, both in appearance and in manner. Otherwise, it seems improbable that a banker would lend him money for a business when he was still legally a minor, or that older and more experienced men would agree to work for him on his newspaper. Yet, for all his savoir faire in the business world, the twenty-four-year-old publisher was struck speechless when the pretty Miss Iphigenia presented herself in the parlor and said, "I'm Effie Miriam Wise. Who are you?"

My father, flustered by her sudden appearance and struck by her good looks, stumbled in his answer. Groping for conversation, he could think of nothing to talk about except horse racing. He had just seen two famous horses, Longfellow and Harry Bassett, in heated competition, and he described the race to Effie with great enthusiasm.

My mother, to whom this was not the most interesting of topics, found herself asking, "What was the name of that horse that won?" Something about the young man had impressed her.

"Harry Bassett," replied Adolph.

"Has he ever won a race before?"

Harry Bassett was a winner, and Adolph had picked up a shoe the horse had lost during a recent competition, and the next day he sent the horseshoe to Miss Wise. I think she was pleased with the gift; she rode and was fond of animals.

Thus began Adolph's spirited campaign for the hand of Effie Wise. It would take some doing, since she was engaged to another man. Adolph traveled back and forth between Chattanooga and Cincinnati so often that his free railroad pass, to which he was entitled as publisher, was almost worn to shreds. After many eager invitations, Effie visited Chattanooga. He showed her the newspaper plant, and spoke of how he got into journalism and what he was aiming for in the publishing world, and took her to meet his family.

Effie Wise finally gave in, and on February 28, 1883, they were married in the Plum Street Synagogue in Cincinnati. A special train from Chattanooga brought relatives, friends and leading Chattanooga citizens to the ceremony.

After the honeymoon, which included a tea with President Chester Alan Arthur in Washington, my father brought his wife home to Chattanooga, to a brick house at Cedar and Fifth streets he had purchased a year earlier. In that house lived his father and mother, three sisters, two brothers and a grandfather, as well as assorted cousins, aunts, uncles, friends and whoever happened to be staying over on extended visits.

Most young brides would have taken one look at this house crammed full of in-laws and fled. My mother persevered. Coming from a large family may have made the adjustment easier for her, but in addition to having to cope with this mob, she had to tolerate a very imposing mother-in-law. Bertha Ochs ruled the roost with a firm hand. It never occurred to her that this was Adolph's home and that Effie, as his wife, might like to have a say in running it.

I remember once coming across a photograph of Grandma Bertha and giving it to my mother as a gift. She accepted the present politely, but as she put it down I could tell from her face that she wanted nothing to do with it. I realized then what a trial it must have been for her to live in that house for fifteen years. During all that time she never said a word against her mother-in-law.

My mother's tolerance made a great impression on me. Years later, my regard for Eleanor Roosevelt was affected by her complaining publicly about her mother-in-law.

Perhaps it was because of this matriarchal dominance that my mother became so lazy about household chores. There was a large household staff to carry out Bertha's orders and little left for her to do. As a result, Mama never did learn to attend such matters as marketing, and when my parents first moved to New York, a distant cousin named Blanche Aaron took over that side of the work. She was a fat, amiable young woman who adored my mother and was, apparently, happy to shop for groceries. When Blanche wasn't about, the shopping was left to anyone who happened to be visiting—and there was always someone. Incidentally, Blanche had great admiration for my father, too. Against her family's advice she bought shares in his fledgling New York newspaper. It was an investment that eventually made her rich.

I can't recall my father's ever offering the slightest criticism of my mother's housekeeping, though I know it affected his day-to-day arrangements. I remember asking him once why he entertained important luncheon guests at the office instead of at home, where I could meet them.

"It's perfectly simple," he said. "At the office I have someone to do the housekeeping. At home I would have to plan the meal, order the food, arrange the flowers, and so on, myself. Not that your mama isn't a charming hostess." And she was—if someone else did the work.

My mother spoke little to me about her years in the Cedar Street house. All I have are letters and comments from my aunts. I gather that she used to stay in bed all morning, catching up on her reading. Then, just before noon, there was always a mad rush as my grandmother and aunts made her presentable for my father. At noon he would arrive for lunch.

She spent much of her time reading. She had books by Tennyson, George Eliot and other great authors of the day, but her greatest love was history. I imagine she found a wonderful retreat in the pages of history from the difficult circumstances she lived in. The stories she told me when I was a child so captured my imagination that I, too, have always been a history buff.

Nearly every evening after dinner my mother would accompany my father back to the office. There, by a flickering gas lamp, she would write book reviews and occasional verses about books or people in public life. The late nights gave her a perfect excuse for staying in bed the next morning. She spent a lot of time in her room.

Years later, I found a letter my father wrote her, asking her why she spent so much time alone. Being both a loving husband and a dutiful son, he probably never realized there was cause for friction every time his dear Effie came downstairs. It wouldn't be an open conflict; Mama never got into fights. She was very gentle and very sweet and was loved by the whole family. My grandfather was so devoted to her that he would come home with little gifts for her, a flower or some trinket—something he didn't do for his own daughters.

Perhaps my mother would have been less of a recluse in that house if she had had a child to raise earlier in her marriage. Her first child was stillborn. She was soon pregnant again and, after a very difficult labor, gave birth to a daughter. When only two and a half months old, the child developed a mouth infection. The doctor who attended her was not competent—medical skill was a rare commodity in Chattanooga in those days—and the infant died.

Bitterly distraught, Mother developed a painful condition in her leg muscles. They became cramped and sore; soon she couldn't even walk. The doctor prescribed drugs, but though they relieved the pain, my mother still couldn't walk, and now she couldn't get through the day without medication. She was becoming an addict. It was my father who realized it first. I remember Mama telling me how Papa had stayed with her, shut up in their room, for two days in a row, while she screamed and swore and called him every kind of name and implored him for relief—just a little bit of the medication. He endured her ravings. Telling me of the experience, she said, "How grateful I've always been to him that he did it!"

My mother was freed of her addiction, but not of the trouble with her legs. Her youngest brother, Harry, who was a pharmacist, thought she needed a good rest. He arranged for a lengthy stay at a Texas ranch owned by his parents-in-law, the Landas. As it happened, living near the ranch was a masseur who had a local reputation as a healer. His name was Fleming. He was a huge man who claimed that he had been struck three times by lightning and now possessed lightning in his fingertips. The Landas asked him to look at my mother. Mr. Fleming went to work on her. He massaged and manipulated her legs. After three months of daily treatment, my mother was cured. And she never had any difficulty with her legs again. Needless to say, she became a believer in Mr. Fleming's electricity and was forever grateful to the Landas.

Shortly before her ninth wedding anniversary, my mother was pregnant again, and this time my father decided the medical facilities in Chattanooga would not do. When the delivery day was near, she boarded the train for Cincinnati. There she stayed in a hotel next to her doctor's home. It was called the Alms Hotel after its owner, Frederick Alms. The doctor's name was Stark.

I was born in that hotel on September 19, 1892. My parents always delighted in telling people that I was born in an almshouse. And, because of the way they pronounced the doctor's name, I believed for many years that I had been brought by Dr. Stork, which I thought was very nice. Papa described me in a letter to his mother as "a great big baby with much dark hair, eyes between blue and grey, and a nose that seems inclined to be puggy. She has a double chin, the cutest of hands and nails."

I can't say I suffered neglect in my early childhood. Rather, I was quite the attraction. I was the only child in a house full of adults, and everyone was enchanted with me and called me Baby. I think I would have been spoiled utterly had it not been for my younger cousin Julius. Julius lived only a block from our house, so the family was able to spread their devotion between two children.

Julius, the son of Ada Ochs and Harry Adler, was two and a half months my junior and my dearest childhood companion. I always regarded him as a brother. I recall our big moment at the wedding of my father's youngest sister, Aunt Mattie. I was three and a half and was decked out in a lace-trimmed dress with a bridal veil, and my cousin Julius wore a white satin suit, like a page at the court of Louis XVI. Side by side we walked down the aisle ahead of the bride, and I was told that people climbed on their seats in the synagogue to see us better. But what I remember even more clearly was when my father's young cousin, George David, took away my ice cream at the reception. He meant it as a joke, but I wept so loudly I was put to bed.

I was only four when we left Chattanooga, so I don't have many memories of my life there. I do remember that when I was eight I put a stop to people calling me Baby. Thereafter, I was Iphigene to the family and Iphie to my friends.

3

During my early childhood, my father struggled to survive one of the most costly mistakes of his life. He had made the blunder when he was about thirty, four years before I was born. The *Chattanooga Times* was making $25,000 a year—a good profit in any business in those days—and was considered the leading newspaper in the South. He had made a name for himself, and the city of Chattanooga regarded him as one of its outstanding citizens. For the very first time, he had money in the bank. In fact, he had a great deal of money.

At that point, a land craze hit the South. It was thought that America's future lay in its cotton fields and virgin forests. Real estate agents were beseiged. Acreage was ravenously bought up by investors. The hottest commodity was city land. Cities like Chattanooga, people were sure, would become the great railway hubs, the centers of business and heavy industry. Chattanooga would be the Pittsburgh of the South.

My father, like so many of his friends, got carried away in the excitement and invested everything he had or could borrow in Chattanooga real estate. Then the land boom collapsed, and he was left with a lot of all-but-worthless property. (I still have one or two small lots. They're not of much value, but I pay taxes on them.) He was also left with mortgages and loans to repay. By any standard, he was deeply in debt.

Friends advised him to declare bankruptcy and pay off the debts at fifty cents or even ten cents on the dollar. It was the sensible thing to do—sensible to everyone but my father. He thought the idea dishonorable, and resolved to pay his debts in full.

It was a noble goal, but extremely difficult to achieve. The profit from the *Times* hardly made a dent in his indebtedness. The amount he had to raise was enormous—at least $100,000. There was only one way to make that kind of money, he told me years later, and that was by expanding.

I think he had a bit of genius and a bit of insanity in him, since he concluded that the solution lay in buying another newspaper. It would mean borrowing a great deal of money, going even deeper into debt. He realized the potentially disastrous consequences, I'm sure. At the same time, he must have had faith in his Midas touch with newspapers. He had brought one to life when it was dying. Never again would he invest his money or his mind in anything but journalism.

He searched for loans and for another paper. A publication called the *Nashville American* was up for sale, and he went to Nashville to negotiate, but the deal fell through. He then went to New York looking for loans. He'd go from bank to bank, on foot to save carfare, borrowing a thousand dollars here and a thousand dollars there, but it was never enough to meet his repayment schedules and he sank deeper into debt.

It was a great blow to his pride that he had to pledge the new *Chattanooga Times* plant as collateral. That building symbolized all he'd achieved since his days as a chore boy for Captain Rule. A spectacular structure it was, with its great gold dome and a view that topped any in the city. My father had laid the cornerstone himself, a few days after I was born, and ten thousand people had attended the opening ceremonies.

For more than seven years, Father struggled to find a way out of his financial difficulties. The solution came in an unexpected way.

He had been very active in the newspaper world on a national level—in fact, the night I was born he was in New York, fighting to get the smaller papers accepted in the Associated Press—and one of the journalists he came to know was Harry Alloway, a reporter for the *New York Times*. They had met while Mr. Alloway was on a reporting assignment in Chattanooga. They liked each other and kept in touch. On March 12, 1896—my father's thirty-eighth birthday—Harry Alloway sent him a telegram that turned around the Ochs family's entire life. Mr. Alloway said his paper was headed for the graveyard and would most likely be up for sale at a very reasonable price.

The telegram must have filled my father with excitement and trepidation. The *New York Times* was a paper he had long admired. Founded in 1851 by Henry J. Raymond, one of my father's journalistic heroes, and George Jones, the daily had grown continually in the public esteem. Mr. Raymond was a brilliant editor; when he died in 1869 the *Times* was second to none in New York and very sound financially, and Mr. Jones carried it to even greater heights.

The *New York Times* broke the notorious Boss Tweed ring. William Marcy Tweed was unabashedly stealing from the municipal coffers. Everyone knew it, but no one had the courage to stop him and his corrupt gang. While other newspapers remained neutral or sympathetic toward Boss Tweed, the *Times* began to attack his insidious involvement with graft. On July 22, 1871, the *Times* devoted its entire front page to an itemized account of Mr. Tweed's graft and corruption. The city of New York had been defrauded of between ten and fifty million dollars—the exact amount was never determined.

The *Times* was staunchly Republican, with a largely Republican readership. But in 1884, Mr. Jones decided to support the Democratic Presidential candidate, Grover Cleveland, against the Republican James Blaine. Many Republicans stopped buying the paper. Profits went down.

That was the beginning of an avalanche of bad luck. In the late 1880's the *Times* spent a lot of money—in hindsight, too much—putting up a new building on Park Row in Lower Manhattan. George Jones, it seemed, tended to take on more than he could handle. When he died in 1891, a new company was formed, headed by Charles Miller, who had been editor-in-chief of the *Times*. But the reorganization did not solve the paper's difficulties, and the depression of the early 1890's and the panic of 1893 made them worse.

Mr. Miller and his associates pooled their personal holdings in the company and sold them in an attempt to rescue the paper. They raised a million dollars, but it wasn't enough. By March 1896, when my father got the telegram from Harry Alloway, the *Times* had hit rock bottom. Its circulation was down to 9,000 and it was losing about $1,500 a week. This was the heyday of yellow journalism, and newspapers such as the *World*, the *Journal* and the *Herald* profited from sensationalism. It was difficult to impress advertisers to invest in a serious paper that concerned itself with politics and news events.

Yet this was the very kind of newspaper my father wanted. Here was a journal that had shown it could take corruption by the tail and shake it until only the truth was left. The philosophy the *Times* was born with was the very one Father wanted to preserve and foster. Financially, it was a great risk; he didn't know if he could put the paper back on its feet. But he did know that unless he tried, the *Chattanooga Times* would go down, too.

Papa did not rush off to New York after receiving Mr. Alloway's telegram. I know that because of a little story he told me. He went instead to Chicago, taking this out-of-the-way route to seek the advice of a longtime friend.

Herman Kohlsaat was a newspaperman who published the *Chicago Times-Herald* and a paper called *Inter-Ocean*. He had gone into journalism after making his fortune in the bakery business. My father outlined the situation to him. He must have seemed awfully nervous, because Mr. Kohlsaat interrupted him.

"Now tell me, Adolph, what is it that's really bothering you?"

"Well, Mr. Kohlsaat," my father confessed, "I'm not sure I'm a big enough man for the job."

Mr. Kohlsaat reflected for a moment and said, "Don't tell anybody, and perhaps they'll never find out."

My father proceeded to New York. A few days later, he sat in the drawing room of Charles R. Miller, president of the New York Times Company and the paper's editor-in-chief.

Mr. Miller was glad to see him. The major stockholders of the *Times* wanted to be free of the newspaper before they went further into debt. In their opinion, this man from the South had appeared at just the right time. He had revived a dying paper in Chattanooga. Perhaps he could do the same with the *New York Times*.

The appointment, arranged by Mr. Alloway, had been for a short meeting after dinner; Mr. Miller planned to take his family to the theater. The two men started talking. Theater time came, and Mr. Miller sent his family on, saying he'd catch up with them shortly. He never made it to the performance. The men talked far into the night. That was the beginning of their formal negotiations. My father had his foot in the door of the *New York Times*. Moreover, he had rekindled Mr. Miller's hope that the once-great journal could be brought back to life.

My father was away in New York for three whole months. I think that was the longest period he was ever separated from my mother, and she, waiting, became even more of a recluse. Yet, busy as he was, he found time to write her almost every day. His letters were full of enthusiasm and optimism: He was determined to be publisher of the *New York Times*.

Within the family in Chattanooga, only my mother believed in this new plan of his. She had and always would have complete faith in him. The others thought he had taken leave of his senses. The general feeling, my Uncle George later told me, was that "with all the problems Adolph already has, the last thing he needs is to go and buy the *New York Times*." The family pleaded with Uncle

George to go after him and make sure he didn't do anything crazy. George refused.

In New York, the negotiations were delicate and complicated, but by now Mr. Miller and the other controlling stockholders wanted my father to have the paper. He had a fine reputation as a journalist and businessman, and he supported the gold standard—and that was important to the owners of the *New York Times*.

The controlling interest in the firm lay in the hands of Wall Street bankers—among them Charles Flint and Spencer Trask—who very much wanted a New York paper that backed gold. The bankers were nervous about the Presidential election, now less than six months away. The Democratic candidate, William Jennings Bryan, was running on a platform of free silver, and the bankers feared that if he won and got his policy enacted, the value of the dollar would be drastically reduced. Adolph Ochs, although a Democrat, regarded Bryan as a demagogue whose ideas on the free coining of silver could wreck the economy, and the *Chattanooga Times* supported the Republican candidate, William McKinley, who stood firm on gold.

The bankers offered my father the management of the *New York Times* on $50,000 a year—a salary that would greatly ease his financial difficulties, and even eliminate them in time. It was an amount that would have made anyone else in his place giddy with delight. My father turned it down. A fixed salary, no matter how generous, was not his objective. His ambition was to own and operate the most influential newspaper in New York City—perhaps, someday, in the entire United States—and he saw potential for that kind of greatness in the *New York Times*.

He presented the stockholders with a plan for rebuilding the *Times* under which he would acquire ownership of the paper if he succeeded in operating it at a profit for three consecutive years. It was a very complicated financial scheme that involved converting old *Times* stock into new *Times* stock and giving free shares as a bonus with the purchase of bonds. The plan was adopted. The new New York Times Company was formed. My father bought a great number of these bonds—$75,000 worth. Where he came up with that kind of money, I don't know. With this purchase he automatically received 1,125 shares of stock, out of the new company's total of 10,000 shares. An additional 3,876 shares would give him controlling interest. These 3,876 shares were put into escrow—to be sold to him after the three-year trial period.

I, of course, was far too young to remember any of this. My one childhood recollection was overhearing some talk about an "angel" named Charles Flint. I also heard people talking about "escrow." To me it sounded very much like "escarole," which was a word I knew. Why all these grownups were putting stock in salad I couldn't figure out. And I always pictured Mr. Flint as a man with wings. It was deeply disappointing when I met him and found him to be just a short man with a pointed beard and no wings at all.

Years later, my father told me how nervous he had been while going around town to see those stockholders. There was one in particular who made his knees tremble. He was a giant in the world of finance, a man ruthless in his decisions. His name was J. P. Morgan.

Papa told me he put himself through mental torture as he rode the elevated one day to Mr. Morgan's Wall Street office. The financier had $25,000 worth of old *Times* stock. My father had to persuade him to exchange the amount for new shares, and he had his sales pitch carefully prepared. He entered Mr. Morgan's office. They exchanged greetings. Then Mr. Morgan simply said, "Where do I sign?" In five minutes the transaction was completed.

Mr. Morgan had already been sold on the plan. It was one of Papa's favorite stories.

On August 18, 1896, five months after his first meeting with Mr. Miller, my father became the new publisher of the *New York Times*. He was thirty-eight years old. In the next day's issue the editorial page carried an announcement of the change of management and a statement by the new publisher that began:

"It will be my earnest aim that the *New York Times* give the news, all the news, in concise and attractive form, in language that is parliamentary in good society, and give it as early, if not earlier, than it can be learned through any reliable medium; to give the news impartially, without fear or favor, regardless of party, sect, or interest involved; to make the columns of the *New York Times* a forum for the consideration of all questions of public importance, and to that end to invite intelligent discussion from all shades of opinion."

It was a rather ringing statement. What chance, people asked, did this man from Tennessee have with this respectable but dying newspaper? He was competing with flamboyant characters like William Randolph Hearst, Joseph Pulitzer and James Gordon Bennett who had all the money they needed and were putting out extras with flaming headlines every hour on the hour.

The newspaper world was very skeptical. How were they to know that the principles my father set forth in his first issue of the *New York Times* weren't just rhetoric—that Adolph Simon Ochs meant what he said?

4

The Gerald was a second-rate hotel in New York City's theatrical district, catering mostly to vaudeville people. The rooms were musty and the toilets were at the end of the hall. I doubt that we would have stayed at the Gerald if my father had known what it was like, but he was too engrossed with his new venture to make the arrangements for our arrival and the rooms had been booked by his cousin Ben Franck, who worked as his assistant at the office.

My mother and I moved into the hotel from our Cedar Street house, and my father, who had been living at the Astor House on Broadway and Barclay Street, near the *New York Times* building, joined us there shortly afterward. I was four years old and I thought the Gerald was simply grand. I remember playing in the hallway with another little girl, running up and down and having a wonderful time, but we stayed there for only two weeks before moving into a house on East Thirty-ninth Street, near Lexington Avenue.

This was a very narrow house, several stories high, and, once you were inside, it seemed as though there was only one direction to go—up. There were so many stairs that it was like a wooden mountain. The house stood on a little hill, and down the block I could see the Third Avenue El. My father rode to work on the train. Every evening I would watch and wait for him, and when I saw him I'd race down the hill to meet him. We'd walk back home together for dinner.

We rented there for one year. Two of the Chattanooga house staff lived with us—my nurse, Susan Arnold, who was very black and whom I loved very much, and her son, Willie. Mrs. Arnold did the cooking and housekeeping. Willie did odd chores. Occasionally he'd take me to Central Park. I remember going there because I got some valuable information from a policeman who patrolled the park. He told me I must never step on the cracks in the pavement because that's where the candy grew.

Almost every Sunday my father would take me for a walk around the reservoir at Forty-second Street and Fifth Avenue— where the New York Public Library now stands—and into the adjoining Bryant Park. One Sunday, when we were on Madison Avenue on our way home, we came upon a large crowd and a great deal of commotion. Papa hoisted me on his shoulders. It was such a thrill, for there were the President of the United States, William McKinley, and his wife.

Our lease expired in the fall of 1897 and we moved into the Majestic Hotel, at Seventy-second Street and Central Park West, and from there into our next home. Somehow my father had discovered a family by the name of Read who had a brownstone at 14 West Seventy-second Street and wanted to rent the second floor. What made the offer particularly attractive was that the Reads had six children. My father, who had been raised in a family of six children, and my mother, who had fourteen in her family, worried about my being an only child. They felt that in the Read house I would have instant brothers and sisters.

Mr. Read was an Englishman. He was small and pleasant and

had the most unusual occupation—he was a tea taster. Mrs. Read was an enormous woman who was always bossing people around. The children were fine, as far as I was concerned, and one of them, Hermia, eighteen months my senior, became my playmate in the park after school. Hermia was my dearest friend until we were eleven or twelve.

The Reads had another family for boarders, a Mrs. Newhouse and her grown son and daughter. Mrs. Newhouse used to call me the "human interrogation point," because I was always asking questions. She was the daughter of a rich Louisville brewer and the first woman I ever met who had gone to college. She was a Vassar graduate, but acted more like a tavern keeper's daughter, talking freely about divorcing her first husband because he was a crook who wound up in jail, and about how, when her second husband died, she lost all his money on Wall Street. I liked the old gal. She had a spark in her and was very much alive.

About a year after we moved into the brownstone, the Reads bought another town house on the same street, at No. 144, and all three families transferred to the new location. How we all fitted into these houses is a mystery to me. After another two years my parents decided to move into a more spacious apartment at 2030 Broadway, at the corner of Seventieth Street. It was on the fourth floor of a brand-new ten-story building and had ten rooms. Although it was poorly planned by today's standards, it had one modern luxury we'd never had before—electric lights.

One thing I shall never forget about that apartment was the den. My mother decorated it in a most extraordinary manner. There was a big couch with a tent-like canopy over it. The tent was adorned with swords and daggers and pistols. The weapons were fakes, but you'd never know it by looking at them. In front of the couch were tables inlaid with mother-of-pearl, and the draperies were embroidered in an exotic Oriental design. This entire arrangement was meant to resemble a Turkish corner. That was the going fad; my mother purchased the complete affair from a shop called Flint's.

To me it was a most marvelous place. I used to crawl under the tent onto the couch, and in my imagination I would be Ali Baba riding through the desert chasing the forty thieves, the sun scorching my back. Sometimes the couch was made up as an extra guest bed. Our visitors must have had to be very courageous to sleep there.

Some of my friends who lived in that building had most unusual names. One playmate was Chella Otisa Ingals, another was Zulu Gaddis, and one little girl, who was American of Irish descent, had the misfortune of being born in Egypt and named Egypta Nila Slavin. With friends like these, I could never be too self-conscious about having an unusual name like Iphigene.

Broadway in those days was called "the boulevard." On Sundays, people would stroll or ride their bicycles; my father and his friends used to bicycle out as far as Coney Island. Then construction of the IRT subway began, and I remember leaning out the window and watching the men dig a tunnel beside our building. One time I leaned out too far and might have fallen out if one of the Read boys hadn't caught me. After that, my parents had guards fitted on all the windows.

After several years we moved again. My parents met a Mrs. Bondi, an enterprising woman who invited them to dinner at her house at the corner of West End Avenue and Eighty-third Street—with, apparently, rental in mind. By the time my parents left that night, they had rented the house and all the furnishings. There was less space at Mrs. Bondi's, and the Turkish corner had to go. However, one advantage to the house was that it had a bathroom on each of the three upper floors.

One of the greatest trials of my childhood was taking piano lessons from Nelly Levy. Nelly was one of my father's cousins, and I disliked her thoroughly. Moreover, I had little aptitude for music, and the piano was in the front parlor, a dark and unfriendly room full of furniture carved with angels and gargoyles. Eventually, my parents realized that Nelly was wasting her time, and the lessons were stopped.

The cultural institutions of New York were my classroom. From the time I was five or six, my mother was frequently taking me on excursions about the city.

From our home on Seventy-second Street we would walk across Central Park to the Metropolitan Museum of Art. It would always be on a Monday, because we liked to watch the young artists who were allowed into the museum that day with their paints and easels.

By copying the great masters, the artist would learn painting techniques. Mastering skills was necessary in those days, when "self-expression" without technique was unheard of.

As we wandered about the museum, my mother saw a story in each canvas. The more dramatic the story she told, the more the painting would appeal to me. One of my favorite paintings was "The Last Token." A beautiful Christian girl stood in a Roman arena. A rose lay at her feet. The girl gazed mournfully into the crowd to see what last friend had tossed her the rose. Close beside her, a black leopard was crawling out of its den.

Later, the painting was stored away in the museum's cellar. Most of the other pictures I grew up with, many from the Huntington and Vanderbilt collections—then the height of fashion—suffered a similarly sad fate. Many of them were sold to other museums or remain buried in the Metropolitan's archives. "The Last Token," I was glad to see, was recently put back on exhibit. It was like seeing an old friend. I was told this was the picture most admired by one of the first delegations from the People's Republic of China to tour the museum. It seems that the Chinese and I share a preference for realism.

Another painting that made a great impression on me as a child was of John Brown being led to his execution. His hands are tied behind his back, and, as he passes a crowd of onlookers, a black woman holds up her baby for him to kiss. Mama was deeply troubled by injustices inflicted on Negroes and I too became upset. I remember seeing a stage performance of *Uncle Tom's Cabin*—Eliza running across the ice floes, her baby clutched in her arms, the men and bloodhounds in pursuit—all of it very real to me, and pretty terrifying.

My mother started taking me to the theater from the time I was five. Nearly every Saturday we'd see a matinee. We'd see musical comedies, melodrama, new plays and Shakespeare and other classics. Both my parents were avid theatergoers. Back in Chattanooga my father had helped to raise money to build an opera house, and traveling companies would perform there.

My father particularly enjoyed musical comedies. He saw *Beauty and the Beast* five or six times. When he took me to one of the performances, I was left cold, since the Prince was played by a lady with a large bosom and big hips and the King and Queen were played by two comedians, both men.

My father's taste in music extended about as far as *Floradora*. My mother, however, was devoted to classical music, went to concerts frequently and enjoyed the Metropolitan Opera. Papa bought her season tickets for Monday nights in the orchestra section, and Aunt Nannie or I would often accompany her. (Papa would do so only as a social duty, on each season's opening night.)

I saw my first opera, *Siegfried*, at the age of ten, and was thrilled. I also loved the Italian and French operas in which Enrico Caruso appeared. He had the most fantastic voice—I've never heard it equaled. When the new Met was built at Lincoln Center, I endowed seats A101 and A102—the same seat numbers Mama always had—in memory of Mama and Aunt Nannie.

My mother would also take me on shopping excursions. Ready-to-wear clothes were introduced just about then, and Mama would insist that I make the selections. "You're the one who is going to wear it," she would say. I thought this showed a certain respect for my intelligence, and was grateful. I was also relieved to be free of the frilly clothes I had been dressed in as a young child. I grew up in the Little Lord Fauntleroy era, so I had had far too much lace, which didn't suit me at all. I remember having dresses that were trimmed with the laces and embroidery of my mother's trousseau underwear.

Sometimes, when my mother wanted to shop for herself at the department stores on Twenty-third Street, she would leave a friend and me off at the nearby Eden Musée waxworks. There, in the basement, lighted in a gloomy red, was the chamber of horrors. One scene depicted an old Hindu practice—an Indian woman being burned alive on her husband's funeral pyre. Her head and eyes rolled back in agony, and the mechanism that made her head move made a frightful groaning sound. Another scene, called "Execution in Siam," showed an enormous elephant with its foot poised over a man's head, about to crush it. A scene from the Spanish Inquisition exhibit had a man being tortured with hot irons.

That chamber of horrors was a truly terrifying place, and it left me with an abhorrence of cruelty. Ever since, I have avoided looking at the horror scenes in movies and plays. When the nasty bits come up, I simply close my eyes and cover my ears. I have also avoided prizefights and bullfights. The one time my husband Arthur invited me to accompany him to a prizefight, I refused, saying, "Since I would sit with my eyes shut, it would be cheaper and more comfortable to do it at home."

Those times I spent with my mother when I was a child hold many happy memories. She had a keen sense of humor, and there was a great deal of pixie in her. My father once told me he didn't think he could have made such a success of his business had he had any other kind of wife. She demanded so little. Many of the women of their acquaintance had social ambitions and were always dragging their husbands to parties. Mama, on the other hand, preferred to stay at home, letting my father devote himself to his work without wasting energy on meaningless socializing.

My mother was not an easy person to characterize. I remember telling her when I was a young woman that she reminded me of one of those little Chinese toys that always straighten up when you knock them down. She was an individualist and a freethinker, yet she was not the type to ruffle any feathers, and she got along well with everyone. Her habit of sleeping late in the mornings was one she retained all her life. I used to tell her that she would have made a good charwoman, for in the middle of the night, while everyone else was sleeping, she would get up and wander about the house to see if things were in order. She would move the furniture, check the icebox—do all the things that most people do during the day. Then she would go back to bed and sleep till noon.

When I wasn't following my mother around the city, there would be excursions with my father. Sometimes we'd just go to the *Times* office on Park Row or for a walk in Central Park. On occasion, he would take me somewhere more special.

One evening we were to hear Booker T. Washington speak at Carnegie Hall. My grandmother Ochs was visiting, and this plan outraged her. "How can you be taking your child out to hear that darkie!"

Papa responded very calmly but very firmly: "Mr. Washington is a great man, and Iphigene should hear him."

Those words made quite an impression on me. My father was

· 34 ·

the very first person I ever heard say that a Negro could be a great man.

We went to Carnegie Hall. Before the lecture, a choral group from the Tuskegee Institute performed, and I liked them. But Mr. Washington was a great disappointment. I had imagined him a heroic figure with jet-black skin, but he turned out to be quite light and no different in dress or manner from the white gentlemen who came around the house.

The evening was saved for me by an unexpected meeting. Among the whites who had come to hear Mr. Washington was a man in a white suit, with a shock of white hair and a great white mustache. My father introduced me to him as the future publisher of the *New York Times*. I forgave him the levity. It was a great moment for me. I was shaking the hand of one of my favorite authors—Mark Twain.

It is interesting today to recall what an uproar there was when President Theodore Roosevelt invited Booker T. Washington to lunch at the White House. It almost tore the country apart. My father was involved in a similar situation on a local scale when he invited the Negro singer Roland Hayes, a fellow Chattanoogan, to lunch at the *New York Times*. Mr. Hayes's Carnegie Hall concert was sold out, but my father's social invitation was widely regarded as scandalous.

Accompanying my father, I met many interesting people. On Sundays we'd often call on Andrew Carnegie. He lived in a big house on Ninety-first Street and Fifth Avenue. I would sit in his library while the two men discussed world affairs and business matters. Most of their conversation was over my head, but I'd listen carefully and try to understand. I remember Mr. Carnegie talking to me once at great length about his ideas for a new phonetic system of spelling. I was agreeing enthusiastically when Papa interrupted us and said that I couldn't spell any other way. I was humiliated.

On some Sundays we'd visit the Daniel Guggenheims, or the Sterns of Stern's department store (who had one of the first big advertising accounts with the *Times*) or the Jacob Schiffs or other prominent New Yorkers. Papa took me along because he wanted me to share in matters that interested him. And he wanted to be close to his little girl.

My father concerned himself with my studies and was always encouraging me to improve. "I think you could do it better," he would say. This was disheartening when I had been making a great effort, but I soon realized that he just wanted me to do my best. He had the highest expectations of me. He believed in my ability, and that gave me a great deal of confidence when I was growing up.

My favorite time with Father was when we'd walk together in Central Park. Because of him I've had a lifetime of enjoyment from walking. We'd set out, he in his high silk hat, stiff collar and cut-away coat—the dress all gentlemen wore when strolling in the park on Sunday—and I wearing a black velvet coat, a hat plumed with ostrich feathers, and a muff that hung from a ribbon around my neck. To complete the outfit, I wore black stockings and black high-laced shoes. We must have made a nice picture, Papa and I.

As we strolled along, Papa would entertain me with stories he'd make up. Every Sunday I'd hear a different episode of some marvelous saga. When my governess, Mademoiselle Christine Hegi, left to get married, he improvised a whole new series. "Once there was this beautiful Swiss governess," he began, "and a very rich young man who wanted to marry her." For reasons that now escape me, she wouldn't consent to being his wife.

Each Sunday would begin a new adventure, as the young man tried one scheme after another to change her mind. The episode I remember best was the last one. The suitor had himself wrapped in a brown-paper parcel and mailed to his love. The postman delivered him to her door, and she had to accept the parcel because the postman refused to return it. So they were married and lived happily ever after.

The stories would always end just as we'd reach the Carousel or the Sheep Meadow. There were actual sheep grazing in those days, and I loved to watch them. Near the meadow was a small building where they sold bubbly Saratoga spring water flavored with syrup, and we would stop to sample some.

One day Papa hired an electric hansom cab for a Sunday-afternoon ride. There was great excitement. I had never ridden in a horseless carriage before. We were still living with the Reads at that time, and three Read children came along with us. The driver operated the vehicle from the rear and the passengers sat up front, so we had a wonderful view as we drove from Seventy-second Street up to Grant's Tomb and back.

Everything was fine until we got home and my father told me to say good night to Mrs. Read. I was tired, and cross because I didn't want to go to bed, so I refused to say good night. At that, my father took me over his knee and gave me a spanking. I was enraged. I felt that he was violating my sense of dignity and propriety. He was also taking advantage of my size. I remember screaming that I hated him. I vowed I would have nothing more to do with him, not ever again.

That declaration took all the spirit out of him, and he spent the next three weeks apologizing. From then on, I had him wrapped around my little finger.

5

When I was five, my parents engaged a Swiss governess to teach me French. Her name was Mlle Hortense. Though not what one expects of a governess—there were never any scheduled lessons— she spoke and read to me in French, and this gave me a good foundation in the language. But Mlle Hortense left to be married and my parents hired another French-speaking governess. Her name was Hélène, and she was from Belgium. We were spending that summer in Atlantic City, and Hélène and her boyfriend took my cousin Julius and me to a striptease joint on the boardwalk. I was only seven and didn't understand why these women should be taking off all their clothes in front of so many people. I asked my parents about it, and that, of course, was the end of Mlle Hélène.

My third governess, Christine Hegi, was from Lausanne. She stayed with us until I was about eleven, and under her tutelage I became fluent in French. She used to read me the most wonderful stories—Jules Verne and a series of books called the *Bibliothèque Rose*, by the Countess of Segur. A particular favorite of mine was a book called *Sans Famille*, which told of the adventures of a wandering trio—an abandoned child, a kind old man and a dog that did tricks. After all their hardships, it was discovered that the child was the missing heir of a member of the British royalty. Christine was young, attractive and charming, and would have stayed with us longer if it hadn't been for the reappearance of her long-lost boyfriend, Fritz Keller.

We were living in Mrs. Bondi's house when Fritz cabled Christine from Basel and said he wanted to marry her. This was the first Christine had heard from Fritz in the three years she'd been with us, and she didn't know what to do. She liked the young architect but wasn't sure about marrying him. My mother, my aunts and the various visitors in the house all had opinions. They chittered and chattered all that day, giving Mademoiselle all kinds of advice, and it wasn't until my father came home that the matter was settled. Christine, he pointed out, could decide after seeing Fritz again. In the excitement, everyone had forgotten that we were soon to go on a trip to Switzerland.

The couple was reunited in Chamonix. After two hours they announced their engagement. Mademoiselle's seventeen-year-old brother, Edward, was there as chaperon. My father, afraid of Edward's being in the way, took him aside and engaged him in conversation. Papa ended up by offering the young man a job at the *Times*. Edward joined the paper later that year, and eventually became chief cashier.

Christine and Fritz settled in Switzerland and had four sons. I would always visit them when traveling abroad.

My mother also took her turn at tutoring me. When I was seven or so, she gave me a set of history books written especially for children learning to read—all the words divided into syllables. I had little chance to read them, however, because my mother so enjoyed reading aloud to me.

She usually selected stories from history, mythology and the Bible—she was passionately fond of all three. Then there were stories like Hawthorne's *Wonder-Book* and *Tanglewood Tales*.

Dickens's *Child's History of England* made a great impression on me. It was the horror of those times that struck me—Bloody Mary burning Protestants at the stake, and the Protestants hanging or drawing and quartering the Catholics when they regained power. I used to have nightmares about it. Other stories that gave me horrible dreams were by the Brothers Grimm. Children are subjected to a lot of frightening material when they are growing up.

My occasional lessons at home hadn't prepared me for the rigors of Dr. Sachs's School for Girls. I was eight then, and that was the first school I attended. My record there was far from distinguished. I was constantly in trouble. I misspelled words and made careless mistakes in mathematics. Assignments took longer for me than for any of the other students. I would never finish on time, and then I'd have to do the work over again as punishment. Only when I was allowed to do the assignments at my own slow pace, or when it was a question of memorizing something, was my work satisfactory.

My teachers thought I wasn't paying proper attention. No one suspected that I had a mild eye disorder that caused me to reverse the positions of letters and numbers. No one realized that my father had the same problem. When he read aloud, he always hesitated, as though having to study each word before pronouncing it. This eye dysfunction wasn't understood in those days, and the school kept sending notes to my mother saying, "Please do not read aloud to this child any longer. She must learn to read by herself." These notes didn't worry my parents; they thought I was brilliant. When I didn't get good marks, they thought it was the school's fault, not mine.

At Dr. Sachs's School for Girls we studied reading, writing, arithmetic, history, French and German. The German teacher was Madame Zeek. I got to know her quite well because of my ineptitude with the language. I suppose I was a bit tired of conjugating German verbs the day I brought a mechanical mouse to school and sent it scampering across her classroom floor. Madame Zeek really let out some shriek. I thought I'd be reported, but she went easy on me.

I never did develop any fluency in German. In fact, Dr. Sachs's school didn't do much for my educational development as a whole. But then, the school did have inadequacies. My parents first began to take notice of them when I developed eyestrain.

The school was housed in an old narrow office building at 116 West Fifty-ninth Street. There were few windows, so many of the classrooms had artificial lighting. Even so, the lighting was dim and made reading very difficult. My eyes became red and sore, and when I had to go to the optometrist, my mother insisted that Dr. Sachs change the lighting arrangements in his classroom. He did. He repartitioned the rooms so that no classroom would be left without a window. Each now had half a window. It was even darker than before.

My parents assumed that the situation had been corrected and never came to the school to see. It wasn't that they didn't care; they just had faith that all was well.

The nearest my parents ever got to that school was when my father left me at the entrance in the mornings. Although he was working hard and keeping long hours, he would walk me to school nearly every morning. We used to go down Broadway, and one winter we kept meeting the same two children every day. One was a little girl who looked Germanic and had long braids. With her was a little black boy who had the brightest of smiles. We used to nod and wave to each other. When Christmastime came, my father bought some candy for them. I remember running up to them and saying, "Merry Christmas!" and giving them the present. Never again will I see two more startled children.

After five years, my days at Dr. Sachs's came to an abrupt and explosive end. Dr. Sachs was highly regarded as an educator, and later became a professor at Columbia Teachers College. He was also German, and his temper would flare whenever a student violated his stern disciplinary approach to learning. One day he entered our classroom and started shouting about something, terrifying us all, then suddenly stopped and pointed his finger at me. He was red with rage.

"You're laughing!" he bellowed.

"No, sir," I said. I was certainly too terrified to laugh, but he was not convinced.

"I want to see you after class."

I went to his office. While he was lecturing me and shouting at me, I said nothing. I just looked at him. Evidently, the expression on my face was not properly contrite, for he stopped his raving and demanded, "What are you thinking about?"

A burst of truth and courage overcame me and I said, "I think you have no business talking to me the way you are." It was my undoing.

Dr. Sachs was still in a fit of anger when my governess arrived to collect me. He related the episode, and so embellished my retort that it sounded like a treatise and not the passions of a twelve-year-old girl. That infuriated me. I burst into a flood of tears and yelled at the top of my voice: "He's a liar!"

When my mother heard the story she was sympathetic. Nothing her little angel did could be wrong. Besides, she had never been very fond of the school or of Dr. Sachs. Be that as it may, she never uttered an unkind thing about anyone. Not that she didn't have her opinions. But she used to tell me, "If people aren't worth liking, they aren't worth thinking about, and certainly not worth talking about."

When my father heard my version, he was a little more skeptical. He insisted that I finish out the year; there were only two or three weeks left. Somehow he got Dr. Sachs to agree. And so it was that I left Dr. Sachs's school, expelled for impertinence at the age of twelve.

After my rather checkered career as a student, my father felt I needed a governess who could teach me a bit of discipline. Christine had just left to be married, and he engaged another Swiss woman. Her name was Mlle Berle. She was a tyrant. She had been governess to descendants of the Baron von Münchhausen and had acquired a rigid Germanic idea of discipline. She had two dresses—uniforms really. They were tailored exactly alike. The black one she wore on weekdays and the white one on Sundays. She did her best to regiment me, and I rebelled. I constantly staged bad-temper scenes. Fortunately, her regimentation began to disturb my parents, and after she spent a summer with us in Europe my father let her go. The only redeeming thing about Mlle Berle was that she introduced me to the Baron von Münchhausen stories.

They were fantastic nonsense tales about the Baron's travels. I remember one in which he was riding through the Siberian snow looking for a lost village and came upon some sticks propped upright in the snow. He tied his horse to one of the sticks and went to sleep. When he awoke, the snow had melted, and he found himself lying in a village square. The poor horse was hanging by its harness in midair. The stick it was tied to turned out to be the steeple of the village church.

After Mlle Berle left, I felt I no longer needed a governess. My father thought otherwise and hired an Irishwoman through a London agency. Henrietta MacDonnell must have been in her fifties when she joined our household. She was a handsome woman with a retroussé nose and vivid blue eyes. I imagine that she was very pretty when she was young. She had been educated in France and spoke French perfectly. Before she came to us she had been employed as governess by the family of the French Minister to Persia. I was still in a rebellious mood toward governesses and did my best to provoke Miss MacDonnell into leaving. Being a calm, intelligent woman, she took me into her room one day and said, "You know, I've never been in America before. I've left all my family in England. I'd hoped that you'd take the place of my favorite niece." With that, my attitude softened. I soon realized that she was gentle and kind, and we became great friends.

Miss MacDonnell was horrified to find that, though twelve, I read so poorly. She would sit me down and say, "Now, you read one paragraph, and I'll read you the next." Because of her patience I finally did learn to read. From then on I was never without a book in my hand, even when I was brushing my hair. I had long hair and would sit for hours in front of the mirror, brushing with one hand while with the other I'd be turning the pages of Dickens, Thackeray or any other author I could find in my parents' library.

Miss MacDonnell was very proper. She wouldn't let me soak in the bathtub, as I liked to, because she said it was indulging the flesh. She got this notion from the convent school she'd attended as a young girl. There, when they bathed, they had to wear nightgowns. At least I didn't have to do that.

I have no doubt that Miss MacDonnell could have taken full charge of my education, for she was an excellent teacher. But there was no escaping school, and my parents enrolled me with the Misses Ely, who ran a boarding school in an old-fashioned wooden building on Riverside Drive, between Eighty-fifth and Eighty-sixth streets. I had been attending that school as a day pupil for one year when the Misses Ely moved to the suburbs. I wanted very much to go with them, so I suggested to my parents that I become a boarder. My parents thought that unnecessary.

I was enrolled next at our neighborhood school, Benjamin Dean, run by a Mrs. Benjamin and a Mrs. Dean. I spent four years there— the equivalent of high school—and they were four years pretty much wasted. It was a poor school. I was bored. I disliked most of the teachers and most of the girls. I spent a large part of my time daydreaming, wishing I were somewhere else.

It was Miss MacDonnell's encouragement that kept me from turning my back on education altogether. She'd find me books that made otherwise dull material interesting. And it was Miss Mac-Donnell's support that helped me gain my independence from my father. That was a struggle, because my father didn't want me to grow up. I was his little girl, and I had to fight to be treated like an adult. When I needed support on one petition or another, I would turn to Miss MacDonnell, not to my mother. Mama simply wasn't a fair critic; in her eyes whatever I did was right.

So, as I grew older, Miss MacDonnell's position changed subtly from that of governess to that of ally. And when by everyone's consent I finally outgrew the need for a governess, Miss MacDon-nell stayed on with the family to run the house. The efficiency she brought to that task enabled my parents to start entertaining at home. She became practically a member of the family. All of us had deep respect and affection for her. Yet she always remained "Miss MacDonnell." My parents were very formal that way.

6

It was August 1896, and the days were stifling hot. In the offices and composing room of the *New York Times* at 41 Park Row, the staff moved about sullenly. They feared that the paper was on the point of failure, and that the collapse would come once this unknown Southerner, Adolph Ochs, took charge. This was the melancholy atmosphere in which my father began to pull the *Times* back from the grave.

The task before him was Herculean. He handed over to his two brothers the operation of the Chattanooga paper. During the first few weeks on the new job, he slept only five or six hours a night. He spent every waking hour at the *Times*, interviewing its editors, reporters, printers, newsboys, advertising salesmen—everyone involved in the operation of the paper. He sought their opinions and kept his office door open to all. He knew what he wanted done—he was very positive that way—but he was never autocratic in his approach. He worked *with* people, not over them; he made them feel good about what they were doing, and won their confidence. They began to put everything they had into their work, and their depression vanished.

The paper got a face-lift. My father changed the typeface and bought new ink and newsprint, making the paper cleaner and easier to read, as he had done with the *Chattanooga Times* eighteen years earlier. While cutting back on operational expenses, he added an illustrated Sunday supplement and a Saturday book-review section, which brought in new advertising. And he kept his promise to give the news straight. While the other New York papers fought a ruthless and unscrupulous battle for circulation by means of outrageous headlines and sensational stories, the *Times* sought to expand readership with sober and comprehensive reporting.

Two months into his new career, my father launched a big promotional campaign to implant his policy in the public mind. He offered a hundred dollars to anyone who could make up a better ten-word slogan for the paper than the one he himself had coined, the seven-word "All the News That's Fit to Print." Thousands of entries poured in from around the nation, and the prize went to D. M. Redfield, of New Haven, Connecticut, for "All the World News, But Not a School for Scandal." In the end, settling on the slogan to run in the top left-hand corner of the front page, my father decided—wisely, I think—to stay with his own creation. It quickly became a household phrase, and it still is.

My father's competitors scoffed at his objectives, never thinking that a sober newspaper that printed "dull" news would survive. The *Sun*, an urbane and brilliantly written paper, expressed that view to perfection when it entered my father's competition with the slogan "Why is the *New York Times* published? God only knows."

The *Sun* was famous for its wisecracks. One day a water main burst in front of the *Times* building, flooding the pressroom and holding up publication for several hours. It wasn't a serious accident, but the *Sun*, caricaturing the *Times*'s comprehensive style, published a lengthy story enumerating every detail and making a minor mishap into a major event. The story ended, "We are glad to reassure our readers that the *New York Times* will come out tomorrow as dry as ever." My father was delighted with this little satire and took great pleasure in recounting it over the years.

The new leadership began paying off almost immediately. Circulation and advertising revenue started a steady climb, and in a mere twelve months the profits were higher than they had been for fifteen years. Support and congratulations came from all over the country, even from the White House. What my father achieved in the fierce competition of a complex metropolis made journalistic history. For two years the *Times* surged forward at an extraordinary pace. Then, in the autumn of 1898, the paper's circulation began slipping.

The Spanish-American War had broken out, and there was a lust in the nation to know every gruesome detail of the battle. The giants of turn-of-the-century journalism, William Randolph Hearst and Joseph Pulitzer, had been fostering that lust with bloodcurdling stories about Spanish oppression in Cuba. Now they went all out to feed the morbid curiosity they had created in their readers. They could afford to send their own correspondents, including famous writers like Richard Harding Davis, to every front, while the *Times* couldn't and had to rely on the Associated Press. It was America's most jingoistic era, and Hearst's *Journal*, Pulitzer's *World* and James Gordon Bennett's *Herald* boomed, taking readership away from the *Times*.

My father regained some of the readers by expanding business and financial coverage, but, by itself, this wasn't enough to save the paper. He knew he had to do something radical—and he did. He cut the price of the *Times* from three cents to one penny. It was an enormous gamble financially and much criticized on another ground: The hallmark of yellow journalism was the one-cent paper, and it was feared that the *Times*'s prestige would drop with the price.

My father, insisting that "a person's intelligence can't be measured by his pocketbook," stood firm. Within a year, circulation tripled. The *Times* had come through; he had won.

To celebrate the end of the Spanish-American War, a gala

parade took place in New York. It went directly past our home on Seventy-second street. In those days, people would have their own private reviewing stands built over the front stoops of their brownstones, and my father had a stand erected and draped with red, white and blue bunting. For me, at the age of six, it was thrilling to watch the soldiers march past and to give them fruit and sandwiches when they came to a halt in front of the house. But my proudest moment came when the distinguished citizens of New York City rode by in their landaus. One of the honored participants in that parade of horse-drawn open carriages was Papa.

On occasion, my father would take me for a day's excursion to the *Times* building on Park Row. The street was usually referred to as Printers' Row, or Newspaper Row, because that's where most New York papers had their offices. Across the street was City Hall.

Sometimes I would attend editorial conferences, and would have to sit quietly for what seemed like years. What I liked best was visiting the composing room. The printers would let me push buttons on the linotype machines, and they'd set my name in type. Some of the men there had been old friends of my father ever since his days as a printer in Knoxville. Printers, reporters or editors, my father considered all of them his family, and his proudest boast was that he had maintained the same staff from those desperate days when the paper had been hopelessly in debt.

Now the paper's profits increased year by year, and on August 14, 1899, the stocks that had been held in escrow were released and Adolph S. Ochs obtained full control of the *New York Times*. His greatest dream had come true—and, to make it even better, the *Chattanooga Times* was out of debt, just as he had predicted.

By 1901, after six years under my father's leadership, the circulation of the *New York Times* had grown from 9,000 to over 100,000. It was truly astounding, and even his sharpest critics applauded his success. My father responded, "I merely proved that, given the chance, the reading public would choose a newspaper that presented the news without coloring. I knew it would work out that way."

By 1902, the *Times* was outgrowing the Park Row building, and my father was looking for a new site. Once again he went against the grain of the city's newspaper publishing tradition. Only one other paper, the *Herald*, had left Printers' Row, moving out of the general business district to Thirty-fifth Street and Sixth Avenue. My father went even farther uptown and found a location at a place then called Longacre Square, at Forty-second Street and Broadway.

Before making a final decision, he sought the advice of his old friend and severest critic—the *Times*'s counsel, Leopold Wallach. Mr. Wallach considered most Ochs schemes reckless and excessively costly. The two men arrived at the site one Sunday morning, and my father told him of his grand plan, which involved demolishing the buildings occupying the site (the Pabst Hotel and four brownstones) and provided for delivering the papers by subway, which was still under construction.

Mr. Wallach's reaction was completely out of character. He kept saying, "Great idea. Excellent. Fine idea, Adolph."

My father was miffed. At last he turned to his friend and said, "What's the matter with you? You've never approved of anything I've done before. What's come over you?"

To this, Wallach replied, "Adolph, you're never happy unless you're in trouble. If you put up this building, you'll be in trouble up to your neck!"

I laid the cornerstone of the new Times Tower at Forty-second Street and Broadway on January 18, 1904. It was a frightfully cold day, and to my humiliation, and despite my tears, my mother insisted that I wear long underwear. There was a small crowd assembled for the occasion, some dignitaries and the people from the *Times*. Bishop Henry Potter gave the invocation, then Charles Miller made a short speech. I was next.

Carefully coached in my part, I stepped up to the cornerstone and recited the dedication speech that my father had written. I had it well memorized; I can still recite it.

"I dedicate this building to the uses of the *New York Times*. May those who labor herein see the right and serve it with courage and intelligence for the welfare of mankind, the best interests of the United States and its people, and for decent and dignified journalism, and may the blessings of God ever rest upon them."

The stone was lowered. As I patted it with a silver trowel, I concluded:

"I declare this stone to be plump, level and square."

There was a great deal of mirth around me. I had said "plump" instead of "plumb." I was a little upset about that, but the building stood.

7

New York bustled with vitality and strained with growth. The first of the uptown skyscrapers, the Flatiron Building, was being built. Gasoline buggies were replacing horse-drawn carriages. New bridges over the East River were under construction, and Brooklyn and Queens were being built up to take in the overflow of people streaming into Manhattan. The brisk tempo brought further expansion to the *Times*. New businesses advertised, and the circulation grew steadily. Success came to our family in dollars as well as prestige.

The household was in a turmoil of excitement the day an invitation arrived from the White House. My father was invited to lunch with President Theodore Roosevelt. I was nine years old, and upon my father's return I cross-examined him on every detail of the visit. He said that the President had spoken proudly of his own children, and that he had responded by boasting about me.

What completely overwhelmed me was the arrival, a few days later, of a package from the President of the United States, addressed to me. Inside was a photograph of the President, inscribed: "To Miss Iphigene Ochs with regards of Theodore Roosevelt." I wrote to thank him for the gift and ended the note: "With love and kisses." I'm sure the President, having young children of his own, understood my salutations.

A few years later, when my uncle Jim Molony took his daughter and me to Washington, we called on the President in his White House office. I remember nothing of the conversation, but I do recall we were interrupted by a group of visitors who were ushered into the room to shake hands with the President. He greeted them cordially, one by one; the last was a little girl of about six, holding her father's hand. President Roosevelt took a rose from a vase on his desk and gave it to the child. The group left, and the President, turning to Uncle Jim, winked and said, "Only half a minute to get 'em for life."

I also remember when Mr. Roosevelt's successor, William Howard Taft, came to our house at 308 West Seventy-fifth Street for a lunch with the editors of the *Times*. Secret Service men stationed themselves all about the house. The butlers from Sherry's catering service stood at attention. There were flowers everywhere. Miss MacDonnell seemed satisfied, as she stood with Mother and me waiting for the President at the living-room door. She had orchestrated the entire event.

In walked the President. I said, "How do you do?" I remember being struck by his enormous size. He was a great, round bulk of a man. He seemed most affable, altogether a pleasant person. The men proceeded into the dining room. It was a men's lunch. None of the editors' wives were invited. That was the last I saw of the President. But I did get a new dress for the occasion.

In those days, children were not invited to formal lunches or dinners until they were at least eighteen; until then, they were considered part of the nursery. However, although I was only sixteen when Guglielmo Marconi came to a party at our Seventy-fifth Street home, I was invited to the dinner. I was to partner a boy about my age named Marcel Isaacs, who was the son of Marconi's business manager.

My father had close business ties with Mr. Marconi. As soon as the inventor had perfected his wireless telegraph, the *Times* arranged with him to transmit dispatches from Europe. It was the first newspaper to use the new invention. The foreign-news pages were headed: "By Marconi Wireless Telegraph to The New York Times." My father's enthusiasm was such that he bought some stock in Marconi's company. But then he recollected the enormous debt he had incurred by investing in Chattanooga real estate, and he sold the shares, taking a small loss but reaffirming his old vow not to put money into any company but his own.

Our dinner party for Mr. Marconi didn't go at all well as far as the guest of honor was concerned. He was seated between my mother and another very attractive but older woman, and seemed totally disinterested in their attempts at conversation. He was gracious enough when the company raised their glasses to him, responding that he couldn't have succeeded if it had not been for the work of his predecessors, but the rest of the time he slouched in his chair, looking bored and miserable.

After dinner, when the gentlemen joined the ladies in the living room, Mr. Marconi came up to me and said, "I like them young. Is there any place we can get off alone?" I was ecstatic. Mr. Marconi was then in his thirties and a handsome, attractive man. I said, "Yes. There's a library upstairs."

We disappeared—unnoticed, I thought. But Miss MacDonnell never missed a trick, and soon appeared in the library with my dinner partner, Marcel Isaacs, in tow. We were ushered back downstairs to the party.

Mr. Marconi's next visit to New York was much more successful. My father had realized that the inventor was not too interested in older people, no matter how prominent, and we went to Coney Island. I brought four friends along and we rode all the rides—"Shoot-the-Chute" was the best—and Mr. Marconi had a whale of a time. He had never had an ice-cream soda. We ordered one and drank from two straws. I was rather enamored of him. But my ardor was soon to be dampened. The next time he came to New York he was accompanied by a very good-looking Irishwoman—his wife.

Many famous people were to come through the front door of

our house to share a meal, discuss business and become our friends. But acquaintance with the powerful and important people of the world didn't alter my parents' ways. My mother wasn't overwhelmed by all the invitations to join the elite of society; she remained her gentle, aloof self, with no leanings toward social prominence. My father, while courted by business leaders, intellectuals and the powerful rich, never let that interfere with his concentration on rebuilding the *Times*. Having put the paper back on its feet, he now fastened on a new dream—to make the *Times* the most important newspaper in the country and in the world. He shunned the notoriety of Hearst, Pulitzer and Bennett, who used their newspapers to emblazon their family names. In fact, he forbade personal references to himself in the *Times*.

The deluge of social demands was met by Louis Wiley, the *Times*'s business manager. Mr. Wiley was a popular speaker, extraordinarily witty, and a reporter by instinct. He kept his ear to the ground and would often return from a social engagement with a lead to a news story. Audiences knew him as "Mr. Wiley of the *Times*." That he was only four feet seven inches tall and had a shiny bald head didn't interfere with his air of authority.

One evening my father was attending a social function when his dinner partner informed him of some newsworthy event. My father said he'd get a reporter on the story right away.

"Oh, don't bother," his companion said. "I know how to get it published. I'll just tell Mr. Wiley."

My father kept a straight face. "That's all the connection you need."

My father guided the *Times* to success by adhering steadfastly to lofty principles. Sometimes his allegiance to these principles interfered with his friendships and upset his family.

One longtime friend of his, Samuel Untermyer, a prominent and wealthy lawyer, was extremely offended when the *Times* printed a quotation about him that was quite unflattering. My father understood how he felt and offered to publish his rebuttal. Mr. Untermyer refused, and broke off relations. My father regretted the incident, but as he explained in a letter to his friend, "I have to print the news as long as it is accurate and worthy of interest. I can't suppress the facts to protect people—not even my friends." A year or so later Mr. Untermyer told my father he had come to understand his position, and their friendship was resumed. This incident made me an admirer of Samuel Untermyer for life. It takes a lot of courage to admit you were wrong.

One day when I was sixteen, I set my heart on a fur coat. But the maker of that coat, the Hudson Bay Fur Company, didn't advertise in the *Times*, and my father ruled out the purchase for that reason. I told the manufacturers of my predicament, and the next day a big ad appeared in the paper. I now had permission to buy the coat and did so at once.

The ad ran for only one day; the *Times* refused to print it again because upon investigation it found the company unreliable. My father's policy was to reject advertising that was dishonest or misleading. Shortly afterward, Hudson Bay Furs went out of business. And not too long after that, my coat fell apart. Papa was sympathetic. He bought me another one.

The *Times* influenced my life, and in an indirect way I influenced the *Times*. Because of me, the *New York Times*, for the first and last time in its history, ran a comic strip.

Papa disparaged the hours I would spend reading the "Katzenjammer Kids," "Foxy Grandpa" and other strips in the *World*, the *Journal* and the *Herald*. He thought them vulgar and not worth his daughter's time. He tried to encourage me to read the news instead, but I wasn't interested. Then he stopped having those Sunday papers delivered to the house. That didn't thwart me: I used my allowance to buy comic books. So he thought the best thing would be for the *Times* to run high-class comic strips for children. That's how "The Roosevelt Bears" came into being.

But they didn't stay long. The drawings were all right, but the verses relating the bears' adventures were wordy and uninteresting. I dutifully tried reading them, but it was too boring and I gave up. Papa gave up too. "The Roosevelt Bears" went into oblivion after only one and a half years.

Living up to the declaration my father made when he became publisher of the *Times*—"to give the news impartially, without fear or favor, regardless of any party, sect, or interest involved"—

meant many a hard struggle over the years. Friendships would have to be sacrificed, family matters would have to take a back seat. There would be times—many times—when the paper would suffer financially in order to uphold this ideal.

Early during my father's stewardship, the paper lost two of its largest advertising accounts because of stories it had published.

Wanamaker's, then one of the leading New York department stores, withdrew its advertising when the *Times* reported that John Wanamaker had spent large sums of money on his campaign for public office. The expenditure was not illegal, and the *Times* story made that clear. Nonetheless, Mr. Wanamaker was most upset. He asked my father for an apology. My father refused, and the account was lost.

A couple of years later, our family happened to meet Mr. Wanamaker's son during an ocean crossing to Europe. The young man came to like my father, and when he returned home he suggested that the store resume its advertising in the *Times*. Sure enough, the ads started reappearing. The demand for an apology was forgotten.

The other lost account involved an elevator accident that took place in Macy's around 1900. The *Times* reported the occurrence, and Nathan Straus, the owner of the store, was enraged by the bad publicity and pulled out all his ads. Nathan's brother Oscar was my father's close friend, and the episode nearly ruined the brothers' relationship. The subject was so volatile that a third Straus brother, Isidor, made it a rule that the name Adolph Ochs never be mentioned at a Straus family gathering.

Macy's kept its ads out of the *Times* for I don't know how many years. The feud was still going on when I became acquainted with old Nathan's son, Nathan, Jr. We had mutual friends, and some of them must have spoken well of me, for I was invited to Nathan's twenty-first birthday party. It was a dinner dance at the Harmonie Club, on Sixtieth Street off Fifth Avenue, and it was held in an upstairs room next to a roof garden, where we could go for a breath of fresh air between waltzes. The year was 1910 and Halley's comet was in the sky—a superb sight, a great tail of light that stretched across the heavens.

Nathan was amusing and bright, and I liked him right away.

We saw a lot of each other after that. I went to parties at his house and became acquainted with his father. Gradually, the old man came to like me in spite of his intense feelings about my father. I'm sure there must have been sound business reasons as well, but it was sometime around then that Macy's resumed advertising in the *Times*. There was no change, however, in old Nathan Straus's attitude toward my father. He still held his grudge.

Many years later the two men met by accident in Coronado Beach, in San Diego. My father had gone there to recover from an illness. Nathan was there on vacation. They talked, and Nathan took a shine to my father. They played golf together, and my father was amused by the old gentleman's retinue on the course— besides the caddie, he was escorted by a boy who carried an ice pack and another boy who shaded him with an umbrella. Nathan Straus became my father's devoted friend. When he died some years later, his papers contained the request that one of the pall-bearers at his funeral be Adolph Simon Ochs.

8

Our summers were lived to the full. The summer of 1898, the year after my mother, my father and I left the Ochs household in Chattanooga, was given over to a family reunion in a summer house my father rented in Atlantic City. The next eight summer vacations were spent either at this then fashionable resort or touring Europe or the United States.

In Atlantic City, my mother resumed her Chattanooga ways. She slept late in the mornings, had a dip in the ocean before lunch, and enjoyed shopping in the attractive stores along the boardwalk in the afternoons and going to the theater or a concert in the evening. With many friends about, life was never dull, and Mother found it far easier to cope with her mother-in-law than when they lived under the same roof on Cedar Street.

Grandma Bertha took command the day we arrived. Though her health had deteriorated over the years, and particularly after

Grandpa Julius's death in 1888, she was in good form during the first few summers in Atlantic City. She supervised the housekeeping and did the marketing. Dressed always in black and wearing a bonnet with a crepe veil, like Queen Victoria during her years of widowhood, she would drive to the stores in the fringed-top, horse-drawn surrey we would rent each season. Most afternoons, as a break from her chores, she went for a chair ride on the boardwalk. When she became more feeble and was confined to the house, she took to wearing wrappers instead of dresses and, from her rocking chair on the porch, would delegate chores to her daughters Nannie, Ada and Mattie, and to my mother. Only one thing could make her move in a hurry, and that was a thunderstorm. At the first clap, she'd prop herself up on her cane and shuffle as quickly as she could into her room, where she would remain until the storm had passed. My mother, on the other hand, would take me under the portico to show me the beauty of the lightning as it cut patterns in the black sky.

Grandma Ochs would read the *Chattanooga Times* and the *New York Times* every day, and she was an avid card player. She liked a game called Flinch that went on endlessly. I and my cousin Julius, who spent those summers with us, had the job of entertaining her at cards. We soon discovered that Grandma hated to lose, so we always let her win.

While we entertained Grandma at cards, she kept a watchful eye on the household activities. Her daughter Nannie was assigned to supervise the help. One of Nannie's duties was to lock all the kitchen cabinets after the dinner hour. The blacks who were employed for household work in those days were given so little money that I can easily understand why thefts were not uncommon. A week's salary, with room and board, was five dollars for a cook and three dollars for a maid. Our help came up with us from Chattanooga, and that was the going rate of pay in the South.

As Aunt Nannie went about unlocking the cabinets every morning, Julius and I would be at her heels like a pair of pups, ready for the cookies and sweets that came our way as she distributed supplies to the cook. Julius and I adored Aunt Nannie. I remember Aunt Mattie saying to me, "I think you like your Aunt Nannie better than you do me." And I said, "Well, yes. Isn't it true that everybody in the family loves her best?" Aunt Mattie had to admit that I was right.

Aunt Nannie was not a beauty, but she was the best-looking of the three sisters. Like all the Ochses, she had lovely blue eyes. I always wondered why, with her wonderful disposition, she had never married. It wasn't until just a few years ago, while going through some family papers, that I discovered the reason. Aunt Nannie had been engaged to a young man from Atlanta who, I believe, ran a food store. Grandma Ochs disapproved of the fiancé's occupation and conducted a little campaign to discourage the match. She succeeded; the engagement was broken off. As it happened, Nannie's ex-suitor became very successful, one of Atlanta's leading citizens.

A few years later, Grandma tried to disrupt her daughter Ada's romance with Harry Adler. I think, again, it was the young man's line of work that she found unsuitable: He worked for a Chattanooga clothing store. But Ada was more assertive than gentle Nannie and married the man of her choice.

Ada had learned to stand up for her own rights after an experience she'd had as a young woman. Ada had a lovely soprano voice, which the family encouraged her to cultivate. They even permitted her to take lessons in New York. But when Ada announced her ambition of performing professionally on the stage, the family objected strongly. She yielded to their protests and settled for singing at amateur concerts, charity affairs and the synagogue. As the years passed, she came to be disappointed in herself for not having pursued a stage career. Never again would her family be able to pressure her into decisions.

Poor Aunt Ada developed Parkinson's disease in her later years. By then she was living in the Pierre Hotel in New York, to be near Julius and his family. I used to visit her. Her husband had died, and she hadn't hit it off with her daughter-in-law or her grandchildren. She was a good patient toward the end; she didn't complain. Considering what she went through, that showed a lot of character.

Aunt Mattie, the youngest of the three sisters, also had her share of misfortune. She married Harry Adler's first cousin, Bernard Talimer, a Philadelphia lawyer who went to work for my father when my father purchased the *Philadelphia Public Ledger*.

Their first and only child was stillborn. Then, after ten or twelve years of marriage, Bernard, though still quite young, suffered a stroke. He was crippled by pain, and mentally reverted to childhood. Aunt Mattie took him all over Europe for treatments, but his condition never improved. After some years as an invalid—gentle, undemanding and decent—he died.

With all the tragedy in her life, Aunt Mattie never lost her fun-loving disposition. She was a sociable, popular woman, with a parlor always full of friends. Her friends were a diverse lot; one of her companions was Lillian Gish; another was the chaplain of the United States Congress. After her husband's death, she widened her social activities by joining the Daughters of the Confederacy in her hometown, Philadelphia, Pennsylvania. Her membership was accepted on the basis of her mother's loyalties. But when the club learned that Mattie's father had pledged allegiance to the Union cause, Aunt Mattie's membership was on the line. There is little doubt that she would have been expelled if it hadn't been for her personality. They liked her so much they allowed her to stay.

When Aunt Mattie was getting on in years (she lived to be ninety-one or ninety-two), I'd visit her every month in Philadelphia. To pass the time on the train trip, I'd read a book; one day I arrived with a detective story in hand. When Aunt Mattie saw the book, she said, "How can you waste your time reading that stuff? You should be improving your mind!" She was in her eighties then. After that, I would always read serious literature on that train trip.

The summer commute from New York to Atlantic City took three hours. People worked on Saturdays in those days, and my father would arrive late on a Saturday afternoon for his one-day "weekend" with us on the shore. He stepped off the train in high spirits, bringing boxes and boxes of candy for Julius and me. By Monday morning we had eaten so much candy that we were in bed with stomach aches. But with Papa there on Saturday nights and Sundays, Julius and I saw almost everything there was to see in Atlantic City. He took us to minstrel shows, melodramas and Gilbert and Sullivan operettas, and to hear John Philip Sousa's band on the Steel Pier.

I remember seeing my first movie, *The Great Train Robbery*. We went to shooting galleries on the boardwalk; we went swimming; we went fishing off Young's Pier.

Julius and I were captivated by the mysterious veiled Turkish lady who read palms. We imagined her an exotic Middle Eastern beauty, and we'd give anything to see her face. We went to her repeatedly to have our fortunes read, hoping each time that she'd agree to unveil her face, but she always refused. Not until the last session of the summer did she give in to our pleas. She told us to follow her into the back room, which we did with breathless expectation. Slowly and with great drama, she lifted her veil. What we saw shocked us. Our Middle Eastern beauty was an old lady with a wrinkled, ugly face. We tried our best to look honored and delighted, but I have a feeling that she knew what we were thinking.

The only thing that was a trial to me in Atlantic City was attending temple every Saturday morning with my aunts. It was always so hot, and in those days women had to dress up more than they do today. Invariably I'd have to sit squeezed between my well-padded aunts. I distinctly remember the feel of their steel-corseted hips.

Fortunately for me, my religious training did not include a kosher household. My mother thought the tradition unnecessary. Mama said that her soul was not in her stomach, so anything that agreed with her was acceptable food. Her approach made our social contact with non-Jews much easier. Mama had been taught by her father, the eminent Rabbi Wise, to be liberal in her interpretation of religion and she followed the path, developing her own philosophy, whereas Papa was more conservative, though not on the question of diet.

In 1901, after three summers in Atlantic City, my parents took me with them on their first grand tour of Europe. I was then eight years old.

We sailed on the *Deutschland*, then the fastest ocean liner in the world. It made Plymouth, England, in five and a half days' sailing time from New York. Traveling with us was Mlle Christine Hegi, my cousin Alice Bernheim, and my mother's half sister, Regina. My father had the best time on the dance floor. He was a good dancer and would dance with young women, old women, or any women in sight. He loved being with women and would have been blissfully happy with a large harem.

Of course, being just a little girl, I missed all this excitement. Mlle Christine would tuck me in bed early each evening in the cabin I shared with my parents. I remember one night when it was late, and I lay in my upper bunk listening to my parents talking. They had just returned from the captain's dinner, where my father had had more than the usual amount of champagne. He was determined to put on his opera cloak and silk hat and go for a promenade around the deck. My mother didn't approve. It was too late, and the wrong attire. He went ahead anyway.

I never heard my parents quarrel when they had a difference of opinion. Occasionally my father would chide Mama about her indolent habits, but more often he'd take a quiet delight in her idiosyncrasies. He used to call her Peter Pan.

My parents toured Europe with the eagerness of children. Their curiosity was boundless, their energy unlimited. Wherever we went, my father wanted to be sure he missed nothing. If it was a dungeon, we went down into it; if it was a tower, we'd climb to the turrets. My mother was equally energetic in the art galleries, museums and shops. I went along everywhere on those ceaseless expeditions to châteaus, cathedrals, monuments, battlefields, torture chambers—everything conceivable.

One summer we hiked across the Mer de Glace at Chamonix, an adventure that cost my mother a day of recuperation in bed. Another summer, when I was thirteen, my father and I climbed Mount Vesuvius shortly after a major eruption. As we ascended the slope to the crater, clouds enveloped us. Then it began to thunder and rain. Two boulders rolled past us in the gloomy mist, and that put me into a panic. I raced downhill, tripped, and fell into wet volcanic ash. I was completely black with soot. We gave up hope of making it to the crater and headed home.

In 1901, we returned to America aboard the *Fürst Bismarck*. The steerage deck, which circled the first-class dining room, was packed solid with families emigrating to the States from the poorer European countries, and while we were served our appallingly large dinners, those poor people would hold their babies up to the portholes for us to see. I became very upset, and when no one was looking I would take what I could from the table—a roll or a piece of fruit—and sneak it out to the hands that were always waiting on the other side of the porthole.

Some summers we went on excursions around the United States. One year we made a motor tour of the New England states in a secondhand Mercedes. It was an open car, which meant that we had to wear dusters and goggles, and when it rained we would cover up the luggage with a rubber sheet and ourselves in waterproof gear. My father had never learned to drive, so he hired a German chauffeur who had worked in a Mercedes factory. It was good to have a mechanic on hand, because the tires kept blowing out. That chauffeur stayed with us for years, though he was by all odds the most disagreeable man who ever lived. Only my father liked him. The man did, however, manage to drive us all the way to Halifax, Nova Scotia, and back. That was quite an achievement, because when we got to Maine the only routes were trails through the woods and farms.

The summer of 1909 we made a trip out West to Colorado Springs, Yellowstone Park, Salt Lake City, Yosemite, Los Angeles, San Francisco and Portland. The most enjoyable were our excursions into Yellowstone and Yosemite. No cars were allowed, and we toured on horseback and in horse-drawn wagons. In Yellowstone, the mosquitoes were so fierce that we had to wear dusters, hats with mosquito netting and high boots. In Seattle, we boarded a ship for a two-week cruise to Alaska by way of the Inland Passage. I remember the superbly beautiful mountains and glaciers, and the salmon run at Ketchikan, and the visit to the town where the gold rush of 1898 began.

There was no stopping my mother and father. My mother even rode a mule down the Grand Canyon. Halfway down, she started muttering what a fool she was, but she stuck it out.

My parents gave me children's books about the places we visited, and my father had me memorize our itineraries. On our first European trip in 1901, I learned to recite, in order, the places we'd seen, the towns we'd stopped in, where we went, how we got there, and what we did once we arrived. That was eighty years ago at this writing; if pressed, I could still recite that itinerary.

During one Atlantic crossing, when I was sixteen years old, I met a Hungarian portrait painter named Kopay. He was apparently quite impressed with me, for he wrote to my father a few weeks later, saying that I was the most beautiful girl he'd ever seen and that he would never be fulfilled as an artist until he painted my portrait. "The joy of capturing such beauty will be payment enough," he wrote. "The painting shall be yours free of charge."

My father was flattered, and consented. I posed for Mr. Kopay. When the work was completed, my father received a bill for one thousand dollars. When he remonstrated, Mr. Kopay replied, "Your daughter has such a beautiful face, it was a joy to paint it. But the body was dull and bored me. It is for this that I charge you one thousand dollars."

I still have the portrait. It hangs in the living room of my country house, and I must say that the family has had more than one thousand dollars' worth of pleasure and fun from it. Shortly after the Kopay incident, another artist wrote to my father, saying that he had seen me, and so forth, but Papa had learned his lesson.

9

Despite his success in journalism, my father harbored a sense of inadequacy about his limited schooling. He had quit school at the age of fourteen and never returned. Having forfeited the opportunity to complete his own education, he developed enormous respect for scholarship. He was determined that I, his only child, should get a higher education and win the academic standing he so regretted not having achieved for himself.

If my father had not pressured me, I would not have taken the college entrance exams. Though I worked hard in high school, my performance was no more than mediocre. I was a slow reader, spelled miserably and continually made seemingly careless mistakes in mathematics. I didn't know why I had such difficulty, and I began to believe that it was because I was less intelligent than most people. Discouraged and feeling inferior, I gave up trying.

I didn't learn the reason for my ineptitude until thirty years later, when my eldest child, Marian, had a similar problem in school and I took her to Philadelphia, on the advice of a psychiatrist friend of my father's, to see a prominent analyst who specialized in children. He found that Marian had a mild form of a visual disorder called dyslexia, which resulted in inaccurate vision when she became nervous or tired. He said that the disorder was hereditary and that I undoubtedly had dyslexia as a young girl.

Upon returning to New York, I followed the analyst's advice and arranged for Marian to see a psychiatrist named Dr. Levy, hoping the doctor would prescribe a treatment that would remedy the problem. In those days dyslexia was thought to be triggered by emotional problems. Although little is still known about dyslexia, it has since been explained as a neurophysiological condition. In the course of the first interview, the doctor asked Marian, who was fourteen, how she got along with her mother. Marian was enraged. She told the doctor it was none of his business and refused to go on seeing him.

Marian adjusted to the malfunction when she was about eighteen and no longer subjected to the pressures of high school, but for many of her school years she suffered from an inferiority complex. When my son Arthur developed dyslexia, I was able to recognize it as a visual difficulty, and he was spared those awful feelings of inferiority; and my children learned enough to recognize dyslexia when it appeared in their children.

During my high-school years, unaware that I had this vision problem, I became so discouraged that I wanted more than anything else to escape the demands of a formal education. I was getting poor grades, I had failed in German, and there was nothing in the school's unimaginative curriculum to stimulate me to special effort. Latin was my Waterloo. My teacher, Mrs. Dean, had me in tears. To this day, I skip Latin quotations with joy; I don't know what they mean, I don't care what they mean, and no one can compel me to try to understand them.

The results of the college entrance exams were disastrous. I flunked every subject except, surprisingly, German. This disqualified me from entering most colleges, but it left me the option of applying for the "two-year specials" at Barnard College, the women's division of Columbia University. The program was designed for students who were not very bright or who were inadequately prepared for the regular college courses.

The entrance exams for the Barnard program were to be held at the end of September, and my father had arranged for us to tour New England in June and July. That left me less than two months to study. On August 1, under the supervision of a tutor, I settled down to the task. The hours I put in were so long and strenuous that by the beginning of September my vision was blurred; the words on the page before me were a jumble of lines. My mother rushed me to a New York eye specialist, who diagnosed the trouble as eyestrain and prescribed complete rest.

So my studies came to an abrupt halt and I recuperated, regaining perfect vision by the end of September, just in time to take the exams. To my surprise, I passed, and was admitted into Barnard that fall.

I didn't expect to like the program. Yet I found the atmosphere of the school congenial, the students friendly and the teachers excellent, and I became interested and decided to work for a degree. To be admitted as a four-year student I would have to pass the entrance exams I had so miserably failed. I started the grueling preparation by boning up on high-school Latin. My Latin tutor had little patience with my carelessness. She was hot-tempered, and every time I made a silly mistake she would snap a pencil in half, so that by the lesson's end her desk would usually be covered with broken pencil stubs. Somehow I managed to pass the entrance exams, but I went on to fail the first term of freshman Latin and had to repeat the course.

It took me until my junior year before I had passed all the requirements to become a full-fledged member of my class. By the time I graduated in 1914 I had become a good student, getting A's in nearly every course—geology, history, economics and sociology. My major was in economics and in American and modern European history.

My interest in economics had been aroused by a young and delicate-looking professor, Benjamin Anderson. We all fell in love with him. I remember my father's surprise when I got an A on the subject of the "Aldrich Plan for a Federal Bank." As for my fascination with American history, that came about as a result of a course I took with Professor William Sheppard. It was the first time I had studied the subject, since it wasn't offered in my high school. I remember that during one of our classes, Professor Sheppard said that all newspapers took fraudulent ads. "Professor," I said, "I think you are mistaken. Some newspapers do not."

"Do you really believe that?" he asked.

"Yes, sir," I answered. "In fact, I'm sure of it. I know that the *New York Times* takes no such advertising."

Professor Sheppard didn't know of my connection to the paper —few people at Barnard did—and he disputed the point unconstrainedly. His arguments distressed me and I repeated them to my father. It didn't occur to me that he would send a representative to tell my professor that the *Times* went to great pains and expense to sift out fraudulent advertising, and to ask him what specific ad he thought fraudulent. Poor Professor Sheppard couldn't produce any examples, and admitted his mistake.

A few days later, before starting his lecture, Professor Sheppard pointed to me and said, "I want to see you after class."

I was a little apprehensive when I walked up to the lecture platform. He was a big, tall man, and standing on the platform he seemed an overpowering figure. His good-looking face was stern as he peered down at me and shook his finger. "You're a naughty girl," he said. "You told on me." He paused, and his scowl faded into a warm smile as he asked me if I wouldn't join his wife and him for tea that afternoon. It was the beginning of a lasting friendship.

There was another professor who knew that my father was publisher of the *Times*. His name was James Harvey Robinson. He was an eminent historian and later became one of the cofounders of the New School for Social Research. He taught a course called "History of the Intellectual Classes of Europe." During his lectures, he'd occasionally say, "I want to show you a perfect modern example of the medieval mind." Then he would read one of Charles Miller's editorials in the *Times*, while I sat shrinking with humiliation. I rarely agreed with Mr. Miller's editorials—they were too conservative for me—but I was torn between my loyalty to the paper and my agreement with Professor Robinson's ideas. I never totally resolved my dilemma, but this time I didn't mention the professor's criticisms to my father.

For one of our assignments, Professor Robinson had us read a book that I found very dull going until I came across the sentence "The art of reading is the art of skipping." At that, I said to myself, "Here, old boy, I take you at your word," and closed the book and skipped the rest.

As luck would have it, a question about the book appeared in our next exam. I decided that the only thing I could do was be truthful, and I wrote that I had found the book exceedingly dull and a complete waste of time. Much to my astonishment, I got an A.

Four or five years passed. I attended a Barnard reunion, and introduced myself to Miss Hutman, my freshman history teacher.

"Iphigene Ochs!" exclaimed Miss Hutman. "I'll never forget you! After grading hundreds of Professor Robinson's tests, in which he always included a question on this one book I hated, I read your answer and went no further. I gave you an A because you were the only student who didn't praise that tedious author."

I've always remembered that as a perfect example of the rewards of telling the truth.

Another of my favorite teachers was Professor Vladimir Simkhovitch. I took two of his courses—on the history of socialism and "Radicalism and Social Reform as Reflected in the Literature of the Nineteenth Century"—and solemnly declared that I was a socialist.

This made quite an impression at home. During dinner I would burst forth to discourse on social injustices. I'm sure my father was often tempted to call me a damn fool, but instead he'd respond calmly: "On what do you base your opinion?" or "Are you sure of your facts?" or "Where did you read that?" He made me look into the basis for my statements. When I found no evidence to substantiate something I had said, I learned to admit that I was wrong.

To impress upon me the danger of making dogmatic statements, my father had me memorize this passage from Benjamin Franklin's autobiography:

"I made it a rule to forbear all direct contradiction to the sentiments of others and all positive assertion of my own. I even forbid myself . . . the use of every word or expression in the language that imported a fix'd opinion, such as *certainly, undoubtedly,* etc., and I adopted instead of them, *I conceive, I apprehend* or *I imagine* a thing to be so and so; or *it appears to me at present* . . . And this mode, which I at first put on with some violence to natural inclination, became at length so easy, and so habitual to me, that perhaps for these fifty years past no one has ever heard a dogmatical expression escape me."

That passage appeared on page 95 of my father's copy of the autobiography, so whenever I violated its precepts, my father would exclaim, "Page 95, Iphigene!" If I persisted in being dogmatic, he'd make me recite the entire passage.

My father taught me to keep an open mind, for which I've always been grateful. I tried passing the same wisdom on to my children. When they made a dogmatic remark, I'd exclaim, "Benjamin Franklin!" Those words made them shriek in exasperation, yet they raised their own children on Benjamin Franklin. I am now busy spreading the gospel to my grandchildren. They, too, wriggle uncomfortably when I say, "Always qualify what you say; don't be too positive. It's much less embarrassing when you find out you're wrong."

While going to Barnard, I spent Thursday afternoons at the Henry Street Settlement on the Lower East Side. It was my first encounter with poverty. Until then I had seen slums only at a distance, looking down from the Manhattan Bridge on our way to Coney Island. The congestion and dirt of the neighborhood appalled me, but what saddened me most were the children.

It was my job to run a club for ten-year-old girls. I wasn't a harsh disciplinarian, and the unruly youngsters took advantage of me. At last I found an ally in a little girl named Sadie Horowitz. To this day I think of her fondly, for as the children ran wild and I threw up my hands in despair, she'd yell, "Shut up, kids! Give her a chance!"

My experience at the settlement confirmed my socialist sentiments, and I imagined leading a mob against the capitalist exploiters.
But Benjamin Franklin's words always overrode the ideas put into
my head by Karl Marx and other proponents of social revolution;
I wasn't "absolutely sure."

I was passionately involved in one cause or another as a student.
After hearing a speech against women's suffrage by Anne Nathan
Meyer, who was not a convincing speaker, I immediately espoused
the suffragette cause. From then on, I delighted in bringing up the
subject at dinner. My mother and Miss MacDonnell were both
sympathetic to the idea of giving women the vote, though they
kept their opinions within the confines of the house. My father
had the old-fashioned, chivalrous Southern attitude toward women.
He and I had heated discussions about *Times* editorials opposing
the suffragettes, and both of us held fast to our opinions. I didn't
go so far as to embarrass my father by marching in suffragette
parades, but I used to sneak my allowance to the women's-suffrage
committee at school.

In 1913, I became entranced with the progressive ideas of
Walter Lippmann. He had just published a book called *A Preface
to Politics*, which I thought was gospel. When, in the following
year, he helped found the *New Republic*, I knew the magazine
was gospel. I was convinced that Walter Lippmann ought to have
been on the *Times*. He could write editorials that wouldn't make
me blush with shame.

I set out on a campaign to bring Mr. Lippmann to the *Times*.
I persuaded Eustace Seligman, one of my intellectual friends, who
knew Mr. Lippmann, to recommend the idea to my father. Eustace
was happy to do so and succeeded in his mission; Eustace was to
invite Mr. Lippmann to the *Times* for lunch.

"But for goodness' sake," warned my father, "don't tell him
I want him to be an editor."

Eustace relayed the message to Mr. Lippmann. "He told me,"
Eustace reported back to me, "that he'd go to the *Times* only if he
was given a completely free hand." I relayed his words to my father.

"Well, I guess that's that, Iphigene," he said. "So much for your
Walter Lippmann." My father took back his invitation; I was
crushed.

A few years later I met Walter Lippmann. I recounted the incident and asked him if he recalled it. "Frankly, no," he said. "But if I made such a fool remark, which I might have, I don't blame your father for not inviting me to lunch."

10

On July 31, 1914, while I was vacationing with my mother and my cousin Julius at the Oberhof Resort in the Thuringen Forest in Germany, we received an alarming cable from my father in the United States: "Come home immediately. Europe is on the brink of war." The following morning, our party, which included Miss MacDonnell and my mother's French maid, Henriette, hurried to the nearby railroad station at Erfurt to board a train for Holland. The same day Austria and Germany declared war.

The train from Amsterdam wasn't to depart until the next day, so we had to find lodging in a hotel in Erfurt. Somehow amid the confusion we managed to get rooms. I remember the hotel lobby overflowing with soldiers. Julius left immediately for Munich to take his mother and Aunt Mattie out of the war zone.

The train to Holland was packed. As we pulled out of the station, I saw that our luggage was still on the platform.

I shouted to a porter, "Our trunks! You forgot to load our trunks!"

"They'll follow you," he yelled back. He kept his word; our belongings caught up with us in Amsterdam.

The train crawled toward the Dutch border, stopping at every station to pick up passengers. There were scenes of tearful farewell. People stood packed together in the train's corridors. Since there were just four of us in a first-class compartment that could seat eight, we offered to share our accommodations. A German officer who was traveling with his wife and baby accepted our invitation. When they disembarked, three young German men about my own age accepted the seats. They were students at a forestry school and were volunteering for the army. "Why volunteer now?" I asked. "Everyone says the war will be over in six weeks." One of the men, who was very good-looking and very charming, said it was their patriotic duty. "If your country is at war, you can't watch your brothers go and not go yourself."

I spent only a few hours with those young men, but I felt we had become friends. A few years after the war, when reading Erich Maria Remarque's *All Quiet on the Western Front*, I remembered that meeting. The book opens with a professor at a forestry school telling his students it is their duty to enlist and defend their country, and as I read, I was convinced that the novel's hero was the attractive young German who shared our railroad compartment in 1914.

The book was so compelling that I stayed up most of the night reading. After the heartbreaking ending, when the boy is killed on the last day of the war, I fell asleep. An hour or two later I awoke and burst into tears.

"For heaven's sake, what's the matter?" asked my husband, Arthur, waking up too.

All I could do was sob, "He's dead . . . he's dead . . ."

"Who's dead, Iphigene?"

"The boy I met on the train!"

Finally I calmed down enough to tell him the story.

At the German border, the guards asked to see our passports. Since passports were then required only in Russia and, I believe, Turkey, we didn't have any. Fortunately, my mother was carrying a letter of credit that established our American citizenship.

We held our breaths as the guard inspected the document. My mother had claimed that Henriette, the French maid, was also her daughter, and we were afraid that the guard would discover her identity. The French were not being permitted to leave Germany. Henriette and I stood quietly, side by side. We were the same size and coloring, and Henriette was dressed in one of my previous year's outfits.

The guard didn't ask any questions. In fact, he would have stamped the letter of credit as if it were a passport if my mother hadn't managed to retrieve it.

Miss MacDonnell, who was a British subject, got by border control without incident. The Germans began detaining the British only two or three days later, when Britain entered the war.

We got back on our train. The German engine was exchanged for a Dutch one. We were instructed to close all the windows and not to smoke until the train had crossed the bridge into Holland: There were rumors that the bridge had been mined. I don't think a word was spoken during the crossing. Such moments of fear make breathing difficult. As the train inched onto firm land, we realized we had made it.

The Amstel Hotel in Amsterdam was in an uproar. A money panic had seized the city. Paper currency was not being accepted because of fears that it might become worthless overnight, and gold alone could buy our passage to England. Being a seasoned traveler, my mother had a hundred dollars' worth of gold coins in a little bag she kept hidden in her clothing. It was just enough to secure accommodations for us four women.

As we steamed into Harwich, England, I remember the seamen lining the rails of the warships putting out to sea. On the wharves, people stood cheering and weeping. It was two weeks before we could arrange for three transatlantic passages to New York. (Miss MacDonnell had decided to remain in England.) On August 15, we left on a ship that had been condemned for scrap. The ship was British, which meant that it could be attacked by the Germans. Nonetheless, we felt ourselves lucky to be aboard. Our crossing was uncomfortable, but also uneventful.

I returned to the United States strongly pro-German. My travels in Germany had influenced me, as had the course on modern European history I had taken at Barnard under Professor W. M. Sloan, an American educated in Germany. In learning about the Germans, I had been impressed by their advanced legislation in regard to old-age pensions, unemployment insurance and other social issues. Professor Sloan was skeptical about whether the Allies, and Czarist Russia in particular, represented the cause of freedom against that of autocracy, and I shared his reasoning.

My anti-Russian, pro-German feelings were not very popular at home. They conflicted with my father's pro-British sympathies. In his opinion, the war had little to do with the Russians; the British, he felt, were the dominant Allied power, and he was all for them. The *Times*'s editorials were strongly pro-British. This provoked some rough criticism from German sympathizers. I remember my father receiving anonymous letters asking him why he didn't change his name to John Bull. Letters addressed to me asked how I liked living off British blood money.

Someone started a rumor that the *New York Times* was the puppet of Lord Northcliffe, owner of *The Times* of London. The rumor was taken so seriously that in March 1915 a Senate investigating committee summoned Charles Miller, the editor-in-chief, and Carr Van Anda, the managing editor, to testify on behalf of the paper. The committee alleged that the *Times* was controlled by English money and was acting as a propaganda organ for British interests in the United States. Mr. Miller and Mr. Van Anda denounced the claims as hallucinations. The entire story was nonsense, they said—and the investigation bore them out. The accusations were, nonetheless, a blow to my father. He was deeply upset to see the *Times*'s integrity questioned.

After the first few months of war, my sympathies changed over to the Allied side. This switch came as a result of my father's urgings that I read all the official documents the *Times* printed. I struggled through the British White Papers, the French Yellow Papers, the German Papers. I don't remember if the Russians published any papers, but if they did, I read them, too. Painstakingly reading all those documents and analyses, as events unfolded week by week, made me something of an expert on current affairs.

It also proved useful in the course I was then taking at the Columbia School of Journalism—the first and only time I aspired to become a journalist. I didn't complete the term, though at one point I was the prize student. We had an exam on current world news and I was awarded an A-plus. The perfect grade surprised one of the faculty, whom I overheard asking my professor, "How in the name of common sense can you give a student an A-plus on *anything*?" My professor replied, "I've never had a student who knew a subject as well as that girl." Well, I did know every move of every army, and had read every word of every official paper published by every belligerent Government.

My studies at the school of journalism were cut off in January 1915, when my father intervened in my infatuation with a charming young German, Baron von Seebeck, whom I had met during our homebound transatlantic crossing the previous summer. George, who had been studying banking in London, had moved to the United States to escape being interned. My father did not like George. To get me away from him, he arranged for me to visit friends named Pfeifer in New Orleans, who had an attractive daughter my age. My devotion to George, which was not reciprocated, was not so strong that I could resist the trip South. I stayed a month in Chattanooga, and then a month in New Orleans, where I enjoyed the celebrated Mardi Gras. All thoughts of George soon left my head, and I got myself engaged and disengaged twice.

Though I didn't know it at the time, I had already met the man who was to be the most significant in my life.

I saw Arthur Hays Sulzberger briefly when I was attending Barnard and he was a student at Columbia. Our relationship didn't become serious until Julius Adler introduced us again several years later. Julius was attending a summer officers' training camp in Plattsburgh, New York, not far from where my family was vacationing at Lake George. The camp, known as the First Plattsburgh Businessmen's Camp, was organized by a group of business and professional men. President Wilson, saying the country was "too proud to fight," had refused to mobilize the armed forces, and Congress was of like mind. The camp was attended by twelve hundred volunteers who paid their own expenses. It was such a great success that other "Plattsburghs" sprang up around the country.

Julius volunteered for two summers in the officers' training course. On weekends off, he'd visit us and bring along his friends from the camp. We had so many soldiers around our place it looked at times like an Army club. One of the young men Julius brought with him in 1916 was Arthur Sulzberger.

Arthur had been working for three years in his father's cotton-goods business since his graduation from Columbia, but had decided to take the summer off to prepare himself for the Army. I began seeing him every weekend he could get leave. On the weekends he had to stay at the base I'd go to Plattsburgh, accompanied by a chaperon, and stay at the Lake Champlain Hotel near the camp.

Since the country was not yet at war, soldiering was something of a game, and we were lighthearted and gay. Arthur proposed to me that summer, but I refused him. We were sitting under a big spruce tree and, as Arthur would recount later, I melted into his arms and said, "No." I thought I was in love with another young man, who was highly intellectual. The young man was not as taken with me, thank goodness; I got to know him better in later years and found him a stuffy bore.

Fortunately, Arthur persevered. The following summer, when he was again enrolled in the Plattsburgh Camp, he resumed the courtship and I accepted his proposal.

My father wasn't exactly overjoyed. He said, "I don't understand. You've got a good home. Why do you want to get married?"

He couldn't understand why my mother didn't object to Arthur. When she replied that she found him an unusual young man and liked him in every way, my father just grumbled. I don't doubt that if Arthur had been a newspaperman, my father would have found the match more acceptable. A son-in-law who could become his successor would have been ideal.

Arthur finished his training, received a commission and was sent to Camp Wadsworth, outside Spartanburg, South Carolina. Whenever I went to visit him I was accompanied by Miss MacDonnell, who had rejoined our family. Miss MacDonnell, however, was a good friend and didn't interfere with our privacy.

Arthur looked around town for some romantic place where he could give me the engagement ring, and selected what seemed like the only such place in all of Spartanburg. He thought it was a park. It turned out to be the grounds of the local lunatic asylum. That's where we became engaged.

We were determined to be married before he was shipped overseas. Arthur kept me posted by Western Union, almost daily. He still hadn't been assigned abroad when he was granted ten days' leave. We decided we'd be married during that time.

We had one week to arrange the wedding. Everyone in the family telephoned invitations to friends and relatives, and no one was certain how many guests would appear. Miss MacDonnell supervised, consulting the dressmaker about the gown, arranging for the flowers and ordering the buffet from Sherry's catering service. We decided to have only a few attendants. There were two pages—John Oakes and Cyrus Sulzberger; four groomsmen—Arthur's brothers, Leo and David, and his friends David Heyman and Edward Greenbaum; and the best man—Julius. My only attendant was the little flower girl, Ursula Squier. When the wedding party stood for a photograph, I got a bit hysterical as the photographer's assistant ran around with a candle in order to get the proper lighting. I was sure that my veil would catch on fire.

My father seemed resigned to the inevitable, though he grumbled up to the moment Arthur and I were pronounced man and wife in my parents' Seventy-fifth Street house. We were married by Rabbi Joseph Silberman of Temple Emanu-El on November 17, 1917.

In a moment of nostalgia, my father persuaded us to spend our honeymoon week the way he and my mother had—with a trip to Washington culminating in a private meeting with the President. Arthur and I weren't all that keen on going to the White House, but after a number of daily phone calls from my father to our honeymoon suite, I told Arthur, "We've got to if you want to remain in the family."

The Washington bureau of the *Times* made the arrangements, and upon our arrival at the White House we were ushered into a private waiting room. There we sat for what seemed an awfully long time. When we were summoned, we both got an attack of nerves. We needn't have worried. We were directed to the end of a long line of well-wishers. The line moved to where President Wilson stood, and when we reached him, all I could think to say was: "My father sends his regards."

A quizzical expression crossed Mr. Wilson's face and he said, "Thank you." He didn't have the remotest idea who my father was.

Arthur and I were overwhelmed with mirth. Arthur thought it best not to relate the incident to my father, but when the family questioned me about our visit, the whole story slipped out.

Our first year of married life wasn't without its problems. Arthur's military career as a reserve officer did not progress as he had hoped. His first disappointment was when the Army overlooked his artillery training and placed him in a National Guard unit in Camp Wadsworth at Spartanburg. We arrived at the camp only to discover that the unit had been delayed in the field indefinitely. Arthur got bored waiting for its arrival and requested reassignment. They placed him temporarily in the Quartermaster Corps, to administer supplies, but he made the mistake of doing too good a job, and when the National Guard unit finally arrived his commanding officer wouldn't release him.

His spirits lifted when orders came through assigning him to a unit in Chillicothe, Ohio. But the winter of 1917–18 turned out to be awful. The officers, all old Ohio friends, were cliquish, and Arthur, an outsider and not formally assigned to the regiment, felt like a third wheel. The weather was abominable; we nearly froze to death. Arthur applied for a transfer but nobody paid attention to him, since he was just a second lieutenant in the reserves. The worst for him was when everyone in the regiment was ordered overseas—everyone but the reserve officers.

In June 1918, we were sent to Fort Jackson near Columbia, South Carolina, where Arthur was reinstated in the artillery. In August, he left for further training in Fort Sill, Oklahoma, and I returned to my parents' summer house at Lake George. I was pregnant, and there was fear of my being exposed to the raging flu epidemic. The disease had spread throughout the world, and it was estimated that from 1917 to 1919 between twenty million and thirty million people were killed by it; pregnant women were especially susceptible.

Arthur had an outstanding record at Fort Sill and was recommended for promotion, but before it came through he was transferred back to Fort Jackson, since more artillery officers were needed in combat units. It was disheartening, since during his absence from Fort Jackson all the officers there had already been promoted.

When the war ended and the troops began to prepare for their return to civilian life, Arthur's job was to make up the discharge list for his unit. He put his own name first, an action he was always slightly uncomfortable about later. His discharge came through promptly, ending his thwarted military career. He never saw the war, he never set foot on foreign soil, and he never overcame the disappointment; he resented it for the rest of his life.

Arthur joined me at my parents' Seventy-fifth Street house in New York in December 1918—in time for the best New Year's present of all. On December 31, our first daughter was born. We called her Marian Effie. The baby was the beginning to a new year and our new life as parents, and we tucked those disheartening days of military life into our memories.

11

The war ruled out any more excursions to Europe, so my parents decided to purchase the Lake George house they had rented in the summer of 1918. The house belonged to George Foster Peabody, a longtime friend of my father, and was named Abenia, which means "home of rest" in one of the Indian dialects.

The Lake George community was a fascinating collection. Across the road from Abenia lived Mrs. Charles B. Hewitt, whose husband's family had established the Cooper-Hewitt Museum. Among those with houses along the lake were the Reverend John Henry House, founder of the American Farm School in Greece, and the Reverend Edward M. Parrott, minister of the community's small Episcopal congregation. Reverend Parrott had served for years as the minister of the Grace Church in New York until he contracted tuberculosis. It was essential that he move out of the contaminated city air, and at Mr. Peabody's suggestion he and his wife and daughters settled at Lake George. Reverend Parrott took charge of the parish and began farming some land. It wasn't long before he had completely recovered. The Parrotts became an integral part of the community, and the close friendship between our two families has lasted through these many years. I still see the third daughter, Mrs. Sidney Homer, Jr.

This quiet, scenic area attracted an impressive group of musicians. Madame Marcella Sembrich, the great soprano of the Metropolitan Opera, conducted a voice school for young women. After her pupils' concerts at her house, she would serve tea with the most extraordinary pastries, sandwiches and other treats whipped up by her Viennese cook. I remember the audiences who listened patiently to the girls' trilling—and, when the final high C was sung, scrambled for the delicacies.

Another musician at Lake George was Professor Leopold Auer, in his day perhaps the world's most famous violin teacher. He had taught at the Imperial Conservatory in St. Petersburg; his students had included Jascha Heifetz, Efrem Zimbalist and Mischa Elman. Now he tutored students during his summer holiday at the lake. Professor Auer, a lean, short man, lived with his second wife, a large, imperious woman, and his grandson, Mischa Auer, a solemn-faced beanstalk of a boy who developed into an outstanding movie comedian.

Then there was the famous contralto Louise Homer. She had married her singing teacher, the composer Sidney Homer, and they had six children. Their one son, Sidney, had a wonderful sense of humor, and we kept up our friendship over the years. Sidney became a Wall Street bond expert. When he wrote a book on the history of bonds, he sent me a copy inscribed, "To Iphigene, with strict instructions *not* to read this book."

My father's idea of relaxing at Abenia was to go golfing or boating in the morning and hiking through the woods or mountain climbing in the afternoon. After dinner, we'd sit around the table and he'd supply my friends and me with betting money and then challenge us to twenty-one and poker. He had a passion for gambling, and enjoyed taking us young people along when he played the horses at Saratoga. We'd usually lose the few dollars he'd give each of us; he more often would win.

My father had a lucky streak. One of his favorite stories was about the day he was at a roulette table in Cuba and was following his usual system of playing three numbers—12 (his birthday), 7 (my mother's birthday) and 19 (my birthday). The wheel stopped at one of the numbers, and in the excitement of gathering his winnings he forgot to remove his bet. The wheel spun again and he won again. He won three times in a row on the same number that night.

Abenia was a perfectly hideous old Victorian house, but huge, with plenty of room for my parents' innumerable guests. The house had been built in 1876 and filled with the furnishings of that period—dreadful oversized Victorian pieces, such as great beds carved with pineapples. The house had been bought furnished by Mr. Peabody and had been sold that way to us. My parents kept all the machine-made Victorian furniture and added items of their own choosing, which made the house comfortable, but utterly tasteless.

Mr. Peabody, a tall, handsome gentleman with a Vandyke beard, used to take me for walks in the woods and teach me the names of the birds and the flowers. He was very imaginative and would speak of the birch trees as "maidens of the forest."

Mr. Peabody devoted much of his life to improving the welfare of the underprivileged. He was a member of the board of trustees of the Tuskegee Institute, which promoted Negro education. I asked him once why he was more interested in blacks than in poor whites, and he replied, "If you raise the standard of education and living of blacks, the whites will be inspired to catch up." Among his many public-spirited contributions was the establishment of the Peabody Awards for excellence in radio and television.

Mr. Peabody met my father through Spencer Trask, his partner at Spencer Trask & Co., the Wall Street investment house. My parents had come to know Mr. Trask and his wife, Katrina, during our first years in New York, when my father was struggling to get the *Times* on its feet. Mr. Trask supported the *Times* in those uncertain days, buying a large number of shares in the New York Times Company, and his firm helped with refinancing the paper. More than that, while my parents were still newcomers to New York and all but unknown, the Trasks offered them their friendship and welcomed them into their home, Yaddo, in Saratoga Springs. In those days, it was quite remarkable for Jews to be issued such an invitation by people of wealth and social position; the Trasks were exceptionally liberal.

I remember Mrs. Trask only as a widow. She suffered from a heart condition and had to rest in bed most of the day. I used to visit her in her summer house, Triana, which was situated on one of three little islands on Lake George connected to each other by footbridges. In the course of my visits, she told me of her tragic life.

Years earlier, she was a young mother, proud of her three beautiful children. Then, within one week, two of the children were taken ill with diphtheria and died. Shortly afterward, the third child was stricken with an illness and died, too. Mrs. Trask told me that if she didn't believe in a life after death and in her eventual reunion with her beloved children, she surely would have lost her sanity.

As it was, she and her husband were left with a haunting emptiness in their lives. Their four-hundred-acre estate in Saratoga Springs was unbearably lonely. To ease their grief, Mr. Trask proposed that they build a fifty-four-room mansion on the estate as a home for themselves and a place to entertain Mrs. Trask's literary and musical friends. Mrs. Trask was something of a poet and playwright herself, and was friendly with many of the nation's outstanding artists. They named the mansion in memory of the children, who had always mispronounced the word "shadow" as "yaddo."

Yaddo flourished. Artists, writers and musicians came from all over the world to work or relax at the wooded estate. Mrs. Trask had a flair for the romantic. The young men who visited the retreat she called her knights, and she in turn became known as the Lady of Yaddo. While Mrs. Trask held court at Yaddo, her husband continued his Wall Street career. On New Year's Eve, 1909, he was en route from Saratoga to New York aboard the Montreal Express when the train collided with a freight train. A few passengers suffered minor injuries; Mr. Trask was the only one killed. It was after her husband's death that Katrina Trask developed the heart condition that made her an invalid.

Years later—I was twenty or twenty-one by then—Mrs. Trask invited me to Saratoga for dinner and to spend the night. She was living in a small house next to the mansion, which had been closed down. Her companion, Miss Pardee, who had been the children's governess, greeted me at the door with a book of poems by Henry Van Dyke. It was wrapped in a white ribbon and decorated with a sprig of pine and a rose. Miss Pardee told me that the pine represented Spencer Trask and the rose Katrina Trask. In the book was a poem dedicated to the couple.

Mrs. Trask was bedridden, and each of the guests that evening spent time with her. The man who acted as host was George Peabody.

For many years, Mr. Peabody had been the Trasks' closest friend. After Katrina had lost her entire family, he stayed close to her side. He thought of her as a goddess.

George Peabody had first laid eyes on Katrina some fifty years earlier, when he was a young man and a new partner at Spencer Trask's. He saw her from a distance one summer day while walking in Brooklyn Heights. She was sitting on the high front stoop of a brownstone, and he thought she was the loveliest girl he had ever seen. He fell in love with her at first sight. There, he knew, was the girl he wanted to marry.

A few days later, Spencer Trask introduced George Peabody to his fiancée. It was none other than the girl on the stoop.

Katrina and Spencer were married, and it was a very happy union. George never spoke of his feelings about Katrina until a few years after the marriage, when he entered Mr. Trask's office and said, "Spencer, I feel it is my duty to tell you that I am madly in love with your wife."

"I can easily understand that, George," Mr. Trask replied. "I don't see how anybody could know her and not feel that way about her."

The subject was never mentioned again, and the two men remained friends, sharing good times and bad in later years. When Spencer died, his will appointed George as an executor of his estate.

Katrina Trask related this story to my father when she wrote to tell him that, after ten years of widowhood, she was going to marry George. George was seventy years old then. She had refused his proposal nine years earlier because she felt she should remain faithful to the memory of her husband; this time she accepted. As she said in her letter to my father, it was George's one wish in life to have her as his wife. She wrote:

"I told him, I am old, I am ill. I will be nothing but a burden. He said, 'Not at all. It would complete my life just to know you have been my wife.'"

They were married, and were very happy together for one year, when Katrina died.

George Peabody devoted the rest of his life to developing Yaddo as the artists' haven Katrina had started. Both Spencer Trask's will and Katrina's had deeded the mansion for that purpose, and Mr. Peabody appointed Elizabeth Ames, a widow in her thirties, as executive director of the project. He came to look on Mrs. Ames as a daughter and adopted her legally. Starting with only a half dozen artists, the center has since grown to accommodate more than a hundred guests a year. Those who have stayed there include the composers Leonard Bernstein and Virgil Thomson, the writers Carson McCullers and John Cheever, and the painters Milton Avery and Clifford Still.

George Peabody didn't live to see Yaddo become the internationally known artists' retreat it is today. He died only a few years after the center began operating. He was buried next to the graves of Katrina, Spencer and the Trask children.

Years later, when I accepted the Peabody Award on behalf of Dorothy Gordon for her Youth Forum programs on the *Times*'s radio station, WQXR, I spoke about Mr. Peabody—of his contribution to society and his fine qualities as a human being. I was given five minutes to speak, and I said I didn't want to talk about the *Times*, since everyone in the audience read it, or about Dorothy Gordon, since everyone there knew and admired her accomplishments—I wanted to tell of my old friend George Peabody.

After the lunch, several people came up and said they were glad to hear my talk: They had been coming to these lunches for years and this was the first time they'd heard George Peabody mentioned. That my dear friend, who had contributed so much to the bettering of society, should have slipped into obscurity upset me. I suggested that the *Times* run an article about him. After much persuasion, they acted on my advice. The story was head-lined, "The Man Nobody Remembers," or something equally unflattering. Nonetheless, it was a nice, friendly article. How could anyone help but write a kind article on George Foster Peabody!

12

The *New York Times* spared no expense in covering the First World War. As the armies moved over the map of Europe, *Times* reporters followed, filing dispatches from the battlefields. The enormous costs entailed began to worry the paper's financial advisers. The previous year the *Times* had spent a considerable amount to move from the Times Tower into a more spacious building it had bought on Forty-third Street. Now my father was rejecting advertising to save space for detailed descriptions of battle scenes and full texts of official statements. Cable tolls alone ran to $15,000 a week, or more than $750,000 a year, and there were fears of the paper slipping back into debt.

In the long run, the opposite happened. Getting the story first and getting it accurately proved profitable. By the end of the war, circulation had grown so large that advertising space was eagerly sought. As profits mounted, my father, having no interest in making a private fortune, fed the assets back into the business. This set the *Times* firmly on its feet and paved the way for even more expanded coverage.

My father's approach to covering the war was complemented by the ambitions of his managing editor, Carr Van Anda. My father had a genius for staffing his paper with talented men, and his eye was never so keen as when he hired Carr Vattel Van Anda. The forty-year-old journalist, who had brought acclaim to the New York *Sun* during his sixteen years there, intended to carry the *Times* to new peaks. The two men saw the *Times* not just as a paper of record but as a living history of the world, and under their direction the *Times* became a vital forum for debate of the war issues.

Under them, too, news-gathering techniques were expanded and new areas of journalism were opened up. With Mr. Van Anda at the helm of the news operation and my father allocating the necessary funds, the paper pioneered in reporting on explorations, on scientific discoveries and on developments in aviation. From Charles Lindbergh on, every flyer crossing the Atlantic was under contract with the *Times* for the first rights to his stories. Richard Byrd became so superstitious about *Times* contracts—the *Times* never lost a flyer—that he refused to make a flight without one. He had a flag that he took with him on all his expeditions, and he always gave it to Arthur for safekeeping between trips.

Subjects previously held to be too difficult for the average reader were, for the first time, presented clearly in layman's language. The stories weren't buried in the back pages, either; many ran on the front page. The public was interested and intrigued, and the paper's circulation soared.

Carr Van Anda became a legend. Some say that his ghost still haunts the *Times*. I hope it does. His talents were unending. In mathematics, physics, astronomy and Egyptology, he was on a par with learned scholars. His expertise in Egyptology was demonstrated when he exposed a supposedly 4,000-year-old hieroglyphic as a forgery, earning the envy and admiration of experts in the field. His extraordinary grasp of mathematics alerted him to the genius of Albert Einstein. Einstein was not yet known in America and his complex and revolutionary equations were beyond most physicists. When in 1919 the Royal Astronomical Society announced confirmation of several Einstein theories (findings which led to revision of the Newtonian theory of gravitation) Mr. Van Anda assigned a *Times* reporter to the story. No other newspaper covered the event. It was America's first introduction to him. Within a year it would be hard to find a man in the street who didn't know the name Albert Einstein.

Some years later, Mr. Einstein came to the United States to lecture at Princeton. Mr. Van Anda, who was editing the articles on Einstein, read a transcript of one of the scientist's extraordinarily complicated discussions and discovered a discrepancy in the figures. He alerted Dean Christian Gauss of Princeton to a possible error.

"Van Anda's query," Mr. Gauss related, "came at a time when relativity was understood only by Einstein and the Deity." Mr. Einstein reluctantly agreed to review his notes and was astonished to discover that Mr. Van Anda was right: He had made an error while transcribing the equation on the blackboard. For anyone to have caught the great Einstein in a mistake was astounding. The instance added to the Van Anda legend.

Many people thought Carr Van Anda cold. From all I heard, he must have been a hard man to work for. He believed in getting the job done with no nonsense and no thought to personal considerations. With him, only results counted. Yet he had a sense of humor, and I liked him.

He retired in 1925, after twenty-one years at the newspaper, and he never again set foot in the *Times* plant. He was one of those people who believe that when you finish a job, you close the door and don't reopen it. Thereafter, the only interest he showed in the paper was that of a reader. Nonetheless, he remained a friend, and I used to visit him at his home. He lived alone during his last years—his wife had died—and he coped courageously with his failing health. On one occasion, Gerald Johnson, who was writing a biography of my father, came with me on one of my visits. Mr. Johnson asked the former editor which one of his many contributions led to the paper's success. Mr. Van Anda didn't hesitate in his answer. "I didn't make a success of the *Times*," he said matter-of-factly. "Mr. Ochs did. The paper was a success when I joined it."

Carr Van Anda was managing editor when the false armistice was announced on November 7, 1918, four days before the First World War ended. He looked into the circumstances of the announcement and discovered that it was based on rumor. He was the only editor in town not to jump the gun. The other papers rushed out extras proclaiming the war's end, and the country was plunged into celebration. But the *Times* headline read: "German Delegates on Way to Meet Foch; False Peace Report Rouses All America." The *Times* was one of the few newspapers in the country that told it like it was.

I remember the false armistice celebration well. In my enthusiasm, I went into the streets and mingled with the hysterical crowd. It was pandemonium. Every horn that could blow was blowing, and every voice that could shout was shouting. I recall seeing Enrico Caruso, who used to stay at the Knickerbocker Hotel, throw open his window and sing over the din with his arms outstretched. Four days later, when the *Times* banner headline reported the true armistice, another celebration erupted, but it lacked the sudden spontaneity of the first. No one went on the rooftops on November 11.

A fortnight after Armistice Day, President Wilson prepared to sail for the peace conference in Paris. A Presidential trip abroad had no precedent in American history, and many Americans were against it. The *Times* opposed his going and wrote editorials that raised the question of Presidential authority in Mr. Wilson's absence. Once he sailed beyond the three-mile limit, should the Vice President be sworn to assume the powers of the Chief Executive? This matter stirred up heated debate across the land.

There was also the issue of the President's acting as the chief negotiator when he should, the *Times* reasoned, remain in a position to evaluate the treaty. The paper also criticized the President for not having any leading Republicans in the delegation. It suggested that he take William Howard Taft, the leading sponsor of the League of Nations, or Henry Cabot Lodge, the leading Republican senator. But Mr. Wilson was a conceited man sure of his righteousness, and he stuck to his course. His party included one Republican of no particular consequence; I can't even remember his name. Before leaving for Versailles, Mr. Wilson settled the question of Presidential authority by declaring that he would not forfeit his powers as commander-in-chief.

The relationship between my father and President Wilson was never warm. Mr. Wilson kept himself aloof; not many people could get close to him. He believed that he held a monopoly on truth and wisdom. It was an attitude that eventually defeated his life's work.

The President's uncompromising nature was exemplified by an episode involving my father.

While the paper had taken issue with the President on his decision to attend the Versailles peace conference, it had backed him solidly throughout the war and it backed him in his fight to create the League of Nations. Moreover, the *Times* had supported Woodrow Wilson in both his Presidential campaigns. Only twice during his two terms did the paper run sharply critical editorials— on his economic reform proposals, when the paper thought he was going too far too fast, and on his appointment of the liberal Louis Brandeis to the Supreme Court. A good 75 percent of the time the editorial page approved of his actions. But in 1921, when he was no longer President, Mr. Wilson forgot the 75 percent and remembered only the other 25 percent.

That year, my father celebrated his twenty-fifth anniversary as publisher of the *New York Times*, and to commemorate the occasion some members of the staff put together a book of encomiums and invited prominent people to contribute letters of tribute. The former President was approached by a friend of his and of my father, Bernard Baruch. Mr. Wilson replied in writing that he couldn't possibly say anything praising Adolph Ochs, considering that the *Times* had not supported his domestic reforms.

Mr. Baruch filed the letter away. As far as I know, my father never learned of Mr. Wilson's refusal and the letter was not brought to Arthur's attention until many years later. Mr. Baruch suggested that he destroy it, because it might embarrass the *Times*, but Arthur was of a different opinion. "This letter doesn't reflect badly on my father-in-law or the paper," Arthur said. "The only reason to destroy it is that it speaks badly for President Wilson." The letter was kept.

The year 1921 was a very difficult one in my father's life. The *Times* was doing well—by then it was one of New York's leading papers—but all the years of strain and worry proved too much for him. He had a nervous breakdown.

The collapse was precipitated by an incident a couple of months before the Armistice. My father was in Abenia, keeping in touch with Carr Van Anda by telephone. Between ten and eleven o'clock every evening he would get a direct connection to the office from his study on the top floor of the house, and would discuss the front-page news with the managing editor before the paper went to press. Then he'd come downstairs to the living room, where friends and neighbors would be gathered, and relate the latest news on the war.

On the night of Sunday, September 15, he was called to the phone earlier than usual and heard an excited Van Anda say, "There's an Austrian peace gesture. I think it's the end of the war."

"Better go easy on it," my father said. "How are you handling it?"

Mr. Van Anda answered that Mr. Miller was writing an editorial on it. "Well," my father said, "I'm sure it will be all right."

The editorial that appeared the next day recommended that the Allies take seriously the Austrian proposal for negotiating some kind of peace. It's hard to imagine today the violent reaction that editorial provoked. Feeling was very strong that the Allies should accept nothing short of unconditional surrender of the Central Powers, and newspapers around the country descended on the *Times* like a pack of wolves. The editorial's second paragraph qualified its major theme, and had the order of the paragraphs been reversed the reaction might have been less intense. As it stood, the editorial gave many people the impression that the *Times* was espousing an easing of the Allied terms.

My father's desk was piled high with letters and telegrams accusing the *Times* of throwing away victory and betraying the country. He took it hard. Most distressing to him was when the Union League Club, whose members included many of New York's most prominent citizens, called a special meeting to decide whether to censure the *Times* as lacking in patriotism.

The members were united in disapproving the editorial, but there were a few who nonetheless opposed censure. Our good friend Dr. J. Bentley Squier stood up for the *Times*, saying that the paper had staunchly upheld the Allied side throughout the war and that, in keeping with democracy and freedom of the press, the paper was entitled to express its opinion. After his thoughtful statement, the vote was taken and the resolution lost.

Nonetheless, my father was disheartened by the entire episode. Friends urged him to reveal that he'd had nothing to do with the editorial, but he said, "Mr. Van Anda and Mr. Miller have brought great renown to the *Times*. They are able and conscientious men. I've taken credit for their good deeds. Certainly I should share the blame for any mistake."

Looking back, I think the rival newspapers took advantage of this incident to inflict some blows. The other journals resented the *Times*'s challenge during the war and its increasing success. While they lost ground, the *Times* strengthened its position because of exceptional war coverage. Some newspapers were forced out of business or swallowed up in mergers, while the *Times*'s daily circulation rose between 1914 and 1919 to 170,000. In a last-ditch effort, these papers tried to win back what they had lost by denouncing the *Times*. The *Herald*, for instance, started a circulation drive with the slogan "Read an American paper."

The storm subsided with the war's end, leaving my father distraught and sick. My mother and I went through a terrifying time thinking that he had lost his mental stability. He had delusions of financial difficulties and of having filed a faulty income-tax return. We couldn't persuade him that his fears were imaginary.

According to his doctor, Frederick Tilney, my father's symptoms were typical of a severe case of emotional exhaustion. There was no organic disorder; the only cure was rest. "When your father recovers," the doctor told me, "he will remember nothing of what has been worrying him. All he will know is that he has been ill."

Just as he was overcome by dread of financial ruin, his top men approached him in an untimely request for a bonus. Carr Van Anda, Charles Miller and Louis Wiley asked for $25,000 each for their work during the war. I'm sure their request was justified, but it compounded my father's fears that he was going to lose all his money, and he collapsed under the pressure.

When my father fell ill, there was a great deal of commotion at the paper about who was to take over as publisher, and the question came up before the board of directors. I was only in my late twenties, but my father had put me on the board. The other members, besides my father, included his younger brother George, his cousin Ben Franck, and Mr. Miller.

First, my uncle Harry Adler of Chattanooga expressed his readiness to assume control. He was an attractive man but not a great business mind. Then, after Uncle Harry made his bid, Uncle George volunteered his services for the job.

Uncle George had had leadership positions. At the age of thirty-two he was elected mayor of Chattanooga. During his two terms he managed to balance the city budget and build parks, schools and a hospital without raising taxes. My father dissuaded him from continuing in politics by pointing out that the family's newspapers might be charged with political bias, and he took him into his own publishing business. From 1896 to 1900 George served as general manager of the *Chattanooga Times*. In 1900 he directed the *New York Times* printing plant at the Paris Exposition. Under his supervision, a European edition of the *New York Times* was printed daily. It was such an enormous success that George was awarded the French Legion of Honor.

When my father purchased the *Philadelphia Times* and the *Philadelphia Public Ledger* in 1902, George became publisher of those papers. He remained in that post for thirteen years, until my father sold the properties to Cyrus Curtis of the *Saturday Evening Post* and the *Ladies' Home Journal*. My father felt he was spreading himself too thin and had best concentrate on his first loves— the New York and Chattanooga papers. The sale put a stop to speculation that he was building a publishing empire.

While living in Philadelphia, George married and had two children, George, Jr., and John. About a week after the birth of his second son, his wife, the former Bertie Gans, died of childbed fever. Everyone was bewildered by her sudden death. Her doctor was a leading Philadelphia obstetrician, and her nurse had come highly recommended. The nurse and doctor blamed each other, but nothing was resolved.

About a week after his wife's death, George got word that the nurse had been badly injured in a fire and wanted to see him—there was something she had to tell him. Uncle George hurried over. By the time he reached her bedside she was dead. What she had to say would never be known.

George was not left alone with his two sons. His sister Nannie had moved in to help with the household during Bertie's confinement, and when Bertie died Nannie stayed on and reared the children as if they were her own.

The boys did not bear the name Ochs. During the First World War, Uncle George became so passionately anti-German that he decided to change his name to something less German-sounding. He selected the name Oakes. When no other members of the family followed his example, George modified Oakes to Ochs-Oakes, and he kept that name for the rest of his life. His sons, however, were known as George Oakes, Jr., and John B. Oakes. George became a writer, John a journalist.

This branch of the family was stalked by tragedy. George, Jr., was married and on his own with a family, and seeing his writing career beginning to flourish, when he, his wife, and son were killed in an automobile accident.

At the time the question of a new publisher of the *New York Times* came up in 1921, Uncle George was working in New York as publisher of two *Times*-owned magazines, *Mid-Week Pictorial* and *Current History*. He had founded the latter and was doing well with both publications. He had always had a leaning toward intellectual pursuits. He had had a long career in publishing. All these accomplishments seemed to recommend him as a prime candidate for the post of publisher of the *New York Times*.

I certainly respected his intellect but, more important, I believed that my father would soon recover from his breakdown and that such an important decision was therefore unnecessary.

"The *Times* staff is an extraordinarily capable group," I said at the board meeting. "For the time being, they don't need leadership. They'll produce a quality paper on their own momentum."

Mr. Miller backed me up. The rest of the board came around to agreeing that we should sit tight.

My father was ill for eighteen months. We made him rest, and did our best to keep the worries of the world out of earshot. Dr. Tilney had time for the whole family and helped keep up morale; I remember him with gratitude and affection. Slowly, Papa regained his peace of mind. A year after that decisive board meeting, he was able to return to his office on Forty-third Street. By then, as Dr. Tilney had predicted, he remembered none of the fears that had haunted him. All he knew was that he had been a very sick man.

13

Arthur went to work at the *New York Times* on December 7, 1918, shortly after being discharged from the Army. My father placed him under the supervision of George McAneny, the paper's executive manager. His first day on the job, Arthur was given an office, a part-time secretary and absolutely no work. On my father's instructions, he was let loose in the organized confusion of newspapering. Perhaps the intention was to determine whether he would float or sink. All that was certain was that Father was not inclined to let his son-in-law learn the easy way.

Arthur nearly went frantic looking for useful work. When he expressed an interest in writing for the news and editorial departments, my father assigned him the task of sifting through rejected letters to the editor for possible new leads. That was as near as he came to becoming a reporter.

The annual Hundred Neediest Cases campaign was running in

the *Times* the month Arthur went to work. This Christmas appeal for funds for exceptionally deserving persons among the city's poor had been started by my father in 1912. Arthur discovered that the campaign was not under anyone's personal supervision, and he was permitted to dig into the project. He made careful records of all contributions and worked long hours to make sure that the operation ran smoothly.

When the campaign ended, Arthur went back to roaming the Forty-third Street plant in search of work. The paper was fully staffed by capable and self-sufficient men. Many of the reporters and editors were preeminent in their fields, and at the top were such awesome figures as Carr Van Anda and Charles Miller. They were busy people who didn't have time for a rather lonely, unoccupied young man.

In later years Arthur would joke that a sure way to success was to marry the boss's daughter. The joke irked me, since the success Arthur made of himself at the *Times* was wholly his own. Yet at the beginning that association was a handicap.

He finally got the break he sought. Arthur's supervisor, George McAneny, was a charming, high-minded, lovely person but not, alas, the most efficient executive. When Arthur offered to relieve him of some of his numerous responsibilities, Mr. McAneny offered no objection. One of those responsibilities was the acquisition of newsprint, a serious concern because of the postwar shortage. Arthur proposed to tackle the problem of locating adequate newsprint supplies. Mr. McAneny discussed the request with my father, and they agreed that Arthur should set about familiarizing himself with that part of the operation. The door was open; Arthur had his first major job.

He began by studying wood-pulp processing at the *Times*'s Tidewater Paper Mill on the South Brooklyn waterfront. The mill was short of raw materials and paper production was slowing down. Arthur went on purchasing missions to Finland, Norway and Canada, arranging for enormous shipments that added a hundred tons a day to Tidewater's output. As a result, the *Times* freed itself of newsprint shortages and was assured of future supplies. In the process, Arthur became an expert on newsprint. He had found his way into the *New York Times*.

After that, Arthur made a practice of taking up what others let slide. He tackled such a wide assortment of projects that he became familiar with nearly every aspect of the newspaper business. He met each challenge enthusiastically, applying a highly gifted imagination and a plentiful supply of ideas. For the first time, my father had to admit that I had made an excellent choice when I married Arthur.

In the fall of 1923, there was a pressmen's strike that stopped the publication of all the city newspapers. Volunteer pressmen, newsmen and executives from the various journals joined forces to put out an interim paper called *The Combined New York Morning Newspapers*. The strike lasted only nine days, but there was fear of violence, and Arthur, like the others working long nights, carried a pistol.

One night after a press run, he took a cab home. He didn't know much about pistols, and he took the occasion to inspect the gun and see how it worked. Suddenly he heard the taxi driver cry out, "Is that for me?" The man was terrified. Arthur never carried a pistol again.

Arthur rose higher and higher with the *Times*, and in the mid-1920's my father put him in charge of negotiating an enormous cooperative newsprint venture with the Kimberly-Clark Company of Wisconsin. The company had for years supplied the *Times* with paper for its rotogravure section; now it proposed joint investment in the construction of a new four-machine paper mill, with supporting pulp-making equipment, in Ontario. The provincial government there had granted tree-cutting rights in a vast wilderness.

The proposed mill would be built in the same area where Kimberly-Clark already had a small pulp mill at Kapuskasing, Ontario, a tiny town on a little river that supplied hydroelectric power. The proposal was a tempting one for the *Times;* it would ensure the paper of an abundant supply of top-grade newsprint. But the magnitude of the investment—$30,000,000 between the two companies—called for a thorough investigation.

The president of Kimberly-Clark, F. J. Sensenbrenner, invited Arthur and me to his home in Neenah, Wisconsin, to discuss the venture. I remember Arthur's surprise at the high quality of life in that Midwestern city. Though he had traveled widely in Europe, he clung to the insular New York view that all points west of Chicago were backwoods. His naïveté amused me, and I gave him a good teasing.

Our first evening at the Sensenbrenners' started off in formal, restrained manner. Mr. Sensenbrenner and his daughter Gertrude, who acted as hostess, were very polite, as were the other company officials present, but they didn't make us feel at ease. While pleasantries were being exchanged over a marvelous dinner of German pot roast, Arthur looked up from his plate and said, "Would I be allowed to have an accident and drop some bread in this gravy?"

"Ah, you *dunk!*" exclaimed Gertrude's husband, Jim Bergstrom. Laughter burst forth around the table. The ice was broken.

After a journey to northern Ontario to look over the site, Arthur and the Kimberly-Clark representatives met in Kapuskasing. To harness adequate power for the new mill there would have to be a dam on the Kapuskasing River. In addition, housing for a self-contained community of four thousand employees would have to be built. This would also mean building schools, churches, recreational facilities and a hospital, and providing other normal comforts.

After making an initial survey, the men went on a two-hundred-mile canoe trip down the Kapuskasing River, to James Bay. They were to be flown back to Kapuskasing in small seaplanes, but the fog and rain made takeoffs impossible and the men were stranded. They couldn't send word of the delay, since there was no telephone or telegraph at James Bay, or even a radio. Arthur had forewarned me and my parents of the poor communications and I wasn't worried, not realizing the dangers entailed, but my father was quite alarmed. The return flight a week later proved to be a grueling experience. The seaplanes were puddle-jumping, open-cockpit models used for spotting forest fires, and Arthur's plane had an engine leak and kept landing on lakes in order to replenish its water supply.

Plans for building the paper mill and the communal housing were completed, and work got under way. During the four years it took to build the dam and mill, we made annual September treks to Kapuskasing with our Kimberly-Clark partners. Mr. Sensenbrenner always brought his two daughters, Gertrude and Mrs. Margaret Gilbert, who became my close friends. We were also joined by my father, Louis Wiley and Carr Van Anda, and on one occasion by Aunt Nannie and the Oakes boys. (These wilderness excursions didn't appeal to my mother.) Twenty-five or thirty of us would stay in a little guest house and have a roaring good time. There was no Prohibition in Canada, and spirit, of both the cerebral and liquid kinds, ran high.

One year we were in Canada during my birthday, and Arthur and his friends tried to get hold of enough liquor in that isolated outpost for all of us to celebrate. They were able to rustle up only a few bottles of Scotch, so, to stretch the refreshments, they concocted a most unusual drink—Scotch fruit punch. The party was gay, the cooks made a magnificent cake, and the punch nearly knocked me out.

When the plant at Kapuskasing was completed, it was christened the Spruce Falls Power and Paper Company. It began producing newsprint in 1928, and soon became the *Times*'s chief source of supply. The company is still in operation, with Kimberly-Clark holding the controlling block of shares, and the *New York Times* in possession of the remainder.

In December 1976, my son Arthur asked me if I would like to go to Kapuskasing with him and Walter Mattson, a *Times* executive vice president, for the fiftieth anniversary of the founding of the Spruce Falls Power and Paper Company. I was delighted to accept, and I was the only one of the old crowd to be there. It was 35 or 40 degrees below zero, but the warm reception and the fun of seeing the place again made me happy and comfortable.

My husband liked to tell the story of how the paper decided to enter into agreement with Kimberly-Clark and how he walked into my father's office with the contract and a check for his signature. The check was for something in the neighborhood of a million dollars.

Arthur asked my father if he wanted to look the agreement over. My father answered, "I'm very busy. Have you gone over it with the lawyers?"

"Yes."

"Well, are you satisfied everything's all right?"

"Yes, I've gone over it very carefully and I think it's all in order."

"Well, then," my father said, "I won't waste time reading it." And he signed the check without a glance at the contract.

As Arthur left with the papers, an office boy entered the room and asked my father if he could have a moment to talk about something personal.

"Come in," my father said, leaning back in his chair. "I've plenty of time." The last words Arthur heard as he started down the hall were: "Sit down, my boy, and tell me what your trouble is."

My father couldn't take a few minutes to read a million-dollar contract, but he always had time to listen to an office boy's problem. That's the kind of man he was.

14

Arthur's father, Cyrus L. Sulzberger, watched his son's rise with quiet pride. His boy had not been an outstanding student in high school or college. Arthur had not applied himself until he entered the Army school for artillery officers. His excellent grades confirmed his parents' belief that he was an unusually gifted young man.

Cyrus, like my father, had great respect for scholarly pursuits. He had had to drop out of school at the age of fourteen to go to work as an office boy and assist his family financially. Though he educated himself thoroughly in later years, like Papa he lamented his lack of formal education.

Cyrus was born the same year as Father—1858. Like the Ochses, the Sulzbergers were German Jews who immigrated to America in the mid-nineteenth century. The family settled in Philadelphia, where Cyrus Lindauer Sulzberger was born and where he attended

Central High School. Several members of the family became rabbinical scholars; Cyrus Adler, a nephew, became president of the Jewish Theological Seminary in New York. Cyrus's cousin Meyer Sulzberger became a prominent city judge.

In 1884, Cyrus married Rachel Peixotto Hays. Rachel was a Sephardic Jew, and her family thought it quite beneath her to marry a Jew of German ancestry. Rachel's father let his feelings be known by never pronouncing the name Sulzberger properly.

The Hays family was descended from refugees from the Spanish Inquisition who had fled to Holland and then, in 1700, to the New World. Peter Stuyvesant allowed them to settle in New Amsterdam on the condition that they take care of their own indigents and not be a burden to the community. Other Sephardic Jews chose to settle in Newport, Rhode Island, where the great religious liberal Roger Williams welcomed people of all faiths. The oldest standing synagogue in North America, called Touro, was built in Newport by Sephardic Jews. It is now a national monument, and Arthur at one time served on the committee for its restoration. One of Arthur's ancestors, Benjamin Mendes Seixas, had been a rabbi there, and it was to him that George Washington wrote his famous letter on religious freedom.

The Hays family did well in New York. During the Colonial period, they farmed land in Westchester County. At the time of the Revolution they lived in the Bedford Village-Pleasantville area, and one of them was a captain in the Revolutionary Army. This qualified Rachel to join the Daughters of the American Revolution. She became a member, she said, because she wanted people to remember that Jews had been part of America from the beginning and had joined in the fight for independence.

To Cyrus, however, his wife's membership was a source of annoyance. Whenever the D.A.R. passed one of its outrageous resolutions, he would offer her all kinds of inducements to let him write a letter of resignation over her name. She was never swayed. Arthur agreed with his mother's reasoning and joined the Sons of the Revolution when he was of age.

When Cyrus and Rachel were married, Cyrus was a bookkeeper with N. Erlanger, Blumgart & Company, a New York firm that specialized in importing and converting cotton goods. Among the items the company manufactured was a velveteen edging that was sewn onto the hems of ladies' skirts, which in those days were so long they swept the sidewalks. The velveteen attracted dust, thereby keeping the skirt clean.

Cyrus worked hard and rose from bookkeeper to president of the company by 1902. Though he stayed with Erlanger, Blumgart for the rest of his life, his interests were by no means limited to business. His involvements included backing two Jewish publications, the magazine *American Hebrew* and the *Jewish Encyclopedia*, serving on the boards of Jewish charities and raising money for American and European Jews. In 1900 he helped establish the Industrial Removal Office, which relocated Jewish immigrants to areas outside New York City where there was work for them.

Such help was badly needed. Jewish immigration reached its peak in the early 1900's (due largely to Russian pogroms), congesting New York too quickly with too many aliens to be assimilated into the new culture. The city was saturated with people and industry. Sprawling slums blighted the Lower East Side, where life became hazardous and unhealthy.

For five years Cyrus served as president of the Industrial Removal Office. By 1910, the organization had resettled more than 45,000 Jewish immigrants in towns all over the United States, and tens of thousands more on farms. The project was such a success that the governor of New York, Charles Evans Hughes, appointed Cyrus to a commission for the relief of congestion in cities.

Cyrus's wife was also involved in social welfare. She was second vice president of the New York section of the National Council of Jewish Women, she served as vice president of the United Neighborhood Houses, Inc., and she was a member of the board of the Urban League of New York.

The Sulzbergers had five children. The eldest, Leo (whose son, Cyrus L. Sulzberger, became a foreign-affairs expert for the *Times*), died of pneumonia at the age of forty, a year before the discovery of an effective cure for that disease. The next two children were to have even shorter lives: Cyrus, Jr., died of meningitis at the age of five, and his younger sister, Anna, died of diphtheria when she was one and a half. Arthur Hays, the fourth child, and

David Hays, his younger brother, were the only two children to survive their parents.

At the time of Arthur's birth, in 1891, the Sulzbergers were living in a three-story brownstone on West 120th Street, opposite Mount Morris Park. The house is still standing, but it is a most disreputable-looking building. Arthur once took our children to see the "landmark," telling them on the way that a commemorative plaque had been put on the building. The children were piqued when they realized that their father was teasing. There was indeed a plaque, but it read: "Rooms for Rent."

When Arthur was of school age, the family moved to West Eighty-seventh Street, then bought a house at 516 West End Avenue, at the corner of Eighty-fifth Street. Arthur attended P.S. 166, then transferred to Horace Mann, where he completed his high-school education. He went on to Columbia University and majored in engineering.

Although Arthur's parents were dedicated to Jewish causes, they gradually drifted away from formal practice of Judaism. It was their son Leo who caused them to return to the synagogue. Leo asked them why he couldn't say prayers the way his cousins did. The young parents decided they were depriving their children of their heritage and joined Temple Israel on 120th Street and Lenox Avenue. It was a liberal synagogue, belonging to the Union of American Hebrew Congregations founded by Rabbi Isaac M. Wise.

Cyrus became a fervent believer. His wife, however, retained her more independent views. My mother-in-law was an intelligent woman who always pursued her own interests. Determined to get a higher education, she had been admitted to Hunter College, then called Normal College Training School. After graduating, she taught in the New York City public schools.

Even after her sons were married, the whole family would gather every Friday night for dinner at 516 West End Avenue. Before the meal, my father-in-law would say the prayers, break the bread and drink the wine. My mother-in-law would light the sabbath candles. The dinner was always fish—not a Jewish custom but in the tradition of Rachel's family. Rachel was set in her ways about certain things, and one of them was having fish on Friday.

There was an odd touch one year when Passover fell on Friday. Cyrus, conducting the service, pronounced the words "Bring on the Paschal Lamb"—and the maid brought in the fish.

Arthur had been bar-mitzvahed and, unlike me, always fasted on Yom Kippur, but after we were married we did not attend temple with any regularity. Nonetheless, neither of us ever really drifted away from the faith; Arthur, in fact, served on the boards of Temple Emanu-El and the Jewish Institute of Religion.

However, when I was asked to serve on the board of Hebrew Union College, I hesitated, saying I didn't think I was a true believer. The rabbi of Hebrew Union asked me, "What do you think a true believer is?"

"Following everything that is in the Bible," I replied. "Believing in the scriptures and following all the precepts."

"No," the rabbi said. "The essence of liberal Judaism is believing in the ethics of the religion and keeping your mind open to all aspects of life. Modern science, for example, should not upset your roots. As the prophet Micah said, 'What doth the Lord require of thee, but to do justly, and to love mercy, and to walk humbly with thy God.'"

"Rabbi," I said. "I certainly have no quarrel with that. In fact, I should like to be that kind of person."

I think my early skepticism about Judaism traced back to Miss MacDonnell's notion that Judaism was Roman Catholicism without Jesus. Our faiths were fundamentally alike, she had said, and we must always accept the Bible and never question it. But she believed in a personal God—which I, with what little I knew of science, found hard to believe. Today, I can neither affirm that there is a personal God nor deny it. Today, I feel that in the face of these mysteries, one should be humble.

Though my father-in-law's interests outside his work were mostly related to Jewish causes, he also dabbled in the city's reform politics. In 1903 he ran for borough president of Manhattan. Rachel ordered a cake inscribed with the words "President of the Borough." When the returns told of his defeat, he walked over to the cake and scratched off the *P.* It was the only time he ran for public office.

My father-in-law was something of a biblical scholar, had a

good knowledge of history and held to an idealistic philosophy. He believed that men and nations could attain perfection and that a harmonious world without wars was possible. The outbreak of the First World War was a blow to his beliefs. He became a strong pacifist and for a whole year managed to keep Arthur from going to Officers' Training Camp. But Arthur, believing our entry into the war to be inevitable, wanted to be prepared, and entered the First Plattsburgh Camp against his father's wishes.

Despite their occasional differences of opinion, Arthur and his parents remained devoted to one another. The Sulzbergers, like the Ochses, were a close-knit family, and the two sets of parents-in-law got along well together, although there was never any intimacy between them. As far as temperament went, my mother and my mother-in-law were opposites. My mother was a happy-go-lucky type who rolled with the punches, while my mother-in-law was a doer, active in public affairs. Rachel thought my mother sweet but immature; my mother found Rachel cold and distant. The men—Cyrus and my father—got on better. They saw eye to eye on the question of establishing a Jewish state: They were against it.

Cyrus had had a change of heart on this issue. He had been a delegate to the Third International Zionist Congress in Basel, but became disillusioned with Zionism after the First World War. Like my father, he came to believe that, for Jews, Palestine was the most dangerous place on earth. "Every time you make a new frontier," he would say, "you make a new battle line."

The Sulzbergers had a self-assurance about them that was a bit disconcerting to a new daughter-in-law. I know that David's wife, Louise, felt quite ill at ease when she came into the family in 1921. I broke through their reserve one evening thanks to a biblical quotation.

It was at one of the Friday-night dinners, and the boys were teasing me about something I had done or said. Cyrus came to my defense, saying, "Don't let them upset you too much."

I smiled and answered, "Oh, no. 'Like the crackling thorns under a pot, such is the laughter of fools.'"

He was delighted. "You know that? Wonderful!"

I was in. That was enough to make me a Sulzberger.

15

The 1920's were marked by lawlessness and corruption. Those were the years of Prohibition, when formerly law-abiding citizens succumbed to scandalous behavior, and gangsters like Al Capone ran bootlegging empires and fought bloody gang wars.

We were deeply troubled by this turn of events, but our major concern was with everyday matters, like raising a family and Arthur's job with the paper. The leisure time we had together was spent in entertaining friends and absorbing the city's cultural offerings. This led to a bit of self-discovery.

Arthur and I spent many evenings attending concerts, each of us believing that the other had a deep understanding and love of music. When the truth emerged that I had no great knowledge of classical music and was merely trying to develop an appreciation of it, and that Arthur had no desire to sit out long evenings in the concert hall, our visits to the symphony came to an abrupt halt.

I continued my musical education by trying to foster love of music in my four children. The five of us, along with my friend Meta Markel and her daughter, would go to the children's concerts at Carnegie Hall. The concerts interested Ruth; she is the only one of my children who is musically inclined.

My husband took to listening to music over the radio at home, while relaxing in an easy chair. He derived great enjoyment from this, and in 1944 he decided it would be a sound business venture to buy radio station WQXR for the *New York Times*.

After he bought the station, Elliot Sanger, its general manager, became aware that Arthur had an aversion to one particular composer—Mozart. Mozart became the subject of extended badinage between the two men. They would correspond, more or less in verse, on the question of when Mozart should be broadcast. Arthur thought "never" would be the best time; his second choice was early morning.

Arthur listened to WQXR regularly, and any music he didn't like he would attribute to Mozart. On one occasion he was enchanted by what he was hearing and asked me to sit down and listen. "It's beautiful!" he'd exclaim from time to time. The music happened to be a composition I recognized, and when it ended I asked, "Do you know what you were listening to?"

"No, but it was lovely," Arthur answered.

I smiled and said, "My dear, that was a Mozart symphony."

He was flabbergasted. The banter between him and Mr. Sanger ceased.

Before the *Times* bought WQXR, it used to broadcast news over station WMCA. The news was introduced by the sounding of a gong. When the *Times* and WMCA parted company, Arthur and the station's owner, Nathan Straus, Jr., had a quarrel over the ownership of the gong. I don't remember who kept the gong and who bought a new one, but Arthur and Nathan never quite made up. It was a childish performance, somewhat reminiscent of the more serious feud between old Nathan Straus, Sr., the owner of Macy's, and my father.

Except when Arthur was listening to WQXR, music was not ordinarily sounding through our house. This was a great relief to our friend Leopold Auer, the great violinist we had met at Lake

George and came to know well during the twenties. When he entered our house he would invariably say, "Thank goodness, no music." He had his fill of music every day of the week, and our house was something of a refuge.

In 1924, when Professor Auer received his citizenship papers, a great celebration was held at his house on West Seventy-sixth Street. The guest list included all the important people in the music world—and two unmusical friends, Arthur and me. Mr. Auer asked George Gershwin to play something. Mr. Gershwin sat down at the piano, and a stunning composition filled the house. Professor Auer remarked to us that George Gershwin was bringing something new to music.

What Arthur and I took unqualified pleasure in was the theater. We joined the Theatre Guild and went to opening nights. At least we did until we saw a play—I think it was Paul Claudel's *Tidings Brought to Mary*—whose poetic, soulful artiness was indicative of the trend the Guild was beginning to follow. Finding this type of theater not to our taste, we decided to forgo opening nights and wait for the critics' reviews. We saw approximately one production a week during the theater season and were especially fond of musicals by such composers as Jerome Kern, Richard Rodgers and Cole Porter. In contrast to musicals today, the songs were tuneful, you could hear the lyrics and the singers' voices filled the house without the distorting effect of a microphone.

Social life in those days was subject to the corrupting influence of Prohibition. Like many others, we were in a dilemma. For years no liquor was served in the Ochs or the Sulzberger household, for we felt that laws ought to be observed. Yet the *Times* attacked this particular law as a colossal mistake, and my father and Arthur accepted drinks when visiting friends. (Furthermore, my father wouldn't give up his passion for betting on the horses at the Saratoga race track, which was also against the law. He was in safe company. I remember seeing the governor of New York, Al Smith, placing bets.)

Toward the end of Prohibition, when it was obvious that the law was farcical and an invitation to lawlessness, we abandoned our abstinence and started going to the speakeasy Jack and Charlie's, which is now called "21."

My mother-in-law and an English friend, Mrs. Israel Zangwill, were all excited on their first night at Jack and Charlie's. They had expected to find themselves in a low dive and to be raided by the police. Instead, the place boasted fine decor, and, bribery being common, I don't suppose Jack and Charlie were ever raided. Anyway, the evening went by uneventfully, and you never saw two more disappointed women.

Arthur and I joined in the prevailing mood and became quite free and easy about breaking the drinking law. Some evenings we went to Jack and Charlie's other establishment, a big private house in Armonk, a short drive from New York. There was always an elegant crowd there, drinking and gambling, and if I'm not mistaken there was a policeman guarding the entrance.

One evening, Arthur and I made bathtub gin. A doctor in the medical department of the *Times* had given us a quart of pure alcohol, with instructions on mixing it with distilled water, oil of juniper and oil of something else. The result was awful. Another time we tried spiking Virginia Dare, the nonalcoholic wine, and adding essence of orange bitters, and that concoction was equally unpleasant and brought our adventures in distillery to an end.

We had hoped to see Al Smith elected President in 1928 and get Prohibition repealed. Mr. Smith lost to Herbert Hoover, not, I think, over the Prohibition issue, but because he was Catholic. The Ku Klux Klan was powerful then and ran a strong campaign against him. I also suspect that Al Smith's personality worked against him. He was a good and able man—one of the best governors New York ever had—but he didn't have the manners of a gentleman and he spoke in the down-to-earth language of his Lower East Side upbringing. I never understood why anyone so intelligent would choose to remain so crude. I suppose he thought it good politics in New York City.

I had an amusing encounter with Al Smith when he was serving as the first president of the corporation that built the Empire State Building. I had an appointment to see him (for a reason that now escapes me), and I entered his office to find him in his shirt sleeves, leaning back in his chair, his feet up on the desk, sucking a cigar. He greeted me, "Hi, come in," and waved me to a chair. His feet remained on his desk and he continued to suck his cigar.

I took a seat and started my sales pitch, undoubtedly trying to solicit his support for my latest cause. I don't remember if I was successful, but what sticks in my mind was his annoyance over some newspaper article that described his manners. "They actually implied," he said indignantly, "that I wasn't a perfect gentleman."

I sympathized with him. It was true that his manners were rough and his English atrocious, but in his heart Al Smith *was* a perfect gentleman.

As I said, most of my activities in the 1920's revolved around my family. On March 12, 1921, our second child, Ruth Rachel, was born. We were living in an eight-room apartment on West Eighty-first Street, across from the American Museum of Natural History. We had three live-in staff—a cook, a maid and a nurse for our daughter Marian—and with little Ruth we reached the saturation point. She screamed us out of Eighty-first Street, and we rented a brownstone on West Eighty-eighth between Central Park West and Columbus Avenue. We were living there when our third daughter, Judith Peixotto, was born on December 27, 1923.

Just before our fourth and last child arrived, my father bought us a five-story house, with an elevator and lots of maid's rooms, on East Eightieth Street off Fifth Avenue. The house seemed enormous when we moved in, but it wasn't long before we were using every inch of space and building a playroom on the roof.

We moved into East Eightieth in the fall of 1925, and our son, Arthur Ochs, was born the following February 5. The boy wasn't destined to be called Arthur for very long. Since he came after Judy, my husband couldn't resist nicknaming him Punch. The name stuck, and today, to his family, his friends and his associates, he is, simply, Punch.

We moved in the furnishings we'd acquired during seven years of marriage, but the new house looked empty, and one day I went off in search of a good decorator. It was raining like the end of the world as I made my way from one fancy decorating shop to another. I would splash in and say, "I'm looking for some advice and help. I have a new house." The shopkeepers would take one look at me—I had decked myself out in a raincoat, a large pair of rubbers and my worst hat, a dreadful pink affair, and was carrying a large bright green umbrella, the only one I could find—and would assign me to a junior clerk's junior assistant, who would respond to my interest in an item by saying, "You know, that's very expensive. This is a very high-class shop you're in. I'm afraid you'll find it beyond your means." The condescending remarks would put me off, and I would say, "Thank you very much," and splash out.

In one store, the manager was short of available assistants and had to help me himself. As we made our way from antique to antique, he kept shaking his head and murmuring how expensive this or that was. He clearly thought the likes of me a complete waste of time, until he asked, "Where is this house you've been talking about?" I answered with great poise, "It's number five East Eightieth Street."

"Oh!" he exclaimed, his eyes widening. "That's a very good neighborhood!"

At that point I felt pretty hoity-toity, and I looked him squarely in the eye and said, "Yes, we thought so when we bought the house."

An immediate transformation came over the man, and he was quick to try to impress me. "I decorated Mrs. Hutton's and Mrs. Woolworth's houses just across the street from yours."

Well, his newfound interest in this woman with the awful hat came too late. When he asked if he could have a look at my house, I said, "I'll think it over," and left the store.

Eventually, I found my way into the shop Charles of London. Unlike the other managers, Mr. Charles wasn't put off by my nondescript appearance. Being an Englishman, he was exceedingly polite and helpful. He brought out samples of material, suggested color combinations, and that afternoon we set up an appointment for him to come to the house.

My slogging through the rain paid off. Mr. Charles was the craziest little man, but he was the luckiest thing that ever happened to Arthur and me. He took us in hand and told us we had terrible taste (which was true). To get us started, he would send things to our house on approval. The choices were good and we rarely returned anything. He taught us about different period pieces, and we began to develop a sense of taste and imagination about decorating. In fact, my taste became so refined that while browsing in his shop one day I spotted a beautiful little table and asked, "Mr. Charles, why don't you ever send us furniture like that?"

"Because, Mrs. Sulzberger," he answered, "that is a museum piece. You don't want to live in a museum. You have four children and you want a home. I'll get you another table that's similar, but more suitable for your needs." Sure enough, a few months later an adequate substitute arrived. It was a quarter the price.

As it turned out, we bought nearly all our furnishings from Mr. Charles. We came to know him fairly well over the years and learned that he was the younger brother of Lord Duveen. Apparently the two brothers didn't get along, and someone told me that the Duveens paid Charles not to use the family name in his furniture business. The few things we didn't buy from Charles we got from Hayden's, at Fifty-seventh Street and Park. Like Charles, the manager was English and very polite.

The moral of the story is: Be polite if you want to get ahead in business, no matter how peculiar the appearance of your customer.

16

As the *New York Times* became increasingly influential, I, as the publisher's daughter, was given the opportunity of meeting leading political figures and seeing politics in action.

In 1912, when I was still a student at Barnard, my father arranged for me to see that year's Democratic Convention in Baltimore. I went there with Mrs. Strauss, the wife of his colleague and good friend Samuel (who had been publisher of the New York *Globe*, an evening paper, before coming to the *Times*).

The convention floor was lively with delegates being wooed by backers of the various candidates. The leading candidate was James Beauchamp Clark of Missouri, the Speaker of the House. He had the support of William Jennings Bryan, who had been the Democratic Presidential nominee in 1896, 1900 and 1908. Clark's strongest adversary was Woodrow Wilson, the governor of New Jersey, who was considered a radical in those days. The *Times*, however, had endorsed the dark-horse candidate, Governor Judson Harmon of Ohio. I disagreed with the choice and favored Mr. Wilson.

A few days into the convention, it became apparent that Mr. Harmon was out of the race, and the *Times* came under pressure to switch its endorsement to one of the two front-runners. As the only member of the Ochs family at the convention, I came to the attention of supporters of both sides.

In the Wilson camp were two of my father's close friends—the financier Henry Morgenthau and the owner and publisher of the Baltimore *Sun*, Charles Grasty. Mr. Morgenthau invited Mrs. Strauss and me into his box so we could enjoy an excellent view of the convention, and Mr. Grasty ushered me to the press section, where I was showered with Wilson campaign buttons.

The *Times* did shift its support to Wilson. That had nothing to do with me, of course. Nonetheless, the people who had courted me considered it a great triumph and made more of a fuss over me than ever.

Mr. Wilson and Mr. Clark ran neck and neck. The delegates cast ballot after ballot, but neither candidate could gather the majority he needed to win. Then William Jennings Bryan switched to Wilson. His fire-and-brimstone oratory made a poor impression on me, but his change of allegiance broke the tie on the forty-sixth ballot. Mr. Wilson won the Democratic nomination—and, of course, went on to win the Presidency.

The next time I heard Mr. Bryan speak was at the 1924 Democratic Convention in Madison Square Garden. The contest was between Al Smith and William Gibbs McAdoo, the former Secretary of the Treasury and Woodrow Wilson's son-in-law. Mr. McAdoo wasn't warmly received in New York; the city's Jewish and Irish voters held his Ku Klux Klan support against him. Furthermore, Mr. McAdoo's record was under scrutiny because of his involvement in the oil deals of the Harding Administration.

Mr. Bryan sailed off on one of his oratorical flights in support of Mr. McAdoo, and I could see he felt that the audience was with him. Then he said, "So what difference do three little letters— K.K.K.—make?" and the words ignited the audience into the wildest protest I've ever seen. People stomped and shouted and stood on their chairs and shrieked, "No! No!" A fever swept the convention floor, and I found myself standing on my chair, yelling, "Oil! Oil! Oil!"

I should have controlled myself—Arthur, who was sitting next to me, didn't get carried away—but there was something liberating about it. As part of the crowd, I had a courage I would never have on my own.

Once, when my father, Arthur and I were in Washington during the Coolidge Administration, the President invited us to lunch at the White House. Despite the glamour of the surroundings, the lunch was uninteresting. The President spoke very little. One of his brief comments came in response to my father's attempt to recruit him as a speaker for an Associated Press luncheon. "What date is the luncheon?" he asked. This prompted Mrs. Coolidge to remark, "Oh, then you are going?"

"No," said Mr. Coolidge. "I don't know. I'm just trying to show Mr. Ochs that I'm doing all I can to oblige him."

After the meal, the President, my father and Arthur retired into the President's office, leaving Mrs. Coolidge and me to have coffee in the family living room. She talked of how expensive it was to live in the White House. While the Government absorbed the cost of the servants' salaries, the Coolidges had to take care of the food bills. Evidently this amounted to quite a substantial sum, since the staff was a large one.

Our visit to the White House was, to put it kindly, not particularly stimulating, but when Arthur and I were asked by our friends to relate what happened I didn't want to disappoint them and told the following story:

"After lunch, I started to get into an elevator before the President—assuming, quite naturally, that ladies precede gentlemen —when he stopped me, saying, 'You can't go ahead of me. The President of the United States takes precedence under all circumstances.' The two of us stood there, neither of us moving. We had quite an argument about what to do, while an aide ran off to get a book on etiquette. According to the book, the President was right, so he entered the elevator before me."

I had made up the whole story out of whole cloth on the spur of the moment—and paid the consequences for months afterward.

The story circulated until I thought the entire world had heard it. People kept coming to me and asking, "Why did you do it?" or "Who got into the elevator first?" I only hope my yarn never got back to the President. I never met Mr. Coolidge again, so I'll never know for sure, but my father used to see him quite often and never mentioned his remarking on the supposed episode.

My father did pass on one thing Mr. Coolidge said to him: "My goal as President is to keep things on an even keel so that nobody will go to bed at night worrying about what the President will do the next morning."

Papa visited the President and his wife when they were vacationing on their farm, and a photograph was taken of the three of them on the veranda. Father sent a copy of the photograph to his family in Chattanooga. My uncle Harry Adler, who was running the *Chattanooga Times*, took the picture into the office and showed it to one of the older printers.

"Mighty fine of Mr. Ochs," the printer said. "Who's he with?"

One of my father's favorite President stories was about Warren Harding. When Father was first introduced to the President, Mr. Harding said, "But, Mr. Ochs, don't you remember meeting me?"

"Quite frankly, no," my father admitted.

"Well," the President said, "when I was a young man, I went down to Chattanooga to review the possibilities of starting a Republican newspaper. I decided that the best place to start would be a newspaper office, so I went to see you and related my ideas. I remember your words well. 'It's true there aren't any Republican papers down here,' you said, 'and possibly it could be a good idea to start one. But I do want to call your attention to the fact that practically all the Republicans in town are Negroes and most of them can't read.' So, Mr. Ochs, I decided to give up the project and go back to Marion, Ohio, and set my sights on becoming the President of the United States. I want to thank you."

My father's good friend Charles Grasty, who had showered me with Wilson buttons at the 1912 convention, also introduced me to the man who was to become the thirty-first President of the United

States—Herbert Hoover. Mr. Hoover was a hero in those days because of his dramatic relief work in postwar Belgium. When I told Mr. Grasty of my desire to meet him, he said, "Nothing simpler," and arranged for the three of us to have lunch at the Biltmore Hotel. My mother learned about it and asked if she could join us.

My mother was a good conversationalist, but that day she found talking with Mr. Hoover very difficult. He responded to her questions about his work with short, crisp sentences that didn't invite conversation. Perhaps he was bored with talking about his own achievements, or perhaps he was naturally modest, but my mother gave up and turned her attention to Mr. Grasty, leaving me to struggle with the tight-lipped Mr. Hoover. I knew I had to come up with a more fruitful subject, and on an impulse I said, "Mr. Hoover, I remember having read that you lived for years in China."

Well, I had pronounced the magic words. He launched forth in animated conversation about his experiences in China as a young engineer. He spoke about Chinese culture and art, and about a great deal more that I can't remember. All I know is that he was absolutely fascinating and I had a wonderful lunch. As for my mother, she was terribly annoyed with herself for having given up so soon on Mr. Hoover.

She was, however, able to make up for it subsequently. After he became President in 1929, Mr. Hoover became very friendly with my father, and he and his wife invited my parents to the White House for a dinner party and to stay overnight. It was an especially generous invitation, since the *Times* had supported Al Smith in the 1928 race. My mother had a good time and found the Hoovers very amiable. But the second time she and my father were invited to stay overnight, she refused the invitation. At the White House she didn't get breakfast in bed. It was the one small luxury in life she wouldn't forgo, even for the President.

Arthur and I had little contact with President Hoover. We were once invited to a formal White House dinner, which proved to be extraordinarily dull. The guests were seated according to protocol, and we were way down below the salt. I was placed next to an uninteresting man; I think he was a congressman.

I saw Herbert Hoover on only one other occasion. It was in the late 1930's, when I was invited to an informal dinner party in his New York apartment (Arthur must have been away). Mr. Hoover had just returned from some official business in Germany, and he told of being a lunch guest of Hermann Göring at the Field Marshal's estate in Prussia. He recounted that as his car approached the huge old house, the bronze gates of the driveway were thrown open and green-uniformed trumpeters sounded a regal flourish. Mr. Hoover said he felt he had landed in the middle of a Wagnerian opera. He was escorted to the dining room, where a long table was elaborately set and servants were stationed behind the chairs. In the middle of the table was a gold bust of a woman.

The guests were seated, and Field Marshal and Mrs. Göring took their places at the opposite ends of the table. After the meal began, the Field Marshal turned to Mr. Hoover and asked, "Do you notice the bust in the center of the table?"

"Yes, it's very lovely," Mr. Hoover replied politely.

"It's a solid-gold bust of my first wife," Mr. Göring explained. His second wife did not seem to mind.

Charles Grasty, who was my father's close friend—he was with Papa at the Associated Press meeting in New York on the night I was born, and he often recounted how my father became so excited when he received the telegram announcing my birth that he bought rounds for everyone in the hotel bar—became a close friend of Arthur's and mine.

Mr. Grasty was a true journalist who, in the course of his career, had been publisher of two Baltimore papers, the *News* and the *Sun*. He sold the *Sun* just before the First World War, thereby putting himself into retirement in a very important news era, and, quite predictably, he became depressed. My father persuaded him to come out of retirement and go abroad for the *Times* as a war correspondent. He made his headquarters in Paris. There, when he was already in his mid-fifties, his life took an unusual turn.

While still a young man, he had married a woman quite a bit older than he was. No children were born to them (although she had a daughter by a previous marriage) and this became a source of distress to him. I remember his telling me that he longed to have a child. He said, "I don't think I'm all that handsome"—I thought he was—"but I'd like to see a child with my face, *my* child." He must have felt very strongly about it for years. In Paris during the war he saw a way of making his dream come true.

He had a secretary, a young Englishwoman, and he persuaded her—without too much difficulty, I gather—to bear his child and give him the baby. To explain the baby to his wife he manufactured a story about having persuaded his nephew, who was a minister with six children, to give him their seventh. Mrs. Grasty, I imagine, suspected the truth, for the first thing she asked him was "Charlie Grasty, is this your baby?" He firmly denied it, and they adopted her as their daughter. They named her Joan.

But as Joan grew up, everyone could see that she was Charles Grasty's daughter. I remember being struck by the resemblance when she was brought, one day, to Marian's birthday party.

My parents learned of the secret from Joan's real mother. She called on them while they were on a visit to Paris and told them the whole story. She asked my mother if she could get Mr. Grasty to give the child back to her. "I want her very much," she said. Mama was distressed, but felt there was nothing she could do.

When Joan Grasty was about seven, Mr. Grasty fell ill and died. Under the terms of his will, Mrs. Grasty inherited the bulk of the estate, and Joan was to inherit it upon Mrs. Grasty's death. But the will contained the proviso that the estate be withheld from Joan if she were returned to her mother; instead, the money would go to Mr. Grasty's stepdaughter. The identity of Joan's real mother was thus avowed.

Shortly after Mr. Grasty's death, Mrs. Grasty died and Joan's mother went to Baltimore to claim her daughter. This left the three trustees of the Grasty estate with a very difficult problem. Joan was a minor, and needed a home. Hence, if she were not to be given to her mother—and thus denied her inheritance—she would have to be adopted by someone else. Yet none of the three trustees was in a position to do so. The first, Julius Adler, had three children of his own. The second, Leah Squier, wife of Dr. J. Bentley Squier, was too old to take on a little girl. The third, Mrs. Cary T. Grayson, wife of a Navy admiral who was Charles

Grasty's cousin, had three boys. The problem was finally resolved when Mr. Grasty's stepdaughter very generously declined to accept the inheritance, saying she thought it only fair that Joan—his true daughter—be the recipient. At that point the trustees decided unanimously to get the will legally changed so that Joan could inherit the estate and be united with her mother, who was by then married to a well-established man and living in California.

This was done. Joan grew up with her mother. Yet she still did not know the true story. Her mother told her that her real father had been killed in the war, and that Mr. Grasty had taken her into his home while her mother was getting resettled. The girl believed this. Both her first and last names were legally changed, breaking all ties with the Grasty family.

I lost track of Joan. Someone told me she had been married and divorced. I suppose it all turned out for the best, but there has always been sadness in my heart for Mr. Grasty—and for all concerned in this all-too-human drama.

17

My father was a modest man who preferred to keep out of the public eye. I don't believe he ever fully appreciated how much fame his success with the *New York Times* had brought him, and he was always astonished by it. Although sought after socially, my parents preferred not to become part of New York society. When it came to Chattanooga, however, they felt differently about these things, and Papa's fiftieth anniversary as publisher of the *Chattanooga Times* was a public event.

On Friday, June 29, 1928, my father and members of our family boarded a train for Chattanooga accompanied by a large group of friends, who included a number of employees of the *New York Times*—some sixty people in all. Among the guests were Darwin Kingsley, president of the New York Life Insurance Company, and his wife; my father's longtime friend Samuel Untermyer; and two representatives of the city of New York—the charming and well-educated Grover Whalen, who was the city's official greeter, and Commissioner Walsh. I don't recall now what Mr. Walsh was commissioner of, but I do remember that he was a tall, distinguished-looking man with a turned-up mustache, an amusing and likable manner and an unabashed bent for murdering the King's English. Mr. Sensenbrenner and his two daughters went to Chattanooga directly from Wisconsin to be on hand for the event.

Of the family, my mother, then sixty-eight, was about the only one absent. She had decided that the trip would be too arduous and would entail too much commotion.

As the train pulled into Chattanooga, the local American Legion band blasted forth with welcoming tunes and a large group of old friends and city officials, led by Mayor E. A. Bass, rolled out the red carpet. We went by motorcade to the new Lookout Mountain Hotel. No alcohol was served during the celebration there, it being Prohibition, but a local friend produced some crème de cacao and we made Alexander cocktails in our rooms.

The people of Chattanooga staged an impressive homecoming for the local boy made good. For two days we were kept busy from morning to late at night with luncheons and dinners and ceremonies. When we weren't attending official presentations, the Jubilee Committee took us on sightseeing excursions to such attractions as the Grand Canyon of the Tennessee River. We went by old-fashioned paddle steamer through the beautiful river gorge, picnicked on the shore and enjoyed the splendid scenery. During one picnic, Mr. Untermyer decided to do a little exploring, and wandered off so far that he didn't get back in time to board the boat for the return trip. There were so many of us we didn't realize he was missing until we were way upriver. We returned to the picnic site to find Mr. Untermyer in a very shaken state. In his wandering he had come upon an illegal still. Fortunately, the moonshiners asked who he was before opening fire, and he managed to convince them he wasn't a revenue officer but a tourist who had strayed from his party.

One of the highlights of the celebration was when Mayor Bass presented my father with a gold key to the city and declared him a Citizen Emeritus of Chattanooga. (My daughter Ruth now has the key in the *Chattanooga Times* office.) The climax was the jubilee dinner at the Lookout Mountain Hotel. Messages and testimonials came from President Coolidge, from governors, mayors and senators, from publishers and from the reading public. They came by mail, telegram and wireless—so many that it took my father days to read them all.

Among the speakers that night was my father's first employer, Captain Rule. It must have been a nostalgic moment for my father when the withered, eighty-year-old man reminisced about the office boy who had put a good shine on his chimney lamp.

I have often wondered what went through my Uncle Milton's mind as he listened to the testimonials. Certainly, his career and that of his brother George would have taken different directions had it not been for their older brother's overpowering personality. As it was, when George was seventeen and Milton fourteen, they became cub reporters at the *Chattanooga Times*, and from then on their lives revolved around journalism.

For a brief spell Milton left the family business and went to Colorado, where he tried his hand at selling insurance. Though he had an outgoing and delightful personality, he was not a successful salesman and returned to the *Times*. It wasn't long thereafter that he took up an independent career again. In 1909 he became part owner and publisher of the *Nashville American*. In 1911, however, my father asked Milton to assist his brother George in running the family-owned Philadelphia newspapers, and Milton left Nashville to become those papers' Sunday editor and later general manager. When those publications were sold in 1913, Milton returned to Chattanooga and became managing editor of the *Times*, a position he held until his retirement.

Milton enjoyed his days in Chattanooga. He became involved in civic affairs, and his colorful and congenial personality made him very popular. When he wasn't working, he turned his hand to gardening and cultivated his hobby, ornithology. He converted a barn into an aviary, in which scores of birds of I don't know how many species sailed and swooped about.

Milton's marriage to Frances Van Dyke (always known as Fanny or Aunt Fan) upset both the Ochs and Van Dyke families.

The match was regarded as highly unsuitable because Milton was a Jew and Fanny a Presbyterian. At the wedding ceremony, the mothers of the couple wept. Grandmother Ochs, in particular, behaved as if she were at a funeral.

The marriage, however, proved to be a good one. The couple celebrated their sixtieth wedding anniversary in 1953 and lived happily together into their nineties. They had three children— William Van Dyke Ochs, Adolph Shelby Ochs and Margaret Ochs (now Mrs. Theodore Palmer). All three were raised as Presbyterians.

Aunt Fan was from a prominent Chattanooga family. Her father was a distinguished lawyer; my father was one of his clients. Her great-grandfather was Ephraim McDowell, the famous surgeon who in 1809 performed the first successful operation involving removal of a woman's ovary. Aunt Fan's great-great-grandmother was, according to the Van Dykes, the first white child born in Kentucky.

Aunt Fan took her Presbyterianism seriously, but Uncle Milton kept some distance between himself and the synagogue. Aunt Fan used to complain to me, "I can't get your uncle to the temple even on the high holy days unless I go with him!" So she took it upon herself to accompany her husband, maintaining that this in no way compromised her as a Presbyterian. "Everyone needs religion," she'd say. "It doesn't matter what kind."

Uncle Milton was, in general, an unpredictable man. As Aunt Fan put it, "Your uncle has the capacity to annoy me, but he never bores me." When he was seventy or thereabouts, he inaugurated a men's club, which he named the Fifty Year Club of Chattanooga, as a practical outlet for his belief in companionship among the elderly. The qualifications for belonging were a fifty-year residence in Chattanooga and membership in the white race (a stipulation that was later dropped). The club's annual activities included a Fourth of July party at Uncle Milton's house on Missionary Ridge and a New Year's Eve party at the Patton Hotel.

These men became devoted companions, visiting one another at times of illness and joining in celebrations on birthdays. When a club member died, all the others attended the funeral service. Uncle Milton once received word from Mississippi that one of the members, who was visiting there, had died impoverished, not even leaving enough money for his burial. However, he left a will asking that his body be turned over to his dear friend Milton Ochs, who would give him a fine funeral. Uncle Milton arranged for the body to be returned to Chattanooga and organized the funeral service, and all the club members came to give their destitute friend a last blowout.

During his final years, Uncle Milton had a falling out with the rabbi and dissociated himself completely from the temple. When he died at the age of ninety-two, he left instructions that he be buried in a nonsectarian cemetery and that two Presbyterian minister friends officiate at the funeral. His children didn't find this objectionable, but his wife was very upset. She said to them, "Your father was a Jew and he was always proud of it. I'm sure there was nothing to that old quarrel. The rabbi will officiate, and the two Presbyterian ministers can each say a prayer." And that, when Uncle Milton was laid to rest, was how it was done.

Milton's many activities never left him with enough time for travel, so Aunt Fan would join my parents on their trips abroad. She and my mother became as close as sisters. Aunt Fan was always beloved in the family, and when my parents died she took over as the matriarch. It was largely through her influence that Milton Ochs's children and grandchildren are still close to me and my children. I don't know how many times she told me, "Now I want you all to exchange Christmas presents. You'll forget birthdays, but as long as you remember each other once a year with a gift, you'll never drift apart."

In July 1928, Arthur and I left for a tour of South America. The purpose of the trip was to establish a news channel from the Latin American countries. Neither the *Times* nor the Associated Press gave nearly enough coverage to South American affairs, and my father wanted Arthur to scout the continent for connections and correspondents.

We boarded a Grace Line ship in New York and sailed through the Panama Canal and down the western coast of South America, stopping at various ports along the way. At Lima we were met by a secretary of the United States Embassy who invited us on behalf of Ambassador Alexander Moore to be his house guests. Mr. Moore, owner and publisher of the *Pittsburgh Leader*, was an old friend of my father and a diamond in the rough. He was the widower of the famous stage beauty Lillian Russell, to whom he always referred as "my dear sainted Lillian." When he had been Ambassador to Spain, he entertained my parents at a party at which members of the royal court were present. Now, in Lima, he gave a dinner party in our honor. Among the guests was the President of Peru, Augusto Leguía.

In chatting with the President, I remarked how interesting we found our visit to the Cathedral of Lima to see Pizarro's tomb. He asked, "Did you notice the chapel across from the sarcophagus?"

"No. Should I have?"

He said he intended to restore the chapel and dedicate it to Atahualpa, the last of the Inca kings.

"But, Mr. President," I objected, "Atahualpa wasn't a Catholic."

The President assured me that I was mistaken. When we returned to our rooms that night, I checked into Prescott's *Conquest of Peru* and learned that when Pizarro decided to execute Atahualpa, he gave the king a choice of being burned as a heathen or garroted as a Christian. Deciding that the second alternative would be the less painful of the two, the king was baptized and garroted.

No visit to Peru would be complete without a visit to Cuzco, the ancient Inca capital in the Andes, 11,000 feet above sea level, and Ambassador Moore decided to go with us. But since he had to be back in Lima by a particular date, we had to shorten our trip. Arthur and I had planned to spend a couple of days in Arequipa, at an altitude of 6,000 feet, to get acclimatized, but now we went directly from sea level to a 15,000-foot-high mountain pass, and into the valley where Cuzco nestles. There were six people in our railroad car—a captain in the American Army Air Corps, his wife, the Ambassador, the Ambassador's Peruvian valet, Arthur and I. I must have been a llama in a previous life, for I was the only one who remained well during our two-day stay in Cuzco. Nonetheless, all agreed that the trip was worth the discomfort. The Inca ruins and the Spanish cathedral were fascinating. The cathedral's altar stretches across the entire nave and is solid silver. I climbed the steps to admire the superb workmanship and was bemused to see a tin spittoon for the priests.

Arthur and I had planned to proceed by train to Bolivia, but the altitude was too much for him, so we returned to Arequipa to recuperate there, while the Ambassador's party went back to Lima.

Before we left Peru, President Leguía made me a present of some interesting pre-Columbian art objects, which I still have. Knowledgeable though he was on his country's history, he was not the most popular of rulers. In 1930, there was a revolution and President Leguía was put into prison, where he was maltreated and died two and one half years later.

If Arthur was chagrined to find himself worsted by the altitude while I, a mere woman, took it in stride, the score between us was soon evened. On the British boat we took down the coast to Valparaiso, I got terribly seasick. Besides, the English with their love of fresh air never closed the doors or windows, which meant that we were in a constant draft. The only way to keep warm was to stay in bed. We spent most of our time under the covers, drinking tea and nibbling toast (the rest of the food being almost inedible).

From Valparaiso we went to Santiago. Arthur had already found a correspondent for the *Times* in Lima, and now he engaged a second one in Santiago. The local newspaper people were very kind to us, and the Embassy most hospitable, and we had a pleasant time.

At Santiago we boarded a train for the thirty-six-hour trip to Buenos Aires. (Airlines had not yet been established in Latin America.) The Chilean railroad was excellent, and as we twisted through the Andes we were overwhelmed by the superb mountain scenery. At the Argentine border town of Mendoza, however, we changed to a train operated by a British company. That train was no credit to Britain. Although it was August 1 and the dead of winter in the Southern Hemisphere, there was no heat, and we sat freezing in our overcoats. The view of the pampas was uninteresting, aside from some cattle and wild ostrich-like birds, so we had nothing to distract us for a miserable twenty-four hours.

In Buenos Aires we were taken in hand by the publishers of the daily *La Nación*, which modeled itself on the *New York Times*. (The other important daily, *La Prensa*, owned by the Alberto Gainza Paz family, was patterned on *The Times* of London.) Between the owners of *La Nación* and American Ambassador Robert Wood Bliss and his wife, we were entertained royally.

The night before we left Buenos Aires, we dined at the American Embassy. I was seated next to the Uruguayan Ambassador, and I told him that the next stop on our itinerary was Montevideo. When he learned that Arthur and I would be sightseeing on our own, he said he would arrange for his brother, Dr. Blanco, to give us a tour of the Uruguayan capital.

The Ambassador was true to his word. No sooner had we arrived in our hotel in Montevideo than Dr. Blanco and his wife phoned to say they were on their way over.

Dr. Blanco turned out to be the leading gynecologist of Montevideo, and his idea of taking in the sights was to show us every hospital and child-care center in town. Fortunately, before dressing for dinner at the American Embassy that evening, we had time to see the capitol, which was outstanding. The Blancos were charming people, but I'd like to return to Montevideo one day and see more of the regular tourist attractions.

We were the only guests at the American Ambassador's home. He was a bachelor, and spent the entire evening explaining how unsuited he was to his job because he spoke no Spanish. Arthur and I had to agree with him.

Our last stop on the tour was Rio de Janeiro. We traveled there on a German luxury liner, stopping for a day at Santos, a Brazilian coffee-shipping port. Rio was glorious, and we spent five wonderful days there before starting our thirteen-day cruise back to New York.

The return trip on the American ship was very relaxing. During a stopover at Bahia, a Brazilian port renowned for its hundred churches, Arthur and I decided to explore the town, even though there were local reports of bubonic plague. It was recommended that all those going ashore wear shoes covering the ankles, since the fleas on the rats that carried the plague couldn't jump any higher than that. Neither of us had such shoes, but we made our tour without a single attack from the fleas.

The excursion around South America took us two months. More than half the time was spent traveling, which is a little different from the kind of touring done nowadays by air. Arthur succeeded in engaging correspondents in Lima, Santiago, Buenos Aires and Rio. Contact with the little-known continent had been established, and the *Times* began to give its readers more news from Latin American countries. It was the beginning of an attempt to cover comprehensively a vast area that had been so long neglected —an objective yet to be fully accomplished.

18

One of the most memorable trips Arthur and I took was in 1929, when we journeyed by way of Berlin and Warsaw to the Soviet Union. Though the United States still had not recognized the Soviet regime, there was, briefly, an easing of hostility between the two Governments, and a few enterprising American tourists were able to get Soviet visas.

We arrived in Berlin to find the city in the grip of a terrible inflation. It was a tragic time for the poorer people and those living on fixed incomes. Arthur restrained me from doing any shopping, saying that to buy items so underpriced would be taking advantage of the country's economic plight, almost like robbery. We couldn't have known that the mark was to plunge even lower, and that our buying would have done the shopkeepers a kindness.

From Berlin we traveled by train to Warsaw, where we were met by the local *New York Times* correspondent, a handsome young Pole. Being Jewish, he was well acquainted with life in the Warsaw ghetto, and as we toured the city he spoke of what a miracle it was that Poland was now free of Russian tyranny and that the country's Jews no longer had to live in terror. "At last," he said, "we are free and equal citizens."

We walked through the ghetto and could see that its inhabitants were buoyed up by hopes of a better life. The streets were clean, the shops were stocked with interesting items and optimism was reflected in people's faces.

Ten years later, Hitler and Stalin divided Poland between them, and the rest of the story is well known. I learned from a Polish friend that our charming correspondent was, fortunately, able to escape the worst of it.

We continued by train to the Soviet Union, and when we reached the border we knew we were entering a country unlike any we had known before. For one thing, we had to surrender our passports to the border officials. "Maybe the guards will want to keep them as souvenirs," Arthur remarked. "After all, they're a nice Communist red color." The police-state atmosphere gave us an odd sense, not of fear exactly, but of foreboding.

We were transferred to an old-fashioned and rather elegant prewar Russian train. The engine was steam-driven, and we were warned not to open the windows because of the coal smoke and dust. But the August heat made our compartment unbearable, and, deciding to take the consequences, we opened the windows. We arrived in Moscow looking like minstrels in blackface.

Our hotel, the Savoy, couldn't have held many more than a hundred guests. (I understand it's still there today and is now called the Hotel Berlin.) We had a small suite, with a sitting room converted practically into a bower by an abundance of potted plants, some hanging from brackets, some resting on the floor. The suite's other rooms were a diminutive bedroom, which we could just about squeeze into, and an adjoining bathroom, where cold water came out of both taps.

We were fortunate to have Walter Duranty as the *Times*'s Moscow correspondent. On our first night, he gave us a delightful dinner party in his small apartment, where we met a young Russian girl whom he subsequently married. He guided us around Moscow and introduced us in diplomatic circles. One evening he took us to a party at the Norwegian Embassy, which was the former home of a Russian industrialist or nobleman and absolutely beautiful. I asked the Ambassador's daughter what had become of the people who had owned the house, and much to my astonishment she said they were living downstairs in the basement.

"You can't imagine how badly we feel," she said. "We suggested to them that we could find another building, but they said, 'Please, don't feel embarrassed about living in our home. We are among the fortunate of our class. At least we have been allowed to stay in our own home, and, unlike so many others, we are all alive.'" They would not accept the Ambassador's invitation to his diplomatic parties, although the two families would get together at other times and had become good friends.

Arthur and I were assigned an Intourist guide, who, according to our foreign friends, was Andrei Vyshinsky's niece and under orders to report all our activities to the secret police. Though we didn't like the idea of her watching our every move, Arthur and I agreed that we were lucky to have such a likable informer.

When not taking in the standard tourist attractions with our guide, we were shown around by Walter Duranty. We went with him to the Kremlin and to the bank where the crown jewels were stored in a huge vault. It was an awesome moment when the guide let us hold some of the precious items, including the dazzling crown and scepter of Catherine the Great. Such an opportunity wasn't to be had by many tourists. The jewels were later moved to the Kremlin, where they were placed under glass and were on view only by special permission. Some of the other royal treasures we saw were Catherine's splendid riding gear, including a saddle encrusted with diamonds given to her by the Sultan of Turkey, and the famed Fabergé Easter eggs of the courts of Alexander III and Nicholas II. The craftsmanship of these extravagant eggs, with their precious gems and delicate gold tracery, was breathtaking. I remember marveling over one in particular, with its miniature railroad train made of pure gold. Viewing all this incredible wealth, I could easily understand why the poverty-stricken masses had staged a revolution.

From Moscow we made an overnight train trip to Nizhni

With Arthur at home in Hillandale in 1961, the year he retired as publisher of *The New York Times*. Under his leadership the *Times* had experienced tremendous growth and we had more time to enjoy each other's company.

With my father at six. We were very close. Almost every Sunday he would take me for a walk. A favorite route was to the Sheep Meadow in Central Park, where we'd get bubbly Saratoga spring water and watch the sheep graze.

I was called, simply, Baby until I was eight, when I put a stop to it. Thereafter, I was Iphigene to my family and Iphie to my friends.

In 1914 I was traveling in Europe with my mother when war was declared between Germany and England. Mama and I were lucky to book passage back to New York on a ship that had previously been condemned for scrap.

Arthur Hays Sulzberger and I were married at my parents' home on November 17, 1917. He was a reserve officer in the Army at the time. (*Left to right*) Arthur's brother Leo, his mother, his brother David, his father, flower girl Ursula Squier, Julius Adler, Arthur, me, David Heyman, Mama, Papa and pages John Oakes and Cyrus Sulzberger II.

My father visited President and Mrs. Coolidge at their vacation home in 1925. Arthur and I had lunch with the Coolidges at the White House, an occasion so quiet that in describing it later I couldn't resist inventing an outrageous story about an argument I had with the President.

Two publishers of the *New York Times*. In this photo, taken in 1930, my son Punch takes a ride on his grandfather's shoulders.

Our children in 1929. (*Left to right*) Punch, Judy, Ruth and Marian.

This portrait was taken in 1935, the year that Arthur became publisher of the *New York Times*. He was forty-four.

As president of the Parks Association, I presented an award in 1935 to Commissioner of Parks Robert Moses for his work on the city's playgrounds. We were often at odds, but he was the best parks commissioner New York City ever had.

With former British Foreign Secretary Anthony Eden and *Times* correspondent Anne O'Hare McCormick at a U.N. correspondents party, 1952.

Arthur and Orvil E. Dryfoos at an Associated Press party in 1960.
Orv became publisher of the *New York Times* the next year.

Punch, when he became publisher of
the *New York Times* in 1963.

In 1961, at the White House. President John Kennedy presented Arthur an award from the American Heart Association in recognition of his excellent recovery from a stroke the year before.

In 1973, at the age of eighty-one, I became one of the first Americans in over twenty-five years to visit the People's Republic of China. Here I'm sharing a meal with Prime Minister Chou En-lai at the Great Hall of the People, Peking. Who knows what other adventures life may bring?

Novgorod (soon to be renamed Gorki, in honor of its most famous native son) for the fair that had been an annual event in that trading center since 1817. On boarding the train we learned that we would be sharing our overnight compartment with two others, an arrangement that was a little more adventurous than Arthur had bargained for. He said to our Intourist guide that since Nizhni Novgorod had managed to hold its fair for a great many years without us, it could doubtless manage without us again; we weren't going to share a compartment with two strangers. Arthur could be very stubborn, and I imagine we wouldn't have made the excursion if one of the guards on the train hadn't offered us the privacy of his compartment.

Among the passengers was the fair director himself. Our Intourist guide introduced us to the old gentleman (being foreigners, we were something of a novelty), and he, speaking to our guide, who was an excellent translator, very kindly invited the three of us to join him for dinner the following evening. The invitation was particularly appealing to us, as this was our first opportunity to meet an official of the Bolshevik Government.

We were famished when we arrived in Nizhni Novgorod the following morning, and we had to wander around the fair until noon, when the restaurants opened. I don't know if the food was as good as we thought it was, but we were so hungry it tasted better than anything we had ever eaten. To this day I can remember the menu. We had sturgeon casserole with cabbage and potatoes, and cheese for dessert. After touring the fair, Arthur and I agreed that the most interesting thing about it was that there was nothing worth seeing. Such halfhearted effort could only mean that the fair, a spectacular event in Czarist days, was being phased out. Our assumption was correct. The fair was discontinued the following year.

We rendezvoused with our friend from the train at a huge banquet hall with long, long tables that could have accommodated hundreds of people. The hall was encircled by a balcony, off which were guest rooms with baths. Our host asked us if we would like to use one of the rooms to rest and freshen up, and Arthur and I gratefully accepted. We followed him to an upstairs room, and when he opened the door a little gasp of horror must have escaped my lips. The room was utterly filthy. When our host asked, "Wouldn't you like to lie down?" I quickly assured him that I wasn't a bit tired. We did use the bathroom, which I'm sure hadn't been cleaned in years, and just enough water dripped through the tap for us to wash our hands.

Considering the condition of the guest room, we couldn't help wondering about the state of the kitchen. We weren't exactly reassured when we sat down at the end of one of the long tables, which was covered by a dirty tablecloth, and saw that we were the only guests. I know I said a little prayer before taking my first mouthful of food. My prayer must have been answered, for neither Arthur nor I was stricken with any terrible disease.

The old gentleman had bright, dancing blue eyes, white hair and pink cheeks, and was an absolute charmer. He spoke of his days as a young Bolshevik, when he, like thousands of others, was arrested by the Czarist police and sentenced to hard labor in a Siberian prison camp. Shackled in chains, trainloads of prisoners were taken to the end of the railroad line and forced to trudge through the bleak, snowy wasteland to the far-off camps. The march took three long months, the old man said, and many died along the way. As the old man recounted the suffering he and his compatriots endured, I was struck by his zest for life. You could tell from the way his eyes sparkled and from the warm smile that lit up his aged face that he was not a bitter man.

He asked us about America, and Arthur and I told him of the prosperity that had come to the people, with the economy booming and everyone making money. As we spoke, the old man shook his head incredulously. "Can't be true," he said. "Things can't be that good." He refused to believe our account, and his skepticism proved warranted. Our glowing reports were inaccurate. While we were dining in Russia, the stock market was on the brink of collapse. By the time we returned to the United States, the country had fallen into the Great Depression. During those black days following the crash, I wanted to write to our friend in the Soviet Union and say, "We were not trying to mislead you; it's just that we were misled ourselves." But I feared that a letter from me might bring him harm.

After returning to Moscow from Nizhni Novgorod, we proceeded to Leningrad, where we visited such historic places as the Hermitage and the Peter and Paul Fortress. On our tour of the fortress prison we were shown the dungeon where Prince Kropotkin, the revolutionary anarchist, was kept in solitary confinement for three years until he escaped disguised as a woman. (Forty-two years later, I was visiting Leningrad with some friends, the Peter and Paul Fortress was one of our stops, and I asked to see that prison cell again. The guide told me in no uncertain terms that there had never been any Prince Kropotkin. Because he had been an anarchist, the Communists now simply denied his existence. "You must be confusing history with fiction," I was told. It was an example of how the Soviet Government rewrote history to depict the Communists as the only revolutionary heroes.)

During our 1929 visit, we also went to Tsarskoye Selo, where we saw the Alexander Palace and the Palace of Catherine the Great. I remember our conversation with the chauffeur who drove us there. He said that because he owned the car, the Government regarded him as a capitalist and had expressed its disapproval by restricting his children's education. I remember thinking that our driver would not remain handicapped by his capitalist status for long, because the ramshackle open-top car was on its last legs. The springs were virtually nonexistent, and we bumped our way out to the palaces in supreme discomfort.

But the Catherine Palace was magnificent. It was being maintained as though the Empress were still living there, with banquet tables set with the finest china and glassware. Connecting the many rooms were great halls lined with mirrors in the style of Versailles. Two of the rooms particularly impressed me. One had gilded walls inlaid with large pieces of amber; the impression was one of bottled sunshine. We were told that Frederick the Great had given that wall to Catherine in exchange for a regiment of soldiers. The other room was a Chinese Chippendale room, which Chippendale himself had come over from England to design and construct. It was absolute perfection.

We had planned to lunch in a Russian restaurant near the palace, but discovering that it was overrun by flies, we opted for a picnic. Our Intourist guide managed to procure some fly-free sandwiches from the kitchen, which was screened, and we found a nice spot in the open.

After lunch we toured the Alexander Palace, where Nicholas and Alexandra and their children had lived, and where they were detained under house arrest by the Bolsheviks before being taken to Siberia and execution. Everything in the palace was carefully preserved, as though the Czar and his family had left moments earlier. There were still clothes hanging in the bedroom closets, and the children's toys were scattered about the floor as if they had just stopped playing with them. There were fresh flowers in every room; photographs of the royal family were dotted about. Some of the pictures were of their foreign relatives—members of the royal houses of England, Denmark, Germany, Rumania, Greece and Spain.

All these personal touches gave us shivers and made us feel we were invading something very private. Nonetheless, we couldn't help being fascinated. Especially intriguing was the Czar's bathroom. He had a huge bath made out of what looked like Tiffany glass, with steps leading up to it; colored lights illuminated the water. (When I saw the Alexander Palace again in 1971 it had been converted into government offices, and our guide flatly denied that Nicholas II and his family had ever lived there.)

After that 1929 visit, I wasn't sure where my sympathies lay. Before coming to Russia I had been ready to believe the best of the revolutionary Government. Seeing the wealth of the Imperial court strengthened my conviction that a revolution had been necessary. On the other hand, revolutions are not pretty things. Who is to say he is so morally superior that his ethics and ideas justify killing people? It seems to me that if you have to kill to convince people of the rightness of your ideas of government, economics or religion, then your ideas are by definition immoral.

Of course, violence and brutality had always been endemic to Russian history, and I remember our Intourist guide pointing at the Kremlin Wall and telling us that Ivan the Terrible used to sit there and watch his enemies being beheaded in the courtyard below. All our sightseeing, all the information imparted to us by our guide, were meant to impress upon us the evils of the Czarist past and the reforms of the Bolshevik present. The guide took great pride in showing us how the Communists had converted the mansions of the "corrupt" upper classes into public facilities.

Some of the reforms were quite impressive. One Institution I particularly remember was a "night clinic." Tuberculosis was rampant in the U.S.S.R. then, and the clinic gave board and treatment to people who were well enough to work during the day but required medical attention in the evening. Another sight that intrigued us was the Palace of Rest and Culture, a former mansion converted into a dance hall, where we watched young people performing Russian folk dances. A relaxed, festive mood filled the hall as the couples swirled around the floor. Men danced together, girls danced together, men and girls danced together—all with the same unrestrained enjoyment you might see among people dancing in any country. In the crowd were two American sailors who didn't know the steps but were having a whale of a time kicking up their heels to the music. Their antics caused some concern among the Russians, and one of the chaperons asked Arthur and me if the sailors were performing that notoriously immoral dance, the fox trot. We assured them that this was not the fox trot, just high spirits, and the boys were permitted to continue with their frivolity.

After visiting a number of these showcases, Arthur and I became pretty well saturated with the party line—Arthur especially. When the Intourist guide informed us that our next visit would be to a chocolate factory, Arthur protested. "I have no interest in chocolate. I know it will be yet another wonderful Bolshevik achievement, and I'm not going." The guide didn't insist.

The Russians were tremendously proud of their achievements. I could not help but sympathize with their enthusiasm. They reminded me of children showing off. So I'd always say how impressed I was. My platitudes annoyed Arthur. He'd chide me. "How can you be such a liar? You know perfectly well we've got superior institutions in the United States."

"When I mention our achievements," I said, "it's waved away as capitalist propaganda. Besides, I haven't the heart to try to break their spirit."

During our travels we met two American girls who had

managed to get across the border without visas. They had stepped off a ship at Odessa and rented a bus. To supplement their meager funds they would pick up hitchhikers, who would agree to pay them something for the transportation. One of the enterprising young ladies turned out to be the granddaughter of J. Pierpont Morgan.

We were in the Soviet Union for about twelve days. We had planned to stay longer, but Arthur became so depressed by the police-state atmosphere that we decided to cut our stay short. Arthur just couldn't tolerate Communism or Fascism or any other kind of totalitarian government. When we were in Italy a few years earlier and saw pictures of Mussolini plastered on every street corner, Arthur's spirits were deeply affected and he said, "Let's get out of here. I can't bear another minute of seeing that man's ugly face every time we turn around." The final blow came when we saw children marching like soldiers in a government parade. Arthur was so undone by the sight of these little ones being in-doctrinated at such an early age that we left Italy the following day.

In 1929, the regimentation we saw in Russia was similar to what we had experienced in Italy. The two countries, one a rightist and the other a leftist dictatorship, were not dissimilar in their lack of freedom and the feeling we had of being under surveillance.

We left Leningrad for Helsinki and had to change trains at the Finnish border. There, in what Arthur said was a "generous moment," the Russians returned our passports. On the way, we had met an attractive American newspaperman whose name I can't recall. When we were changing trains, he joined us for dinner in a little restaurant on the Finnish side of the border. As the three of us walked into the dining room, we exclaimed simultaneously: "No flies!"

The tablecloths were spotless. Everything was so clean, so beautifully clean. A surge of delight swept over us. We were back in the realm of freedom.

In those days, Americans were generally optimistic about the future of the Soviet Union, and in spite of the negative aspects of what we had seen, I was still a little starry-eyed: The Bolsheviks were really trying to improve living standards; they had established schools in centers of illiteracy and had built many new clinics in an effort to provide nationwide medical care. My attitude was soon to change. The 1930's brought Stalin and all his ghastliness—the forced collectivization, the man-made famine, the mass trials. All my hopes for Russia were shattered.

I remember how I worried, when the Stalinist purges began, about our friend at Nizhni Novgorod. As an old Bolshevik who was truly revolutionary and wanted to change things for the good of the masses, he was just the type Stalin would want shot. I hoped and prayed that he was safe, or had died in bed before they got him.

When I toured the Soviet Union again forty-one years later, I found the way of life much the same—secret police, imposed regimentation, the prison system, a denial of many basic freedoms. Economically, people in general were undoubtedly better off than in the Czarist days: They had more to eat, more to buy, more educational opportunities, better medical care. But politically and spiritually, I wonder . . .

19

In the late 1920's the United States was riding high on a financial boom. There was wild gambling on the stock exchange, and prices and real values were totally unrelated to each other. In this surrealistic utopia lived a realistic man by the name of Alexander Dana Noyes. Mr. Noyes was the financial editor of the *New York Times*. In his opinion—an opinion that was shared by only a few people in the country—the booming economy rested on a honeycombed foundation and would soon collapse. He expressed his sense of foreboding repeatedly in his column on the financial page. The articles stirred many readers to hot indignation. Many businessmen and financiers thought Mr. Noyes was being overly dramatic so as to make a name for himself. They called him a male Cassandra, when they were not calling him something worse. His dire warnings, while taken seriously by the *Times*'s editorial page, were disregarded by businessmen and the public at large. The spiraling inflation of the stock prices was too rampant for one man to have stopped it, but if some of the leading financiers had taken heed of Mr. Noyes's warnings, the stock market crash of 1929 might have been less disastrous.

On our family, the effect of the crash and the ensuing Depression was not all that severe. Having never invested in anything outside of his business after losing his shirt in real estate speculation as a young man, my father was not touched directly by the stock market collapse, though the crash did affect advertising and profits.

Neither the Ochses nor the Sulzbergers had to make any fundamental changes in their manner of living. It would be foolish to pretend otherwise. We retained household help. When a position needed filling, there were many applicants for the job. People were desperate for work. One woman who worked for me as a cook hadn't been able to find work in her profession of book reviewer. I asked her why she had chosen cooking as a livelihood, and she replied, "Anyone who can read can cook." I wouldn't say that was generally true, but it was in her case: As a cook, she was a great success.

The *Times* survived the Depression with little hardship, compared to other companies. I remember my father using the term "insensate greed" to explain why so many businesses had failed. The men in charge, he said, had been so captivated by the lure of get-rich-quick that they raked off profits too quickly, neglecting proper management and investment procedures.

Of course, during the worst of the Depression, circulation was down, advertising fell to nearly half the 1929 volume, and profits were at the vanishing point. Something had to be done about the paper's financial situation. Other newspapers in the same fix had whittled their operating staffs down to a bare minimum, but my father could not bring himself to fire anyone. In his mind, *Times* employees were his family, and he wouldn't turn a member of his family out into the street.

When in 1932 the situation became critical, my father had no alternative but to ask his staff to accept a 10 percent pay cut. His request was accepted without a single protest. As a result, not one employee was laid off. And the *Times* stayed out of debt without reducing the scope of its news coverage. The paper's stability during the Depression was a great credit to the sound management practices developed by my father, Arthur and Julius Adler, and to the devotion of an able staff.

Though I did not suffer any particular hardship during the Depression, I was not unaffected by the desperate circumstances of people all around me; no one could have been. Every time you picked up the paper or went out into the streets, you were confronted with distressing sights. You only had to look at the drained reservoir in Central Park (now a playing field) to see the frightful conditions that people were living in. On the reservoir's floor, rickety shacks had been built out of scrap lumber. Similar crude shelters were clustered in vacant lots throughout the city.

On our street corner one freezing December I saw a man selling Christmas trees. He was dressed in a threadbare coat and said he didn't have any other warm clothing, so I gave him one of Arthur's sweaters. When I saw him on the same corner a few days later, he said his child needed clothes, so I gave him some of my children's outfits. A day or two after that, he asked me if I could buy him a horse and wagon so he could make a living as a peddler. I told him I was sorry, but that was more than I could manage. He thanked me anyway, and I never saw him again.

That same winter, only one block from our house, I came upon a crowd of people gathered around a young man who had collapsed on the sidewalk. The lad was semiconscious, and I was able to recruit a bystander to help me pull him to his feet and get him to a drugstore. When I asked the druggist what he could prescribe for the ailing youth, the young man spoke up: "There's nothing wrong with me. It's just that I haven't eaten in two days."

His story was not an unusual one. He had learned of a job opening in New York, but when he arrived in the city the job was filled. After a day of looking elsewhere, he had run out of funds. "I can't even buy my bus ticket home," he said. The druggist sat him down at the lunch counter and gave him a meal, and I gave him money for the bus.

For the most part, Arthur and I contributed what extra money we had to charities and organizations that benefited the community. Our donations were modest, because Arthur's income had been cut and just about covered the upkeep of our home and our other living expenses, though we tried to be prudent with our personal expenditures and never bought anything frivolous.

What free time I had from the children, who were at an age when they demanded a lot of attention, I spent in public service. I served on the Jewish Board of Guardians and on the boards of the New York Child Adoption League and the Girl Scouts. I thought I could be useful in the Girl Scouts because of my experience years earlier in the girls' reformatory—the Cedar Knoll School, run by the Jewish Board of Guardians in Hawthorne, New York.

I remember my work at that school as both rewarding and painful. I taught Bible class once a week (and wasn't very good at it, because I didn't know the Bible very well) and supervised the girls' recreational activities. I would take my class of about thirty girls on walks and drives, and they and I grew to love each other, although their affectionate way of throwing their arms around my neck may have owed something to the fact that I wasn't a great disciplinarian. My classes were relaxed and the girls had fun, even if they learned very little. But there was one girl, ten years old, who kept me on my toes with her bright questions and her inquisitive turn of mind. She still corresponds with me, sixty years later. She said it was because I was the only teacher at Cedar Knoll who treated her as a child and didn't think of her as a bad girl. She said she knew that I loved her—and I did.

My work at Cedar Knoll took its toll of me. One episode in particular made me realize the state I was getting into. I had become worried about a girl who was abnormally short and didn't seem to be growing any taller. I had heard about an orthopedic specialist who treated dwarfed youngsters, and I took the child to him for an examination. After reviewing the girl's case, the doctor told me his treatment would be ineffective because the child was too old. I burst into tears. The doctor took a firm grip of my arm and, looking me squarely in the eye, said, "You're doing more harm to yourself than good to any of these girls. You should quit."

When my second child was born a few months later, I took the doctor's advice. I left the job feeling that my work there had been futile. The majority of the girls had low I.Q.'s (one fourteen-year-old could not tell time) and I had no training in ways to help. I thought I could perhaps make a more significant contribution by working with bright girls who still had hope. That was when I became interested in the Girl Scouts. While never a scout leader, I became an effective fund raiser.

When our children reached school age, Arthur and I enrolled them in private schools. Because I didn't have happy memories of my own early schooling, which clung to strictly traditional patterns, I decided that my children would have a more liberal form of education, and Arthur agreed. The Lincoln School on 120th Street was affiliated with Columbia Teachers College and claimed to be an experimental school employing modern techniques of progressive education. The idea was to let each child develop at his or her own pace, while taking each pupil's individual needs into account. It seemed a sensible approach, especially in the primary grades, when youngsters need a great deal of personal attention, and so we enrolled Marian and Ruth there.

As the children moved from grade to grade, Arthur and I grew increasingly concerned about the system's lack of structure. There was no discipline, and the children weren't required to learn anything. When Marian reached middle-school grades, she was still sadly lacking in the three R's (we later discovered that part of the problem was dyslexia), and I used to go to the school and express my concern. I'd be told not to worry: Marian would learn when she was ready. But time went by and she still didn't seem to be learning anything. I remember one teacher trying to reassure me by saying, "Why do you worry? She's so pretty!" I didn't think my daughter could get through life on that.

It wasn't until Marian was in the ninth grade and Ruth in the seventh that Arthur and I had sense enough to take our children out of Lincoln School. The decision came one day when Arthur asked Ruth a question requiring a simple, factual answer. Ruth replied that she didn't know the answer and didn't have to. "You don't have to know anything," she said. "All you have to know is where to look it up."

The girls were so far behind that we had to have them

privately tutored before we could get them accepted by another school. Ruth studied at home for one semester, then took exams to enter the Brearley School. She flunked every one of them, and we had to have her tutored five days a week for an entire summer before we thought she was ready to take the exams again. This time she passed, but the school made her repeat a class.

Marian presented an even bigger problem. After one year of tutoring, she was accepted at Rosemary Hall School in Greenwich, Connecticut. But we were soon informed that she wasn't measuring up. We got her into Lenox School in Manhattan, but she did no better there.

Marian seemed to have absolutely no interest in studying. When Arthur and I would talk to her about the value of education, shades would come down over her eyes. Somewhere along the line, Arthur suggested that Marian quit school and go to work. I said, "Nonsense. She needs to learn something." One day, in despair over an imminent American history exam, she came to me and I reviewed the course with her. After the exam she came rushing to me, saying, "Mother! You got a B-plus!" She finished school, and a few years later she developed a deep interest in educating herself.

Our third daughter, Judy, didn't have her sisters' academic problems, but neither was she a model student. She attended the primary grades at the Froebel League School, then transferred to Brearley, where she was constantly getting into mischief and being called into the headmistress's office. One incident I remember was when she threw an ice-cream cone at a classmate in a fit of anger. The ice cream splattered the ceiling, and Arthur and I had to pay to have the ceiling repainted.

By ninth grade, however, both Judy and Ruth began to take their studies seriously. Judy became interested in learning when she took a course in biology: It was the start of a lifelong fascination with medicine. The subject that opened Ruth's mind was English. I'll never forget the day she came to me and said, "You know, Mother, you were right; it's fun to know."

When the time came for Punch to go to school, Arthur and I were so disillusioned with educational innovations that we decided on the more traditional system. We enrolled him in St. Bernard's on East Ninety-eighth Street. The school was strictly British, and we hoped Punch would get the kind of grounding the girls had missed. As it turned out, Punch also had dyslexia and couldn't keep up with the work. We felt he needed more personal attention, and when he was in the fifth grade we transferred him to the Laurence Smith School (which later merged with the Browning School and is now known by that name). Punch's performance did not improve, and he grew discouraged and rebellious. Thinking that perhaps he'd do better at a boarding school, we entered him in Loomis, in Connecticut. During his junior year there, when he was seventeen, Punch announced to us that he wanted to join the Marines. At first we were against it, but as he seemed unable to adjust to any kind of schooling, we gave our consent. As it turned out, the Marines were just what Punch needed. "Before I entered the Marines, I was a lazy good-for-nothing," Punch said to me once. "The Marines woke me up."

The Depression lasted six years, some say a decade. Living through it, one tended to be numbed by the many dreadful stories one heard. We did our daily chores and dealt with our own problems, and tried to retain our optimism and not become thoroughly disheartened.

There were times, of course, when we were exposed to the cold reality of the Depression, and it affected us deeply. One such instance occurred during a trip out West, when Arthur and I first saw the Okies heading for California in their broken-down jalopies. Seeing those poor souls living in appalling conditions and looking so hopeless upset us greatly. Their despair was well captured in John Steinbeck's novel *The Grapes of Wrath*, and the movie made from it; both made a lasting impression on me.

The book figured in a conversation I once had with Hobart Taft, President Taft's nephew and the owner of a Cincinnati evening newspaper, when he was my dinner partner at a party given by my cousin Iphigene Molony Bettman in her home in Cincinnati. Iphigene had seated us together in the hope that I could change Hobart Taft's poor opinion of the *New York Times*, which he considered a radical sheet.

I asked Mr. Taft if he had read *The Grapes of Wrath*. He answered that he had read a bit of it, but "the language was so repulsive that I had to put it down."

The remark startled me. "Was it bad? I didn't notice," I murmured. This only confirmed Mr. Taft's opinion about the *Times*. Iph Bettman's plot fell flat.

When Franklin Delano Roosevelt was elected thirty-second President of the United States, there was considerable controversy as to how the Government should cope with the Depression. Some rightists advocated Fascism; some leftists proposed Communism. Mr. Roosevelt, determined to preserve the capitalist system, took the middle of the road. That, however, was enough to categorize him for many conservative Americans as an interloper out to wreck the American way of life. These critics, many of whom were our friends, referred to him as "That Man."

That Mr. Roosevelt actually *preserved* our way of life can hardly be disputed. He put an anxious, restless nation back to work. Under the WPA, hundreds of thousands of Americans were given the incentive to put their skills to use. Laborers were provided with work. Artists were commissioned to paint murals in public buildings. Actors were hired for theatrical productions. Writers were employed to write guidebooks for each of the forty-eight states, books now treasured for their excellence. Then there were the CCC camps, where boys were cared for, fed and educated, and earned their keep by planting trees, reclaiming land and landscaping national parks. The program transformed many of the boys' lives. It lifted their morale and gave them skills for making a living. As one man I know put it, "Those camps saved my brothers' lives."

These New Deal programs were far better, I think, than our welfare system today. But times have changed, and I suppose one can never repeat the past, however much there is to be learned from it.

For those millions of us who lived through the Great Depression—and who cannot ignore the poverty that still exists today—that time is a fearful specter that won't go away. Even after the Second World War, the Korean War, the cold war, Vietnam and all that came afterward, memories of that era still loom in our minds.

20

New York City's parks during John Hylan's administration in the early 1920's were subjected to terrible abuse because of political corruption. Mayor Hylan was an ignorant little politician whose five parks commissioners (one for each borough) were political hacks who failed in their responsibilities and abused their power.

I remember a conversation I had with the parks commissioner from Manhattan, a Mr. John Sheeny, who happened to be sitting next to me at a Board of Estimate hearing on a park problem. "Was there a holiday last Sunday?" he asked.

"Not to my knowledge," I answered.

"That's strange," the commissioner said. "I thought it must have been a holiday. I was in Central Park, and it was absolutely packed."

"Mr. Sheeny," I said, trying to restrain myself, "the park is packed every Sunday!"

"Is that so? I wouldn't know. I never went into the park until I became commissioner."

The attitude of the other parks commissioners wasn't much better. Their uncaring and often self-serving approach to their jobs inspired a concerned group of independent citizens to form an organization for the protection of the parks. The organization was called the Parks and Playgrounds Association, and my old friend Nathan Straus, Jr., was elected president. Nathan, knowing of my interest in parks, invited me to serve on the board of trustees. That was the beginning of my thirty years of active participation in parks councils.

Perhaps the worst abuse of the parklands under the Hylan administration occurred because of the chicanery of the parks commissioners in Staten Island and the Bronx. These two gentlemen had actually rented park acreage to their friends! Some of these rented areas were being used as private property. In Wolf's Pond Park on Staten Island the encroachers had constructed small houses and put up no-trespassing signs. In Orchard Beach in the Bronx they were felling trees for lumber, building summer cottages and closing the beach to the public.

The association filed a taxpayers' suit against the city of New York to ban the Staten Island poachers. The court decided in our favor. While Mayor Hylan's cronies prepared an appeal, the association prepared another suit, this one against the Orchard Beach violators.

A change at City Hall made us optimistic about both cases. We had a new mayor, who had won the 1933 election as a reform candidate. His name was Fiorello La Guardia.

When I first met Mr. La Guardia at a dinner party just after his election, I told him of the parks association's impending suit against the Orchard Beach people, and expressed my concern about the appeal against the Staten Island ruling. He said, "You don't have to worry, Mrs. Sulzberger. I won't be appealing that decision. I'm reorganizing the parks system in this city. There's going to be one commissioner of parks for the whole town, and I'm bringing in the best man in the state to do the job. So your worries are over."

A day or two after Mr. La Guardia's inaugural, I came home to find my household in a state of excitement. The new mayor had telephoned and wanted to talk to me. I called City Hall, and the Mayor's secretary said, "Oh yes, yes. The Mayor's been expecting you." Mr. La Guardia came on the line at once.

"Hello, Mrs. Sulzberger," he said. "This is Fiorello La Guardia. We met at a dinner party a few weeks ago. Possibly you remember me?"

I smiled at the question, and liked him even more for it.

"I just wanted to tell you," he continued, "who I'm bringing in as Commissioner of Parks. He's been Commissioner of Parks for the state, and he is Robert Moses."

I spread the good news among my colleagues at the parks association. "We not only have a mayor who cares about New York's parks and is going to reform their administration but we now have a vigorous commissioner who is a builder and a doer."

Robert Moses went on to become the greatest parks commissioner in the city's history. I couldn't begin to list the many other contributions he made during the three decades he held administrative positions in New York. A map of the city before and after Moses would be enough to show the monumental changes he brought about.

In addition to being noted for his innovations, Robert Moses was known for his headstrong personality. He didn't understand that his aggressive behavior made him enemies. As our friend Edward Greenbaum once put it, Mr. Moses was the kind of man who would cross the street if he saw someone he didn't like walking on the other side—just to tell the fellow what he thought of him.

One of the many people Mr. Moses had words with when he came in as parks commissioner was Nathan Straus, Jr. The two men didn't get along, and Mr. Moses, in his inimitable manner, refused to talk with Nathan about park-related matters. The feud made it difficult for the parks association to operate effectively, and Nathan resigned in frustration. The association elected me as president.

I managed to get along with Bob Moses most of the time. I liked and admired him and didn't take his fits of anger too seriously. When he lost his temper over something, I'd wait until he wore himself out and would then raise the issue again.

I remember a disagreement we had over a restaurant in Central

Park that he wanted to replace with a playground. The Casino, as it was called, had acquired a bad reputation when Mayor Jimmy Walker used it for wild and lavish parties. Mr. Moses thought this expensive restaurant unsuitable for a public park. His other objection was that the building was deteriorating.

The building *was* in poor shape, but I was against his plan to lay out yet another play area. He had just finished constructing playgrounds around the perimeter of Central Park. This had been a worthy project, for until then there was only one play area, the Heckscher Playground at the south end of the park—and even that playground was unusable for most of the winter and spring, since it had little if any drainage and was frequently a field of mud. But now, in my opinion, the Casino site, in the center of the park, would make a fine facility for senior citizens. The older generation had no indoor recreation area, and if the building were renovated it would make a nice place for old people to get together and relax. My board agreed with me and authorized me to present the suggestion to the commissioner.

I wrote to Mr. Moses proposing the idea. It sparked his inflammable temper, and he responded by sending a searing letter to the *Times*, the *Herald Tribune* and the *New Yorker* saying I was a jackass and a fool and didn't know what I was talking about. The letter was reprinted by a number of other publications.

First, Mr. Moses wrote, I was ignorant of the facts: The Casino was not in the exact center of the park but a hundred feet or so off-center. He continued in this same nonsensical fashion, and concluded with the statement that no matter what anybody said, the site was needed as a playground and that's what it was going to be. He signed the letter, "Merry Christmas, Robert Moses."

The letter was typical of Bob's outbursts. Though I didn't enjoy being insulted in print, I decided that if I wrote a counterattack it would only serve to aggravate the quarrel.

No words passed between us until two weeks later, at a New Year's Eve party at the Adolph Lewisohns'. Arthur and I had just arrived when Mrs. Moses spotted us in the crowd. She took her husband by the hand and led him over to me. "Bob," she said, "you were outrageous to Iphigene. You know she's a good friend. Now you tell her you're sorry, ask her to forgive you, and give

· 157 ·

her a little kiss." And Bob, with his head hanging down like a small boy who knows he's been bad, said, "Sorry." Then he leaned over and pecked me on the cheek.

(New Year's Eve at the Lewisohns' was a tradition with us. Then, for several years during the 1930's, we had an annual New Year's morning party in the kitchen of our home at East Eightieth Street. It began one night as the Lewisohns' dance ended and no one felt like going home. About ten of us went to our house and scrambled some eggs. That, too, became a tradition, and before long we were sending out invitations. From about two to seven o'clock in the morning we had perhaps 150 people coming through our kitchen, drinking champagne or highballs, scrambling eggs, frying bacon and having a good time. Every year there were three men we had to throw out bodily at 7 a.m. We gave up these parties during the war, and the Lewisohns discontinued their annual dance. After the war we tried to revive our party, but everyone had grown so much older that no one knew what to do until 2 a.m.)

In the 1940's I made another effort to get indoor facilities for senior citizens. Without consulting Bob, I wrote a letter to the philanthropist Bernard Baruch. It occurred to me that since Mr. Baruch had developed the habit of conducting business transactions in the park—he could often be found sitting on a park bench discussing important matters with a client or a political personage—he should be especially sympathetic toward older people who enjoyed the outdoors as much as he did. In my letter, I described the old-timers who came to the park to play chess and checkers—how, having no tables, they would sit in twisted positions on a bench; how, having nowhere else to play, they would be there even when the weather was cold and uncomfortable. "It's one of the few pleasures these people have," I wrote. "Don't you think they deserve a more congenial setting where they can play the year round?" Enclosed in my letter was a photograph I had cut from the *Times* showing two enchanting old characters hunched over a chessboard on a winter day.

Mr. Baruch's answer took just two words: "How much?" The Parks Department came up with a figure, and he said he would finance a chess house in Central Park. His one stipulation was that the gift remain anonymous.

The news sent me soaring. I telephoned our cantankerous parks commissioner, and he responded in typical Moses fashion: "If it was that easy, why didn't you ask for *two* chess houses? We could use one in Prospect Park."

"You get the second one yourself," I retorted heatedly.

That was Bob Moses. He couldn't even pay a compliment without barbing it with sarcasm.

The chess house was built. It cost $36,000, the *Times* welcomed it and the *Tribune* called it a waste of money. But it was the old people's opinion of the shelter that really mattered to me. Shortly before Bernard Baruch died, I wrote him, telling him of the pleasure the house had provided for so many over the years, and I asked him if he'd permit a picture of him to be hung in the chess house. It was a wonderful photograph I'd come across, showing him sitting on a park bench. Mr. Baruch consented, and the picture went up on the wall.

With Robert Moses as Commissioner of Parks, our once spirited parks association saw little action. Public-interest groups like ours thrive on controversy, corruption, misallocation of funds, official lassitude and the like. Robert Moses was so far above malfeasance or inactivity and had so many ideas and projects going that the association couldn't keep up with him; we had almost no reason to exist. My biggest job as president was to retain and recruit members.

One of Bob's first steps as commissioner was to accumulate land for new parks. In the thirties, a lot of property was claimed by the city for nonpayment of taxes. Bob would study maps showing these properties, mark off areas he thought suitable for parks and file petitions with the city. It was a successful campaign. Acre after acre was earmarked for parkland. When a few years later I told him these new properties were sadly lacking in maintenance, he said, "That's the next generation's problem, Iphigene. If I hadn't gotten the space, they'd have had nothing to fix up."

In addition to expanding park space and constructing and rebuilding playgrounds, Bob Moses constructed many outdoor swimming pools. (The city had had only indoor pools until then.) He was also responsible for rebuilding Jacob Riis Park in the Rockaways, Coney Island in Brooklyn and the park our association fought for—Orchard Beach in the Bronx. With its attractive buildings on the shoreline and its masses of flowers, Orchard Beach was the most beautiful public beach imaginable by the time Bob was finished with it. It has deteriorated a great deal since then.

Another Moses project was rebuilding the Central Park Zoo. He replaced the old firetrap wooden buildings that housed the animals. This eliminated the need for the armed night patrol, whose duty was to shoot any dangerous animals that escaped during a fire. In place of the faulty structures, he put up handsome fireproof buildings.

Though the new zoo was safe, attractive and applauded by the public, I felt the animals had not received fair treatment. They were cramped into small cages, as they had been in the old zoo. I felt it was shameful—I still do. I tried to solicit the support of the Humane Society and the ASPCA, but they gave me no backing, so I resorted to writing another letter to Bob. This time I began by complimenting him on the many improvements, and only then registered my complaint. He responded with a courteous note saying he saw nothing wrong with the zoo.

I don't like zoos to begin with, and I think it is cruel to exhibit live animals in inhumane conditions. Aside from the suffering inflicted on the animals, a poor example is set for the children when they see us tolerate such cruelty. From the time the Central Park zoo was rebuilt, I've been protesting against the cramped cages. It's a battle I've been fighting with no success, but new groups have taken up the cause, so all is not lost.

Among the parks restored by Robert Moses was Riverside Park on the Upper West Side. He more than doubled the recreation area, expanding it to the Hudson River's edge, and installed playgrounds and playing fields. He also had the adjacent railroad tracks covered, so that people in the park would no longer have to hear the bleating and mooing of livestock being shipped downtown for slaughter. Another renovation alongside the park was the building of the Henry Hudson Parkway.

Bob Moses had the good luck to be parks commissioner at the time when WPA labor was available. However, in using that work force, he had to cooperate with the WPA administrator for New York, Victor Ritter. I knew Victor well; he was a good man, doing a fine job, but he was frightfully conservative. As far as personalities went, Victor and Bob were diametrically opposed. A confrontation was inevitable.

I'll never forget the day Mayor La Guardia telephoned and asked me to come down to City Hall and join in a discussion between Mr. Moses and Mr. Ritter. At the time, I was taking care of Judy, who was in quarantine for the mumps, and I told Mr. La Guardia I couldn't leave her. "Oh, we've all had the mumps," he said. "You come along and bring Judy with you."

I entered the Mayor's office, holding Judy by the hand, to find Victor and Bob engaged in such a violent argument that they were almost on the point of blows. The Mayor greeted us, took Judy, sat her on his lap and—seemingly oblivious to the raucous debate—started entertaining her. I wondered why I was there. Perhaps the Mayor thought a lady's presence might have a calming influence, or that my being the president of the parks association and a friend of both men would help move them to a quieter and more sensible discussion. If so, he was wrong. The two men continued their dispute in full force, shouting and waving their arms and sparing no invective.

Victor wanted the WPA to get credit for the work being done in the parks. There had been public allegations that the WPA was made up of loafers, and Victor wanted his men's work acknowledged and appreciated. He wanted to put up big signs in the park saying, "Work Being Done by the WPA." Bob didn't want the disfiguring signs. Besides, the work was being done under the direction of independent architects, engineers and superiors hired by him.

Finally, when there was no sign of an end to the argument, Mr. La Guardia, who had all the while been playing with Judy, stood up and said, "All right. We've had enough of this. I'm mayor of this city and I'm going to make a decision. I expect my commissioners to carry out my instructions." His solution was to put up small signs crediting both Bob's team and the WPA. Victor and Bob accepted the compromise with more or less good grace.

In his post as commissioner, Robert Moses's tenacity was a

virtue. Though the La Guardia administration was the best in the city's history, its bureaucracy was just like any other, and it required power and determination to cut through the red tape. Bob had these qualities to spare. Though he annoyed many people, he got things done. But whether he succeeded or not, he always had the compulsion to get the last word in. There was one parting quip I shall never forget.

The time was during the forties, after the war, when Bob was giving Anne O'Hare McCormick and me a tour of some of the projects he'd engineered. Anne was a star reporter for the *Times* who had made her name as a freelance correspondent. In 1921, when she was based in Italy, she predicted that Mussolini and his Fascist Party would come to power. By 1937 she had her own column in the *Times*, called "In Europe." At the outbreak of the Second World War she became a leading correspondent for the paper, covering front-line action. Her outstanding reporting led Arthur to invite her to join the *Times* editorial board. She became the board's first woman member.

Anne had the map of Ireland on her face, but what stood out most was her innate charm, her femininity, her dynamic personality. Her intelligence was a byword; the younger reporters were constantly seeking her out to discuss the breaking news.

With all her knowledge of the world, Anne knew Manhattan only from Ninety-sixth Street down to Washington Square. Since she now worked and lived in the city, I proposed a tour of the rest of Manhattan and of the four other boroughs, and she eagerly accepted. I phoned Bob to make the arrangements. When he heard that my guest was to be Anne McCormick, he said, "I'll take you around myself."

Bob picked us up in the chauffeur-driven car that went with his job, and graciously and proudly showed us points of interest along our tour. After a while there was a lapse in the conversation, and I took the occasion to discuss something that had been bothering me.

Mrs. Gristede, of the grocery-store-chain family, had recently written Bob to complain about the rats in Central Park. Rats had always been a problem in parks; they still are. Bob had only to give Mrs. Gristede the facts—that the Parks Department had ruled out using poison against the rats for fear of endangering other animal life and that his experts were working on a solution—and she would have been satisfied. Instead, he had written her one of his typically and inexcusably rude letters.

As we drove along, I lectured him on his adolescent behavior. Much to my surprise, he took the scolding without comment, and I took his silence to be an admission of his mistake. When I finished dressing him down, you could have heard a pin drop. Finally Bob broke the silence. We were on the new Belt Parkway, and he asked me how I liked it. "I think it's great," I said, sincerely. "Congratulations!"

"Iphigene," he asked, "do you know when this road was first conceived?"

I shook my head.

"Eighteen ninety-eight. That's when it was thought of. And when was it completed? Last year." He paused and looked me squarely in the eye. "Eighteen ninety-eight, Iphigene."

He turned archly away and looked out on his road. "Those were the days of the polite appeasers."

Another of Bob Moses's Depression-era accomplishments was the city's first public housing project, in Red Hook, Brooklyn, and one day he invited me to go there. Our first stop was a tract of abandoned land where squatters had constructed tumbledown shacks from scraps of wood and other material. Bob's task was to get these people into decent homes as fast as possible, so the housing project was built to be severely practical.

Bob showed me one of the apartments in the project. Like all the others, it was equipped with kitchen and bath, but I noticed that the closets had no doors, just indentations in the walls.

"Doors are expensive," he explained.

"But," I protested, "doors would keep the rooms so much tidier and make housecleaning easier."

"People can put up curtains if they want to. With the money we save on doors we can build another building that we really need."

Perhaps he was right, but there was another aspect of public housing that I objected to even more strongly: The projects forced small shopkeepers to close down or move.

"Instead of taking away these poor people's stores, why doesn't the Government give them space inside the new buildings?" I asked. "It would be a convenience to the tenants, too. The poor have as much right to convenience as the richer classes!"

I got nowhere with my pleas. Bob agreed with the Federal Government that these small shops should not be subsidized. I continue to campaign for the small shopkeepers—though without much success.

As Commissioner of Parks, chairman of the Triborough Bridge and Tunnel Authority, chairman of the State Power Authority, member of the Planning Commission and holder of various other posts, Robert Moses has made contributions to New York that can't be measured. And in the course of his long career as a public administrator, he made many enemies and hurt many people's feelings. Today, while his tempestuous ways are easily recalled, his achievements are being overlooked.

Just a few years ago, a *Times* editorial described Thomas Hoving and August Heckscher, the two parks commissioners under Mayor John Lindsay, as the greatest administrators New York City ever had. I wrote an indignant letter to my cousin John Oakes, then editor of the editorial page, saying that the best parks commissioner in the city's history was Robert Moses.

Whenever I feel strongly about something that appears in the *Times*, I write a letter to the paper. When John Oakes headed the editorial board, I addressed the letters to him. We had an understanding. If what I had to say met the *Times* criteria for letters to the editor, it would be printed in that space. If it fell short, he'd pitch it into the wastebasket. I would write on my own stationery, but to preserve my anonymity I would sign the name of a deceased relative.

My letter about Moses was an exception. I signed it "Iphigene Ochs Sulzberger." John was surprised.

"I can remember, Iphigene," he said, "when Robert Moses called you a fool and all kinds of dreadful names."

"You don't understand, John," I answered. "When Moses said those things, that was his way of saying 'I love you.' Bob Moses was a good friend; and even if he wasn't, he was the best parks commissioner we ever had."

And the letter was printed over my name.

21

If my father could be said to have ever indulged himself, it was at seventy-three, when he bought Hillandale, a magnificent estate in White Plains, built in the 1920's and spread over fifty-seven acres of rolling woodland and meadow. On the property was a lake, a greenhouse, a barn and flower and vegetable gardens. A four-story, white-columned house in the Colonial style stood on the highest hill.

When my father proposed buying the house, my mother wasn't all that keen. The forty-five-minute ride into the city would make it difficult for her to go regularly to the concerts, theater and opera that were a part of her life. The prospect of leaving the West Seventy-fifth Street house upset her. She was used to her surroundings and loath to part with any of her furnishings. Furthermore, the job of decorating a house with twenty-five spacious rooms held no attractions for her. She finally agreed to move if I and a decorator friend of hers did the work and if we used all the furniture in the New York house. Though I saw little artistic merit in many of the pieces, my mother had a sentimental attachment to her early Victorian furniture (circa 1840), which she had purchased so many years before. We consulted her frequently during the moving, and when the White Plains house was completed, both my parents were satisfied.

Aunt Nannie, Mother's frequent opera companion, offered her a guest room in her Manhattan apartment so Mama could stay overnight any time it was too late after the theater to be going back to White Plains. Mama never used that guest room. She found the round trip far easier than she had expected. She went to the theater as frequently as ever, and always returned to Hillandale for the night.

Before long, she found country life agreeing with her. She'd always had a passion for flowers, and now she spent many happy hours in the garden. Another newfound source of pleasure was taking drives along the quiet country roads. White Plains, as all of Westchester County, was mostly country then, not the suburbia it has become in recent years.

Hillandale became a real family homestead. On a typical weekend, Arthur and I would arrive with our four children, the children's guests, a nurse and three dogs. The household would be bursting with friends, and with relatives to the nth generation. My father enjoyed entertaining and having his family around him; there was never a room at Hillandale that was vacant for long. Of all the visitors, the children were the ones Papa enjoyed most. He said he could see the older folks any time, so when the young people arrived he'd take command and lead them in many happy hours of play and laughter.

The children adored him—all children did. He bought them noisy toys and encouraged them to shout and sing, even at the dinner table. Papa had an endless supply of guessing games. I wondered how he was able to make up these riddles, until I discovered a joke book in his library.

The constant stream of guests, the commotion created by my mother's three dogs, the noise of the children—none of this seemed to bother anybody, least of all Mama. She too adored having her family around. She enjoyed reading stories to the children and playing games with them. They affectionately called her Ginny-Ganny. Whatever problems were created by the onslaught of people and animals never concerned her. The credit for maintaining some kind of order and sanity at Hillandale belongs to my cousin Dr. Ruth Bernheim. Cousin Ruth had come to live with my parents after Miss MacDonnell's death in 1921. She not only supervised household affairs but served as physician in case of minor illness. She had had a general medical practice (specializing in obstetrics) until her retirement at sixty, and my parents were very fortunate to have her with them.

The household staff boasted a very proper English butler named Ireland. I shall never forget Ireland because of what happened one wintry day when I took my Scottie, Billy, for a walk. Billy's favorite pastime was chasing the white ducks that flocked around Hillandale's lake. He would bark and run after the birds until they scurried into the water. However, that day the lake was frozen and the ducks gathered on the ice. Billy charged after them, and the ice cracked under his weight. He was just beyond my reach and might have drowned if a gardener hadn't heard my cries for help. He rushed to the lake's edge and scooped the shivering dog out of the water. I took Billy in my arms and raced to the house. Ireland always kept the front door locked, and I rang and called for him. At last he came.

"Quick!" I cried. "Get me some whiskey for Billy!"

"Certainly, madam," he said in his very English manner. "Would Billy prefer Scotch or rye?"

It fills me with sorrow to think that my father had less than four years at Hillandale, and that his health was failing for much of that time. In the summer of 1932, when he was seventy-four years old, his physician and friend, Dr. J. Bentley Squier, told him one of his kidneys was malfunctioning and poisoning his system. He advised an operation. The surgery was performed successfully, there were no complications and my father had a remarkable recovery for a man of his age.

After he was fully recovered, my father had a pretty good

year. He resumed an active schedule as publisher of the *Times*. He also continued to be a critical reader of the paper, though not with the meticulous eye of former years, when he read every single word, including the ads, and distributed memos on any flaws he spotted. He had less vigor now, and began to depend more and more on Arthur and Julius.

February 28, 1933, was my parents' fiftieth wedding anniversary. March 12 of that same year was my father's seventy-fifth birthday. In celebration of the two occasions, my parents decided to spend a relaxing fortnight in Palm Beach, Florida. They wanted to avoid having a big family party. That, however, was something they couldn't escape. Many relatives and some close friends arrived in Palm Beach for a surprise celebration. I remember everyone's remarking on my father's good health. To all outward appearances he seemed in good shape. What we didn't realize was how deeply he was troubled in his mind.

He worried about the Depression. The country wasn't making the recovery he'd hoped for, and he agonized over the state of the economy and the shattering effect it might have on his newspapers. He fretted over the Lindbergh kidnapping and feared for his grandchildren's safety. He was tormented by Hitler's rise in Germany and had the foreboding that this meant another world war. Finally, all these anxieties culminated in a second nervous breakdown.

We called on Dr. Tilney again. I shall always be thankful to him for his kindness, wisdom and good sense. He told us, as he had during Father's collapse twelve years before, that breakdowns of this nature were fairly common in men of tremendous energy who had made highly successful careers. "People like your father," he said, "have a tendency to push themselves beyond their capacity, as if their will were greater than their ability. When the realization comes that they are helpless, there is a kind of internal explosion. There is no medical cure except to give the patient complete rest, and to wait."

On the doctor's advice, I took my children on a trip to Europe, so as to relieve Papa's obsessive fear that one of his grandchildren might be kidnapped. During that period, the summer of 1934, my father convalesced at Hillandale, with nurses around the clock. Saddest of all, he couldn't read his own newspaper; he didn't even want to look at it. Yet the breakdown was less severe than the earlier one, and after eighteen months he was over the worst of it.

By the spring of 1935 he was feeling very well. Most of his old sparkle returned and he was remarkably chipper. He decided to make a trip to Chattanooga. He hadn't been back to his hometown in a number of years. The dogwood was in blossom, and he longed to walk down the familiar streets, visit his old friends and see his beloved *Chattanooga Times*. He also wanted to show his oldest grandchild, my sixteen-year-old Marian, the place where his newspaper career had begun.

On Saturday night, April 6, 1935, Papa took the train at Pennsylvania Station, with Marian and a nurse. Mother, Arthur and I saw them off.

A little after midday on Monday, my father called my mother from the *Chattanooga Times* to report that he had spent the morning touring the newspaper plant with his granddaughter; that his nephew Adolph Shelby Ochs, who was then general manager, had consulted him on some business matters; and that he never felt better or happier.

It was about one o'clock when Father hung up and strolled into the city room to invite R. E. Walker, the editor, to join him and his brother Milton for lunch. At the restaurant a few blocks away they chatted as the waiter handed out the menus. Studying his menu, Uncle Milton asked, "What do you think you'll order, Adolph?" There was no answer.

Uncle Milton looked up. My father was unconscious. He had had a cerebral hemorrhage.

An ambulance rushed him to the Newell Sanatorium. Uncle Milton, Aunt Ada, Uncle Harry, Adolph Shelby Ochs and Marian gathered at his bedside. My father never spoke again. Two hours and ten minutes after being stricken, he was dead.

A funeral was held in Chattanooga. The body was returned to New York. Another funeral service was held in Temple Emanu-El, and on Friday, April 12, 1935, my father was buried in the mausoleum he had had built in Temple Israel Cemetery, in Mount Hope, just a short distance from Hillandale.

Mayor La Guardia ordered the city's flags flown at half-staff. The teletype machines of the Associated Press, the United Press and other international wire services fell silent for a moment all around the world. At the *New York Times*, all work stopped when the funeral service began, and heads were bowed in prayer.

My mother felt the loss keenly but held her grief inside her and went on living as she always had, attending the opera every Monday night, going for drives along the quiet country lanes near Hillandale and spending the summers in Abenia, at Lake George. She loved Abenia and would stay there through October, when the autumn colors were at their best.

But she was having trouble with her heart. The condition was growing worse. On May 6, 1937, my cousin Ruth called me from Hillandale. She said Mama had had a severe attack. Before I could contact Dr. Robert Levy, the heart specialist, Ruth called again to say that my mother was gone.

It was the day before her seventy-seventh birthday. She was laid to rest in Temple Israel Cemetery, next to my father.

22

As the trustees of my father's estate, which held controlling interest in the *New York Times*, Arthur, my cousin Julius Adler and I had to select the next publisher. The question had to be decided at a stressful time for any news-gathering organization. Mussolini was about to attack Ethiopia; Hitler was creating a military force of frightening power; Japan was walking over a stupefied China; Spain was embroiled in civil war. At home, the Depression was still taking its toll, knocking the *Times*'s profits down to one third of what they had been in 1929. The next publisher would be walking into a potentially stormy situation.

My father had all but named Arthur as his successor. But Julius Adler was not prepared to accept the issue as settled. Julius had been trained for management positions for eighteen years, and reared on the philosophy that a man should be a fighter. He now believed he should be the next publisher of the *New York Times*.

From the time he graduated from Princeton, Julius had been sure he would rise to the top. His parents, who were extremely ambitious for him, virtually handed him over to my father, believing that Adolph Ochs would see the boy as the son he never had and would make him his heir apparent.

Just as Julius began his newspaper career, the United States entered the First World War. He was quick to enlist, and to adapt to military life. In short order he was made commander of an infantry company, and he served in combat with distinction. By the end of the war he had been promoted to major and awarded the Distinguished Service Cross, the Silver Star with two oak-leaf clusters, the Purple Heart, the French Legion of Honor, the Croix de Guerre and the Italian Croce de Guerra. I'm sure that if Julius had been left to his own devices, he would have followed an Ochs tradition by making the military his career. Grandfather Ochs had served in the Civil War; Uncle Milton had been a colonel in the National Guard; Milton's son, William Van Dyke Ochs, had chosen the military as his vocation; and Van Dyke's son had been to West Point. But Julius's life had been decided by his parents long before. He resumed work at the *Times*.

My father was quick to see Julius's keen business sense, and when the rotogravure process was invented in Germany in the 1920's he sent his nephew abroad to inspect it. That led, in Berlin, to a surprising encounter. Julius was discussing the new machine with a German sales representative when the conversation happened to turn to the war. Suddenly, the two men discovered a startling coincidence.

One day during the war, after his company had captured a village, Julius was rounding a street corner when he came face to face with an armed German officer. Julius was faster on the draw and got the German to surrender before any shots were fired.

The sales representative of the rotogravure manufacturers was none other than that German officer. From that day on, the two men were great friends. (Immediately, Julius bought the process.)

Julius's capabilities as a businessman led to his eventual promotion to vice president of the New York Times Company. His methodical, precise mind was invaluable in business transactions. Yet these assets worked against him in his quest for the post of publisher. The job required flexibility and openmindedness, and Julius's attitude was often overly conservative, his approach rigid.

Basically, the choice of publisher was up to the trustees of my father's estate—Arthur, Julius and me. Our controlling share of stock would determine the issue. But the decision would have to be ratified by the four members of the Board of Trustees of the New York Times Company—Hoyt Miller (the son of Charles Miller, who was my father's first editor-in-chief), Julius, Arthur and me. Just before the board election, I told Julius I would cast my vote for Arthur. It was only natural, I said, for me to consider my husband the best man for the job, and I hoped Julius would understand my situation. I didn't want to offend him by telling him why I thought him unqualified. He was as close to me as a brother, and one of the most honorable, decent, fine human beings I had ever known.

The news hit him hard. "Frankly," he said, "your decision is a great disappointment to me." He became upset—rather ill, in fact.

On May 7, 1935, the board of trustees elected Arthur president and publisher of the New York Times Company and created the post of general manager for Julius. After the election, Julius came up to Arthur and me and said, "I've got a good job, and I just want to tell you that you won't find a more loyal and devoted second man."

The friendship between Arthur and Julius was sealed. They established a good working relationship. Arthur, like my father, was not the type to throw his weight around. He gave Julius free rein, and Julius responded by acting with dignity and doing a thoroughly good job.

He never lost his taste for military life. In the Reserves, which he joined after the First World War, he rose to brigadier general, and when the Second World War broke out he sought out combat duty. To his delight, he was assigned to New Guinea as second in command of a division. The night his men were preparing for their first assault, Julius came down with a gall bladder malfunction and had to be flown to Walter Reed Hospital in Washington for an operation. There was no question of returning to active service, and he was in the Reserves for the remainder of the war, bitterly disappointed at not having seen action. His final promotion made him major general.

Arthur took on the stewardship of the *Times* with a firm but cautious hand. He felt confident; in effect, he had already been managing the paper during the last two years of my father's illness.

During this period, a new section called the News of the Week in Review had made its debut. The section was the idea of the Sunday editor, Lester Markel. Lester had joined the paper in 1923, and over the next forty years he shaped the package of Sunday sections into the journalistic institution it is today. The Review, which was part of his grand design, at first met with considerable resistance from my father, who felt it was unnecessary. "If you read the daily paper," he'd argue, "you don't need a recapitulation on Sunday."

Arthur supported the project and helped Lester change my father's mind. The decisive factor was the emergence of *Time* magazine. Henry Luce, the publisher and founder of *Time*, told me once that in the early days the magazine relied heavily on the *Times*. He said, "We moved from Cleveland to New York just so we could get hold of the *Times* more quickly."

Lester and Arthur worked well together over the years, though they had periodic fights. But everyone had fights with Lester; he was a most difficult man to get along with. Many of those who worked under him called him a czar, a tyrant and I'm sure a lot of other things. He was an intensely dedicated man who, in the process of building up the Sunday paper, came close to driving himself and everyone else crazy. I remember Anne McCormick telling me that he never accepted a first draft of an article, refusing to believe that any piece of writing could be good on the first try, and that a reporter would often have to revise a piece three or four times. Once, she said, she had gone through two revisions, then submitted her original first draft. He accepted it without change.

Lester was a strange man, often insensitive to others' feelings but terribly touchy when it came to his own. One day he invited me to the Plaza Hotel for a cocktail. (I had known him from my college days; he was at the Columbia School of Journalism and we met at an English literature class. I thought he was a smart aleck and he thought I talked too much.)

I accepted the invitation. We weren't together for five minutes before he demanded: "Why don't you like me?"

"What makes you think I don't like you?"

"You act cold toward me."

"Well, Lester," I said, "do you think I'd be here if I didn't like you?"

He didn't have an answer for that. I finally got it through his head that I liked him fine. After that, we always had a very friendly relationship.

The News of the Week in Review (now called the Week in Review) was one of many innovations that were considered at the *Times* during the two years of my father's illness. Arthur supported many of the proposals, such as selling off old properties like *Mid-Week Pictorial*, and he discussed some of them with my father. But when he became publisher, he held back from initiating them immediately.

The *Times* staff was in mourning. They had lost their patriarch, a man they had respected and loved. Arthur was in a sensitive position. If he were to go ahead with a lot of reforms, it might be construed as criticism of Adolph Ochs. On the other hand, if he gave the impression of imitating my father, he would forfeit the staff's respect for him as an individual and leader in his own right. He had to tread cautiously and to see to it that change, when it came, came gradually.

One of Arthur's first actions as publisher was to reduce operating costs, starting with the rotogravure section.

The rotogravure presses purchased by Julius had printed the clearest photographs ever seen in this country. With improved rotogravure techniques, however, the presses that printed this separate section on extremely expensive, high-gloss paper had become obsolete. It's curious how often things that are important to one generation are useless to the next. On Lester Markel's advice, Arthur merged the rotogravure section with the Sunday magazine.

Other changes came one by one:

My father had made a practice of awarding bonuses for out-standing work. It was an arbitrary system that Arthur felt put the recipient under an obligation. Arthur decided to reward good work with a pay increase. The intention was to create a sense of achievement: A raise was given not as a gift but because it was earned. This tangible incentive had a beneficial effect on morale and on the staff's sense of loyalty. Maintaining staff members' pride in their work was very important to Arthur.

The *Times* had won many awards for its typographic appearance, and Arthur sought to improve the design still further. More photographs were distributed throughout the paper, and more use was made of display headings.

My father had always held that his readers were intelligent enough not to have to be told what to think; hence, that *Times* editorials should not try to influence them but should be interpretive, to help the reader make up his own mind. Arthur, on the other hand, believed that with wars and dictatorships changing the face of the world, the *Times* could no longer be aloof from the fray but had to accept responsibility and state its views. Moreover, he believed that what our readers wanted from our editorials was clarification of issues and clear-cut opinions to help them make their way through the tangled web of world events. So the ivory-tower tone of the editorial page was leavened. Though our editorials were still written with a sense of restraint, they now clearly reflected the *Times*'s position on major issues. In a short while, the paper won a reputation as a crusader for the causes it believed in.

Years later, Arthur confided to me, "I remember how I worried that I was moving too fast, changing things too much. It was clear to me that it was time for change, but I feared I might be ruining the *Times*. The changes had to be made without affecting the basic Ochs formula."

One development that complicated Arthur's life in the forties was the emergence of the Newspaper Guild. My father had had to deal with the mechanical craft unions throughout his career. He understood that the craftsmen needed protection (although he was also aware that some unions were becoming as reactionary as some of their early employers). He'd had a good relationship with the mechanical craft unions, and the union men respected him in turn—remembering, for one thing, that he himself had once been a working printer.

Arthur, too, had had good relations with the craft unions. But when the Newspaper Guild started organizing reporters, he was upset. He did not think that anyone who handled the news should belong to any group, whether labor or any other kind. He felt it would undermine the impartiality on which the paper's reputation was based, and he thought it was wrong for all reporters to share the same point of view on any one issue. "It's because we have reporters with different backgrounds, religions, prejudices and so forth that we've achieved a balanced coverage," he once said during his negotiations with the guild, and he refused to agree to a union shop for the news and editorial departments.

In time, the Newspaper Guild eased up on trying to organize *Times* reporters and turned its attention to the paper's other non-union employees. In 1943 the guild succeeded in bringing elevator men, cleaning women, kitchen help and all maintenance workers under its jurisdiction—while still calling itself the Newspaper Guild.

In addition to his responsibilities on the *Times*, Arthur was confronted with the complicated matter of settling my father's estate. My father had kept all his shares in both the *Chattanooga Times* and the *New York Times* in his own name. Hillandale and Abenia were also registered as his property. Against the advice of his lawyer and friend, Samuel Untermyer, he had not put any of his holdings in my mother's name or mine. He was a self-made man proud of being the family provider. His will left his entire fortune in trust to my four children, with my mother and me as life beneficiaries and Arthur, Julius Adler and me as trustees.

My father's fortune was not as extensive as many imagined, because he had always put two thirds of the *New York Times*'s earnings back into the business. Nevertheless, there was a considerable amount of money and property left in his name, and the inheritance tax was tremendous. The amount due, including lawyers' fees, came to about six million dollars. The only way we could pay this sum was by selling *Times* properties and stocks. And that would put an end to the *Times* as a family-owned paper.

Arthur came up with an ingenious idea. The New York Times Company would offer to purchase its 8 percent preferred stock. In spite of the Depression, the company had substantial capital set aside, and could retire its preferred shares without difficulty. Though the transaction took a $480,000 bite out of the family's annual income, it left the controlling common stock in the family's hands. The arrangement also benefited the *Times* and its stockholders. By retiring the large block of my father's preferred shares, the company had fewer dividends to distribute annually, and this strengthened the remaining outstanding shares.

There seems, however, to have been some question raised within the Federal Government about management selling stock back to its own company, and within a few years the practice was prohibited by law. I don't know if President Roosevelt had a hand in issuing that dictum, but the word in the White House was "We'll get the *Times* next time." Mr. Roosevelt didn't realize that "next time" was a long way off. My children would not have to pay inheritance tax because my father had willed all his stocks directly to them. Not until the grandchildren came into their inheritance would the Government get its cut. By then the inheritance would be split at least thirteen ways, and the tax bracket wouldn't be so high.

Under Arthur, the *Times* experienced tremendous growth. From being a family newspaper it became a public corporation listed on the American Exchange. The evolution was inevitable. Yet when Arthur retired in 1961, he could say that the *Times* was still basically the same paper he took over from my father in 1935. It still adhered to the same principles of journalism and the same doctrine of fairness, and it still had the same spirit that had made it the world's greatest newspaper.

In his affable way, Arthur would still jest that he got where he did by marrying the boss's daughter. Maybe it shouldn't have, but it always infuriated me when he said this. I often rebuked him: "I don't care how many bosses' daughters you marry, you won't get out of the basement unless you climb out. And certainly you could never have remained publisher of the *New York Times* —through the Depression, the Second World War and everything —unless you were a first-rate executive and a man of outstanding character."

23

The White House did not look favorably on the new publisher of the *Times*. First, there was President Roosevelt's disapproval of the inheritance-tax settlement; Arthur learned of that indirectly after only a few months in his new job. Then, less than two years later, there was an open breach over the "court packing" issue.

On February 6, 1937, the *Times* opened fire on the President's plan for enlarging the membership of the Supreme Court, arguing that it would upset the balance of power on which American democracy was founded. The highest court in the land would be dominated by justices sympathetic to the President's policies. Moreover, the paper emphasized, Mr. Roosevelt had not spoken of the plan during his 1936 campaign, and therefore had no mandate for it from the electorate.

Over the next six months, the paper ran editorial after editorial on the question; it became the most intensive editorial crusade in the paper's history. Other papers around the country joined in this editorial barrage.

When, in July, the President abandoned his plan, the *Times* expressed its relief, and added that it would readily support any Roosevelt proposals that were genuinely progressive and in the democratic tradition—as it had during most of the legislative history of the New Deal.

Mr. Roosevelt was not placated. He had become embittered against the *Times* and against Arthur personally. He now vented his anger by making disparaging remarks about the paper's new publisher to congressmen and journalists. His gibes would filter down to Arthur, who would be piqued and would make caustic retorts he knew would reach the President's ears. With every new affront from the White House, Arthur became more and more angry. I had never seen him so bitter.

The injuries mounted without any attempt by either man to negotiate a truce. Had a permanent rift resulted, it would have been seriously damaging to the *Times*, and perhaps to the President. My scheming instincts were aroused. Without consulting Arthur, I initiated a plan of my own.

Henry Morgenthau, Sr., was an old friend of my father and had close ties to Franklin Roosevelt: His son, Henry, Jr., was Secretary of the Treasury. I had known Uncle Henry, as I called him, since I was a girl, and I decided to confide in him. Mr. Morgenthau grasped the gravity of the situation and agreed with me that the two men should meet face to face. "Nothing easier, Iphigene," he said. "I'll get the President to invite you and Arthur to lunch."

I can't imagine how Uncle Henry coaxed the President into inviting us to lunch at Hyde Park. I acted just as surprised as Arthur the day we received the invitation. Arthur decided that since the President had made the first move, he would meet him halfway.

We arrived at Hyde Park full of anticipation. We had met Mr. Roosevelt only once before, at a small White House party. All I remembered about that evening was Mr. Roosevelt's way of making martinis. After taking great pains to measure out precise amounts of gin and vermouth into a pitcher, he added a big splash of gin.

At the luncheon, the President's mother, Sara Delano Roosevelt, acted as hostess, and Arthur was placed on her right. Apparently, Mrs. Roosevelt had not been filled in about her guests, for her first words to Arthur were: "Now let me see, you're with the *Herald Tribune*, aren't you?"

Yet the meeting turned out to be pleasant and healing. When we left, Mr. Roosevelt and Arthur shook hands warmly. Their responsibilities as publisher and President could bring them into opposition again, but that would not affect the new respect they had for each other as human beings.

The feud was over. And neither man was the wiser about my little scheme. I never told Arthur how that luncheon came about.

Mr. Roosevelt took it in stride when, after supporting his candidacy in 1932 and 1936, the *Times* came out for Wendell Willkie in 1940. Neither the editorial board nor Arthur thought it would be good for the country to break with the two-term tradition. But in 1944, conceding that it might be necessary to go against tradition in unusually stressful times, the paper supported Mr. Roosevelt for a fourth term. The Second World War was coming to a climax, and no man seemed better qualified than the incumbent President to guide the nation through the trials ahead. Little did we know how far the President's health had deteriorated, and how little time he had left.

Eleanor Roosevelt was perhaps the most dynamic First Lady in the country's history. I met her several times over the years.

The first occasion was in the mid-twenties, when she called on me at our home on West Eighty-eighth Street to recruit me for some worthy cause. My three small children were keeping me so occupied that I had to turn her down, and the work was taken on by Eleanor Morgenthau, Henry, Jr.'s, wife.

The two Eleanors became lifelong friends. They would go horseback riding (the Morgenthaus had a farm adjoining Hyde Park in Dutchess County), and I wouldn't be surprised if their closeness had something to do with Henry's appointment as Secretary of the Treasury—although the President had a different explanation. Mr. Roosevelt once told Arthur he made the appointment because Henry had no training in economics and was totally trustworthy. This gave the President full control over economic policies.

Henry headed the Treasury with unimpeachable integrity for ten years. He once borrowed a *Times* editorial writer, Charles Merz, to help him with some financial reports. Charlie told us that after they completed the project Henry remarked, "You know, Charlie, since becoming Secretary of the Treasury I've gotten so interested in finance, I think when I'm finished with this job I'll go to Oxford and study it."

My second meeting with Eleanor Roosevelt took place toward the end of 1941 and was initiated by me. I approached her after many unsuccessful attempts to persuade our leading educators to correct a serious flaw in the nation's educational system, a flaw I had become aware of in talking with my children.

At that time, Marian was attending the Froebel League School, studying to be a kindergarten teacher, Ruth was enrolled at Smith College and my two younger ones were in high school. Discussing their studies with them, Arthur and I came to realize that none of their curricula provided a comprehensive course in American history. My children's minds were a blank on the Constitution, the Civil War and the like.

We were stunned to think that you could go through college, acquire a profession, become a voter, and all this with no real knowledge of the democratic foundations of your own country. As Father Robert Gannon, president of Fordham University, put it, the schools were serving a cafeteria form of education. No courses were required; you could elect whatever you wished to study. It struck me as a grave injustice to the nation's youth and a situation that had to be rectified.

I turned to my alma mater, Barnard, and voiced my concern to its dean, Virginia Gildersleeve. I pointed out that knowledge of American history was essential to responsible citizenship. "We have the unique privilege in this country of having a say in our leadership. How can one exercise this important right intelligently without an understanding of our system of government? If you don't know where you came from, how can you know where you're going?"

My speech did not make an overwhelming impression. After politely hearing me out, Dean Gildersleeve suggested I confer with the head of the history department, Professor Eugene Byrnes.

Professor Byrnes proved to be an enthusiastic ally. Together we planned a two-year history program that would be added to the curriculum as a required course. The first year would cover the European origins of democracy, and the second year would concentrate on the growth and development of the American democratic system.

The professor and I regarded our plan as nothing short of magnificent, but the faculty review committee was not of the same mind. The consensus was that two years of required history were unnecessary. Our program was voted down.

Mr. Byrnes persevered nonetheless, and eventually was given a mandate for a required one-year course in history, though not necessarily American history. The votes that swung the decision were cast by the science faculty. The professors in that department had discovered that their students had little concept of continuity. They realized that study of history would strengthen the students' grasp of this fundamental scientific principle.

Professor Byrnes's persistence encouraged me to continue with my own efforts. I wrote more than thirty leading Eastern colleges, asking if American history was required for matriculation or graduation. All thirty, including Harvard, Princeton, Yale and Cornell, replied that it was not. I remember the letter from Robert Angell, president of Yale. He actually said that requiring American history would antagonize students and undermine their patriotism! I always thought of that as an example of high-minded rubbish.

About the only sympathetic response I got was from the president of Harvard, James Conant. Mr. Conant was one of several college presidents who served with Arthur on the board of the Rockefeller Foundation, and when we met at an annual meeting and get-together in Williamsburg, Virginia, I took the opportunity to give my little speech on American history to the university heads present. Mr. Conant was the only one who didn't humor me but took me seriously. However, no change was made in the Harvard curriculum.

I decided to attack from another angle. If history were made obligatory in high schools, it would perhaps become a college requirement in due course. I wrote more letters and talked to school principals and foundation presidents. I didn't strike a spark. Nobody wanted to investigate the situation. Nobody gave a damn.

Then it occurred to me that if there was one person who could promote my cause, it was the First Lady. Mrs. Roosevelt had a knack of getting through to young people. If she could make students realize the flaw in their education, they themselves would demand that they be taught American history. Or so I hoped. I wrote Mrs. Roosevelt, asking for an appointment. She scheduled a meeting for 9 a.m. at her house on East Sixty-fifth Street.

I don't like to have to be anywhere at nine in the morning, but that day I arrived at the Roosevelt house with five minutes to spare. A slovenly looking maid opened the front door and ushered me into a little reception room that looked like a second-rate dentist's office. The furniture was shabby, and in one corner, sitting on an ugly little table, was a vase of dead flowers. I couldn't help but conclude that Eleanor and Franklin were oblivious to interior design.

I must have waited for half an hour before Mrs. Roosevelt breezed in, saying, "Oh, I've been talking to the President. Sorry if I kept you waiting."

From the moment she entered, I could tell she was rushed and I'd have precious little time to state my case. She sat down, and I hurried through my speech, trying to emphasize the need for her personal help.

I got nowhere. "The person you want to see, Mrs. Sulzberger," she said, "is Dr. Studebaker, the head of the Department of Education."

"But, Mrs. Roosevelt," I said, "Dr. Studebaker is on the elementary and high-school level. I was talking about the college level —*that* type of education."

"Oh," she said, "Dr. Studebaker is your man. I'll ask you down to the White House to meet him." Then she stood up and shook my hand and said, "So nice meeting you." And out the door I went.

I was furious. I was sure she hadn't heard a single word I'd said. For the next hour I walked around Central Park, trying to cool off.

I had done everything I could and had failed miserably. I could keep beating my head against the wall, or I could give up. I decided to give up.

It turned out that Mrs. Roosevelt had not been as inattentive as I thought, for about two months later Arthur and I were invited to lunch at the White House. The invitation had to be canceled when the Japanese attacked Pearl Harbor, but it was renewed seven weeks later. Arthur was in bed with the flu and insisted that I go alone. I was astonished to see that Mrs. Roosevelt had remembered and was trying to help, so I arranged for a nurse for Arthur and left for Washington.

The luncheon was held in the family dining room. There were only twelve at the table, and I had the honor of being seated next to the President. He was utterly charming. When the opportunity arose, I asked the gentleman seated on my other side if he would point out Dr. Studebaker; I was there to meet him, I explained. "I'd be happy to introduce you," the gentleman said, "but he's not here."

After the luncheon, the President excused himself and Mrs. Roosevelt took us on a tour of the White House. After seeing the Lincoln Room, we were ushered into one of the parlors and served coffee. I was engaged in pleasant chatter with one of the guests when Mrs. Roosevelt came over and said, "Oh, Mrs. Sulzberger, I haven't had a chance to talk to you. You're interested in kindergartens, aren't you?"

"No, Mrs. Roosevelt," I said. "You invited me here to meet Dr. Studebaker. I'm interested in teaching American history."

"Oh," she said. "So you are. I'll call him and make a date for you."

It was three o'clock on a Sunday afternoon. Nonetheless, Mrs. Roosevelt telephoned Dr. Studebaker's office at the Department of Education, and by coincidence he was there, working. He agreed to see me at four o'clock.

The interview with Dr. Studebaker paid off in an unexpected way. He agreed wholeheartedly that our failure to require American history courses was a serious deficiency in our educational system. The situation, he said, was even worse than I thought; he called it "outrageous."

"It's extraordinary," he said. "The Fascists, the Communists, everybody's indoctrinating their youth. And our young people know nothing about democracy." He encouraged me to continue with my efforts, but advised me not to waste my time with educators and politicians. "If you want to make progress," he said, "go back to the *New York Times*."

When I related Mr. Studebaker's suggestion to Arthur, he was interested and said, "Why not give it a try?" I did just that, and found a confederate in Benjamin Fine, the *Times*'s education editor. Mr. Fine sent a thousand letters to a cross section of schools for higher education—general universities, specialized colleges, engineering and religious schools, teachers' training schools and so forth—asking what their American history requirements were. About three quarters of them replied, and their replies were appallingly revealing. American history was a required subject in only 50 percent of the teachers' colleges, only 17 percent of the average colleges and only 12 or 13 percent of the technical schools, like M.I.T. The startling picture was set out in black and white.

The *Times* printed the findings under a three-column headline on the front page of its Sunday edition. I hadn't known the story would appear, and I felt a great sense of accomplishment. The article aroused widespread interest and support around the country. Among the groups that rallied around were the Daughters of the American Revolution, the American Legion and other veterans' organizations, but the story also made a significant impression on some of the people I was more interested in. A number of high schools altered their curricula, and some states, including New York, made American history a requirement in high schools. Colleges also began to realize the subject's importance, and some of them altered their courses. It was a step in the right direction, and it won the *Times* a Pulitzer prize for public service.

Dr. Studebaker had been right. Going to the newspaper had been much more effective than wooing politicians, educators and historians—to say nothing of First Ladies!

24

The Spanish Civil War was a bitterly divisive issue in America, and the *Times* was under constant political cross fire for trying to cover the war impartially. The paper had two correspondents reporting the fighting: Herbert Matthews filed dispatches from the Loyalist camp, and William Carney covered the Nationalist front. Their stories often ran side by side.

Even so, partisans of both factions accused the paper of slanting the news. The mail was voluminous and indignant. Pro-Loyalists strenuously objected to Mr. Carney's stories, and the Franco supporters protested against Mr. Matthews's reports. The *Times* ran many of these letters, and Arthur would answer some of them himself, sending a copy of a Carney dispatch to soothe a pro-Nationalist and a Matthews clipping to mollify a pro-Loyalist. But the attacks did not abate.

Our editorial writers walked a tightrope. The paper did not

come out in support of either side. The editorials were interpretive, in the Adolph Ochs tradition, since neither Arthur nor the editorial board was convinced that justice was all on one side of the struggle.

One of the editorial writers, Charlie Merz, was particularly responsible for the paper's neutral stance. Charlie had had a long career in journalism. He had worked for *Harper's Weekly* and the *New Republic,* had reported for the New York *World* from Europe and the Far East, had written editorials for that paper when its editorial page was run by Walter Lippmann, and had finally become the paper's associate editor. Charlie joined the *Times* when the *World* ceased publication in 1931 and quickly impressed Arthur with his intelligence. It was said of him that he was so fair-minded he leaned over backward when he walked. (As a matter of fact, Charlie did sort of tilt back when he walked!) Though, like Arthur, a liberal, Charlie thought it would be inadvisable for the paper to take a stand on the Spanish Civil War because the situation was so complex and unclear. In 1938, Arthur named Charlie editor of the editorial page.

Arthur and Charlie became great friends. They thought alike on most matters and had the same interests. I remember they used to spend hours doing crossword puzzles and Double Crostics. Charlie could be full of fun, and he and his wife, Evelyn, were engaging and friendly. They became close friends of the family. They celebrated almost every Christmas with us and were always present at birthdays and anniversaries. My children called them Aunt and Uncle.

My stand on the war was strongly pro-Loyalist. Hitler and Mussolini were backing Franco, and whichever side Hitler backed was the wrong side as far as I was concerned. I didn't need to know anything else. I felt so strongly about the Loyalist cause that I contributed money to its support. The sums were not large, and Arthur never once suggested I shouldn't make the donations. He said it was my money and I could do whatever I wanted with it. Nonetheless, I felt he was slightly irritated. He would argue that the Loyalists were a "rather grubby lot who murdered priests and nuns." I would retort that the atrocities were horrible on both sides. But what frightened me most was the emerging strength of Adolf Hitler.

The first time I learned of Hitler was in the mid-twenties. My father-in-law, Cyrus Sulzberger, was deeply troubled by what he saw in the Nuremberg weekly *Der Stürmer*, published by the notorious Nazi Julius Streicher. The magazine featured violent anti-Semitic articles and cartoons. Arthur and I thought Cyrus was unduly concerned. The Jews had prospered in Germany for centuries. They had overcome prejudice, they were being accepted for good governmental positions, they were prominent in science and medicine. Arthur and I couldn't imagine the Germans letting anti-Semitism go very far. "The people are too intelligent and civilized to be taken in by such rot," we told Arthur's father.

"No, I think you're wrong," he'd say. "This is something to be taken very seriously."

In the thirties we began to get reports of internal rumblings in Germany. Frederick Birchall, the *Times*'s chief European correspondent, filed dispatches describing the spread of Nazi authoritarianism and the violent tactics being used by the S.S. in enforcing Nazi ideology. He wrote an on-the-spot report about the book burning. He was the first reporter for an American publication to tell the world about Nazi concentration camps. His forthright dispatches were sent at considerable risk to his own safety. He was awarded a Pulitzer prize for them, and was asked by the German authorities to leave the country.

There was a sigh of relief in the *Times* newsroom when Mr. Birchall returned. The short, belligerent-looking Englishman, sporting a pointed red beard that seemed to stick straight out in front of him, had become a legend in journalistic circles for having eagerly taken a perilous assignment, though past sixty. At a time in life when most men are ready to relax in an easy chair and put up their feet, Mr. Birchall left his job as acting managing editor in 1932 and went back to field reporting. (He had become managing editor in 1925 when Carr Van Anda retired, but my father altered his title to include the word "acting" because he believed a New York paper shouldn't have an English manager.)

Mr. Birchall's stories caused a sensation in this country, but they did not arouse the fears they should have. We believed the concentration camps were only for indoctrination. No one foresaw what they would eventually become. It could not have been imagined because it was beyond the realm of man's experience. So we read the reports with distaste for the strutting Chancellor and turned our thoughts to the forbidding scene at home. The stock market collapse of 1929 had spread a black shadow over the land. The spread of Nazism overseas was as vague a concern as reading about a hundred people burning to death in a hotel fire: You care, certainly, but you're not in the fire, so you don't understand. It doesn't touch you; it's too abstract.

It's the same today. How calmly we observed the massacre of the Bengalis in Bangladesh and the Hutus in Burundi, the mass slaughter that followed the attempted Communist coup in Indonesia! An estimated half a million people were slaughtered in Indonesia, and I don't remember any criticism on the part of the American Government or the public. Perhaps, to survive, we have to shut our eyes to reality when it becomes too hideous.

Even as late as 1936, few people outside Germany had any concept of the dangers of Nazism. Hitler, it was widely believed, was nothing more than a fanatic trying to salvage a country bled dry by the war and the terms of the Versailles Treaty. It was inconceivable that Germany would become a threat. The show of Hitler's mechanized strength in Spain was underrated.

I, by then, felt that Spain was a testing ground for the Second World War. If I was ahead of most people on that, I owe it partly to my father. It is remarkable, I think, that as early as 1933, mentally exhausted as he was, Father had foreseen the role Hitler would play. When Hitler became Chancellor, my father said, "This will lead to a second world war."

My perceptions were further sharpened in the summer of 1934, when I took the children to Europe. In Switzerland I met a German-Jewish couple and their four children. The wife told me of the unpleasant things that were happening in her homeland. Her husband, she said, had recently been arrested and imprisoned. She was fortunate: With the help of an influential army friend she had managed to get him released. But many Jews were being imprisoned without hope of such intercession. I suggested that it might be wiser for her children not to return to Germany until things calmed down. "Oh, it's all right," she said. "It's just a passing phase."

I returned home to learn that my father's cousin Louis Zinn, who lived in Nuremberg, had been arrested in the middle of the night. Father had often visited his cousin in Germany. Louis was a toy manufacturer and a great collector of old prints. He had quite a number of unusual woodcuts, including a series of prints dating back to the Middle Ages that depicted the history of Nuremberg. He had planned to leave the collection to the city. Louis was seventy when the S.S. arrested him. Some friends managed to get him released, but the strain was too much. Shortly after he returned home, he died.

Louis had two nieces, Elizabeth Abt and Thea Medas. I wrote them, introducing myself and asking if they would like me to look after their children until the threat to their safety passed. They thanked me but said they didn't want to be separated from their children.

About a year later I received a letter from one of the nieces, saying that conditions in Germany had become a lot worse and that the whole family wanted to emigrate to the United States. The immigration regulations, as enacted in 1920, required that a sponsor vouch for the immigrants' good character and accept full financial and legal responsibility for the duration of their stay in America. We signed the necessary papers, and Louis Zinn's relatives moved to the United States. Soon we were getting requests from other distant relatives on both sides of the family to help them leave Germany. Between my aunts, cousin Julius, and Arthur and me, we sponsored some twenty-five or thirty relatives, and relatives of relatives. Though we didn't personally know any of them, our faith was not misplaced. As the various families arrived, we gave them money so they could get themselves settled. When they got on their feet, every one of them reimbursed us, down to the last penny. We didn't want the money back, but they insisted on it. They were a wonderful group of people, and many of them made a great success of their lives.

We also received a flood of letters from German Jews claiming to be blood relations. Apparently there were a few prized New York telephone books in Germany, and in desperation people wrote letters to anyone with a Jewish surname, asking to be sponsored, or at least to be helped in obtaining a visa. Arthur and I couldn't see our way clear to vouching for complete strangers. We rationalized our reluctance by saying that the situation wasn't as bad as people said, and we put the letters aside. Ever since then, I have wished we had taken the chance. I wish I had signed for them all—I wish to God I had.

For those we left behind we have only our terrible guilt. If only we could have realized! There were many other families, like ours, that helped, but could have helped more. I remember discussing this once with Cole Porter. The composer was hospitalized at Columbia Presbyterian at the same time as Arthur. When Arthur was napping I'd go to a sitting room down the hall to read and relax. It was there that I met Mr. Porter, who was recovering from the leg amputation that had been found necessary after his riding accident. He didn't have as many visitors as one might have expected, and we talked for hours. One day we got onto the subject of the war, and I told him of the remorse I felt for not having sponsored more Jews for entry into the United States.

"Do you know," he said, "that's the one thing in life that bothers me. Some lady I didn't know very well wrote to ask me to sign for her. Surely, I thought, she must have closer friends who could help. So I didn't sign. I never heard from her again. I don't know what happened to her, and it often gives me nightmares thinking about it."

When the spring of 1938 came around and Austria was absorbed into the Third Reich, the world at last realized what Hitler had in mind. The response was the appeasement at Munich, which shook the foundations of international morality without bringing the "peace in our time" promised by Neville Chamberlain. Hitler invaded Poland, and on September 3, 1939, France and Britain declared war. My father's worst fears had come true.

Arthur and I were so shaken we decided on a change of scene. We went to Atlantic City, walked along the boardwalk, went to the movies, did whatever we could to divert our minds. We didn't succeed. All we could talk about was the war. After two days we returned home. We had come to realize that you can't run away from fear. All you can do is stick to the job, face up to life and hope for the best. But the best was not to be.

25

On a Sunday afternoon in December 1941, Arthur and I were stretched out in deck chairs, enjoying the mild climate of Pinehurst, North Carolina. We were there on vacation, and that morning we had gone horseback riding along the bridle paths of the resort. After lunch we strolled into the hotel's garden for an afternoon of reading and relaxation.

Soon afterward, Arthur was paged: a long-distance phone call. The *New York Times* was on the line. An editor in the city room said, "The Japanese have bombed Pearl Harbor."

In less than an hour Arthur was on his way to New York. He caught a plane in Raleigh and was back at the paper in time to help out the first edition. That night he slept at the *Times*.

I returned by train Monday evening.

* * *

Arthur had never gotten over his disappointment at missing combat in the First World War. After the Second World War began in September 1939, he grew increasingly restless. He would have liked to enlist again, and this time see battle. Yet he was over fifty. Besides, some fool doctor in the early 1930's had advised him to jog around the Central Park reservoir, and he had strained his heart. No recruiting officer in the country would have passed him. All the same, now that *Times* correspondents were risking their lives in the war zones, Arthur felt badly about being behind his desk in New York.

After Pearl Harbor, his determination to be involved in the war effort became even greater. That same month, he joined the central committee of the American Red Cross and got himself assigned to inspecting Red Cross installations in the war theaters. The way to the battle areas was open.

In the spring of 1943, Arthur made a journey to the Soviet Union. It occurred to him that as publisher of the *New York Times* he could accomplish something besides his Red Cross mission.

Despite their interdependence in the war effort, the Soviet Government and the Western Allies were not on good terms. With the Nazi blitz all but spent and the Soviet counteroffensive gaining in power, it seemed certain that the end of the war would see Russian troops in occupation of much of Europe. Remembering the Soviet-Nazi partition of Poland and the inhumane domestic record of the Stalinist regime, the American and British were suspicious of Moscow's intentions for the postwar era. Their uneasiness was heightened by Stalin's growing secretiveness as his armies drew closer to the borders of Poland and the Balkans. Arthur believed that chances of arriving at a better understanding between the three major allies would be improved if the American and British press were able to report more fully on all aspects of Russian life. He thought he would be in a good position to put that view to the Soviet authorities.

He broached the idea to President Roosevelt. The President liked it. Arthur had asked James (Scotty) Reston, who was then assistant to the publisher, to come with him, and Mr. Roosevelt told the State Department to do what it could to provide them with all possible courtesies by both American and Soviet officials.

Arthur and Scotty proceeded by the roundabout route of flying to South America and across the Atlantic to the African Gold Coast, then to Egypt and Teheran, and finally, eleven days after their departure, to Moscow. Shortly after their arrival, the Soviet authorities arranged for Arthur to inspect a trainload of wounded soldiers evacuated from the front. The poor creatures were lined up at a railway station. Those who could stand were drawn up at attention; those who couldn't, lay on stretchers. Many of them had little bunches of flowers in their hands.

Arthur took one look at them and asked if the stretcher cases couldn't be hospitalized at once. He was told not to worry: They had been there, awaiting his inspection, for only an hour.

"It was a horrible sight," Arthur told me. "Scotty and I had to hold back our tears."

Two weeks later the two Americans were allowed to visit the front. The food rations for the soldiers were appallingly small, but for the visiting dignitaries banquets were laid on every night. Arthur was distressed. Each time they sat down to dishes like suckling pig and vegetable salad—more courses than he could count—he would remember that the soldiers were living on meager rations, often warding off hunger. Yet when he spoke of this, he was assured there was no shortage of food for the troops.

Everywhere he and Scotty went, they got these huge dinners. The meals were always basically the same. Arthur began to get the feeling that they were all the work of one chef, who followed them at a distance.

Arthur and Scotty inspected some ruined cities. They gained a better understanding of Russian psychology. But their attempts to persuade the Soviets to permit a more open dialogue between Russia and the Western Allies were unfruitful. Both newspapermen came to the sad conclusion that Russia wanted to remain aloof. Russia had no interest in closer ties; she would cling to her nationalism and would never invite anything like the kind of trust that existed between America and Britain. That, when they came home, was the gist of the report Arthur made to the President, in addition to his report to the Red Cross.

The following year Arthur went to the Pacific with Turner Catledge, then a national correspondent for the *Times*. One day they were given a tour of one of the islands taken from the Japanese. The colonel escorting them was saying that the area they were in had been completely cleared of the enemy when a shot rang out and a bullet hit a tree next to them. Arthur turned to the colonel and said with aplomb, "It doesn't seem to be completely cleared out, sir." Then he and Turner dived into a ditch.

One thing Arthur did during the war was develop an independent photowire system. He did this with the facsimile equipment he had retained in 1941 after disposing of Wide World Photos, Inc. The equipment involved a new process by which photographs could be transmitted over the phone. The Times Facsimile Corporation, as it was named, operated on the seventh floor of the *Times* building. It was under contract to the armed forces to help develop secret communications equipment for the war effort. Arthur brought in our son-in-law, Orvil E. Dryfoos, to be its executive vice president.

Orvil had married Marian in July 1941. The young man had a seat on the New York Stock Exchange, but Arthur invited him to come to work at the *Times*. Just as my father had given Arthur a chance to show his potential in the newspaper business, so Arthur gave Orvil the same opportunity.

Orvil was pleased to be transferred to the Facsimile Corporation in 1941. He had been turned down by the Army and Navy, and now, at last, he had a hand in war work.

Orvil had volunteered after Pearl Harbor, but the medical exams revealed that he had a defective heart, a consequence of rheumatic fever. He had no recollection of such an illness and checked with his family physician, who confirmed that Orvil had had rheumatic fever as a small child. The doctor said he had never told him about it because he didn't want him growing up worrying about it.

The news of his heart condition was a bitter blow. Not only would he have to give up his dream of joining the Navy, but he couldn't even be sure of his health. The family was torn. We were relieved that he wouldn't be facing the dangers of war. But we were concerned about his heart.

Marian and Orvil had three children—Jacqueline Hays, Robert Ochs and Susan Warms. It was a few years after she married Orv that Marian took to reading and educating herself. Her husband gave her a lot of encouragement. He used to say that none of us fully appreciated Marian's ability. "I consult her on everything," he'd tell me. "She's got more common sense than any of us." In time, Marian's extraordinary talents were recognized by everyone and she became one of the leaders of the New York community.

Today she serves on many boards including Consolidated Edison, Ford Motor Company, Merck & Co., Inc., Rockefeller University and the Dartmouth Medical School. She is also chairman of the Mayor's Council on the Environment in New York. Marian and her husband, Andrew Heiskell, chairman of Time Inc., whom she married two years after Orvil's untimely death in 1963, are involved in so many purposeful projects that I have trouble keeping up with them all. For someone who barely managed to graduate from high school, Marian is a constant source of pride and astonishment to me.

Ruth, too, became a leading citizen—in Chattanooga. After attending Brearley, Ruth went to Smith College, graduating in 1943 and joining the Red Cross the same year. She was stationed at an American air base in England, then transferred to France, and then to Holland. In England she met an American officer, Ben Hale Golden. They were married on June 1, 1946, and settled in Chattanooga. They had four children—Stephen Arthur Ochs, Michael Davis, Lynn Iphigene and Arthur Sulzberger. Ruth became active in community affairs, serving on many boards, including the University of Chattanooga, the Hunter Museum and the Chattanooga Symphony. She was also named chairman of the Area Beautification Committee for the Chamber of Commerce. In 1964 Ruth became publisher of the *Chattanooga Times*. She is today happily married to A. William Holmberg.

Six months after Ruth married Ben, Judy became Mrs. Matthew Rosenchein, Jr. Judy met Matt when they were both students at the College of Physicians and Surgeons in New York. (Judy had enrolled there after graduating from Smith.) They had two children, Daniel Hays and James Matthew. Matt and Judy weren't suited to each other and the marriage ended in divorce. In 1958

Judy married Richard Cohen, an insurance executive, who adopted the two boys. Judy's second marriage lasted fifteen years. She is now married to Budd Levinson, a retired textile executive. She works in various hospital clinics and is a member of the staff of Cornell Medical College. Having a member of the family in the medical profession is a great asset. One of us is always calling on Judy for advice.

Just after the war, as the girls married and started raising families, Punch returned from the Marines and, without my knowing it, set about getting a high-school diploma from Loomis School, from which he had dropped out in his junior year. He took the high-school equivalency test and got such high marks that the school awarded him a diploma. He gave me the news by announcing, "Mother, I'm applying to Columbia." Punch was accepted into Columbia's School of General Studies, which was designed for students who were not qualified to enter the regular program. After one semester he was accepted in the regular university. By the time he graduated, in 1951, he had made the Dean's List several times.

During the summer of his freshman year, Punch married Barbara Grant. They had two children, Arthur Ochs, Jr., and Karen Alden. The marriage ended in divorce, and in 1956 Punch married Carol Fox Furman. Carol had a daughter, Cathy Jean, whom Punch adopted, and in 1964 Punch and Carol had a daughter of their own, Cynthia Fox.

As my children began establishing homes of their own, I was left in the late 1940's with plenty of time on my hands. At Arthur's suggestion, I started doing part-time work at the *New York Times*. I began by filling in for staff members who were on leave, and wound up taking a full-time job in the promotion department. I was to see what I could do to attract more women readers.

The paper was very weak in its coverage of news of particular interest to women. The first woman to be editor of the women's news, Mrs. Eleanor C. Darnton, became so frustrated that she resigned after one year on the job. Most of the ads directed at women buyers were going to the *Herald Tribune*. I began arranging public-affairs programs at women's clubs and inviting the ladies to tea at the *Times*. Occasionally I would approach Edwin

(Jimmy) James, the managing editor, with a suggestion for a story about these groups, so the women could see their names in print, and Jimmy would be infuriated.

Mr. James was a tough, hard-bitten character with a gruff manner that belied his Virginia upbringing. The big cigar he was always smoking, and the way he would talk out of one side of his mouth, conformed to the popular image of a big-city editor. However, once you got to know Jimmy, you realized that his bark was worse than his bite and that the tough exterior hid a kind heart.

"We don't publish stuff like that," he'd say to me. "That's promotion, not news."

According to his lights, to print stories like that would betray the paper's ethical standards.

"Look here," I'd reply firmly. "What are you printing this paper for? For people to read—and here I am working my head off to get readers, and I think the least you can do is cooperate and try to encourage these people to buy our paper."

My arguments carried little weight with Jimmy, so sometimes I'd ask Arthur to put in a good word on my behalf. Arthur got along well with Jimmy and was able to persuade him to run an occasional article, though never of the kind or length I wanted.

At times, Jimmy would get Arthur's goat. When Arthur would offer some mild criticism or suggestion, Jimmy would usually lean back in his chair, take his cigar out of his mouth and say, "Hell, I'm just the hired man around here." Arthur would hit the ceiling.

Jimmy was managing editor of the *Times* for nineteen years. He began his career with the paper in 1915 as a cub reporter. His first assignment was to cover a dinner given at the Astor Hotel by the Consul General of Rumania in honor of the officers of the United States Atlantic Fleet. Jimmy noticed something peculiar about the Consul General's appearance. The man wore a fine jacket covered with an array of medals, but his trousers and shoes were shabby. Suspecting something awry, Jimmy investigated and discovered that Rumania didn't have a Consul General in New York. This was an impostor with a history of psychiatric disorders. Jimmy's exposé was featured in the *Times* and started him off on his career with a splash.

Jimmy worked his way up from reporter to head of the Paris

bureau, and in 1932 my father named him managing editor. In the late 1940's he had a slight stroke. Though he stayed home, his wife, Simone, complained that he refused to rest as he should, so we took him up to Hillandale.

When he arrived, I laid down the law. "You're here to recuperate," I said. "I don't want to see you before eleven a.m. After lunch you're going to take a nap. And at night you're going to bed when I tell you."

"Hell, I'm just the hired man around here," Jimmy protested.

"That's just what you are," I said, "and you're going to behave!"

My disciplinarian tactics worked. Though Jimmy never made a full recovery, he returned to the office in a few weeks' time.

One day several years later, Arthur and I were on our way to Williamsburg, Virginia, for a meeting of the Rockefeller Foundation. When our train stopped in Newark, we received word that Edwin James had died. We decided that Arthur would go on to the meeting while I returned to New York to be with Simone and her children.

Simone's apartment was crowded with Jimmy's friends and colleagues. Simone was exhausted, and I managed to get the visitors to leave. Returning home, I no sooner went to bed than I got a call from some friend of Jimmy's. He was at the funeral parlor and said Simone's youngest daughter, Monique, was refusing to leave her father's coffin. He said she looked very tired, and he was worried.

"Let me talk to her," I said. Monique came to the phone, and I said I would come down to the funeral parlor and stay there until it closed if she would promise to go home. She agreed.

As soon as I arrived, Monique went home. Soon all the other visitors left and I was left alone in the semi-darkness with Jimmy in his open coffin. All of a sudden, I could have sworn I heard Jimmy say, "What the hell are you doing here?"

"But, Jimmy," I found myself saying aloud, "I promised Monique." Hearing my words made me realize my imagination had run wild, and it took all my self-control to keep from laughing.

When I told Arthur about it, he said, "That's just what Jimmy would have said, right out of the side of his mouth."

*   *   *

I stayed in the promotion department for about seven years, and then worked there part-time until Arthur retired. One of the most successful projects I was involved in was a wartime public-service program presented in Times Hall (formerly called the Little Theater) on Forty-fourth Street next to the *Times* building. Our activities ranged from classes on food canning and victory gardens to map reading and evacuation procedures during bomb alerts. When *Times* correspondents returned from abroad, we invited them to speak about their war experiences.

One of the most successful features was a discussion forum for children hosted by the children's entertainer Dorothy Gordon. The discussions, led by *New York Times* experts and a panel of six or eight especially bright children, were held on Saturday mornings. Private, parochial and public schools cooperated in the project, and the auditorium would fill up with children. The discussions were so successful that they were broadcast over radio station WQXR, and later over the NBC television network.

After the war, my work in the promotion department involved both schoolchildren and teachers. I organized discussions among heads of social-study courses and *Times* editors and reporters, and started an "In Service" course for teachers that was accredited by the Board of Education. The first year, the subject was the making of a newspaper; in the years that followed we took up topics in the news. I worked with WQXR to set up a course on music and a contest for child musicians. I also got the *Times* to sponsor book exhibits, first at the American Museum of Natural History and then as a traveling display for schools. As a result of our promotional efforts, the paper's circulation in schools and colleges blossomed.

I was busy outside the *Times*, too. One evening a week during the war I acted as senior hostess for the officers' party at Delmonico's. I'd often invite the guests I met there, both American and foreign, to Sunday lunch at Hillandale. The English-Speaking Union appealed to New Yorkers to provide overnight accommodations for British officers, mostly flyers returning home after training in the States, and Arthur and I did so whenever possible. We had plenty of bedrooms in our East Eightieth Street house, and putting up the soldiers was the least we could do. Most of them would spend a night on the town and show up in the wee hours of the morning, when the night watchman would let them in. I went to work while they were still asleep, and I would often come home to find a good-by note and a little bouquet of flowers.

For a few days, two young Czech officers who were flying for the British were our houseguests. One of them, John Lenhoff, wrote such a charming thank-you note when he left for Britain that I reciprocated by sending him a Red Cross package with food, candy and cigarettes. We corresponded for a while, and that was the last I heard of our good-looking young friend until about two years later, when the war was over. He wrote that on returning to Prague he had learned that his entire family, except for one uncle, had perished in Hitler's gas chambers because they were Jews. During the search that ended with this devastating disclosure, he had met a lovely girl who had survived in a concentration camp with her mother. They were married, moved to England and became British subjects. They adored England, but jobs were scarce and they were moving to Canada. Did we, Johnny Lenhoff asked, know of any engineering jobs in Canada? (He had an engineering degree from the University of Prague.)

As it happened, the day I got the letter, Arthur was leaving for a Kimberly-Clark meeting at the newsprint plant in Kapuskasing. He took the letter with him and read it at the board meeting. Johnny Lenhoff was offered a job on the spot.

Several months later, Johnny and his wife, Hannah, and their baby moved to Kapuskasing. He was soon a father of three, and is still an employee of Kimberly-Clark. I hear from them at least once a year. They now live in Toronto. Their children are all college graduates and doing well.

The *Times*'s coverage of the Second World War was unparalleled in its comprehensiveness. The texts of all the war communiqués and speeches were printed in full, and both the Allied and Axis versions of events were reported whenever possible, even when there were wild discrepancies. The *Times* left it to the reader to decide which was true.

Printing more war news than any other paper imposed a financial sacrifice on the *Times*. Since newsprint was a precious commodity and newspapers were limited to their average prewar supply, expanding the news columns meant sacrificing revenue-producing advertising space.

The decision to turn away advertisers was the same decision my father had made during the First World War, and once again it proved a wise move. While the *Times*'s chief competition, the *Herald Tribune*, grabbed up all the ads it could, the *Times* accepted a temporary loss in revenue. As more and more readers began to rely on the *Times* for the news, circulation grew. By the end of the war the paper had gained such a large following that when the newsprint restrictions were lifted, many of the *Tribune*'s advertisers came to the *Times*. From then on, the *Tribune* began coasting downhill.

I can't say that our circumstances were drastically altered by the war. We had to cope with minor inconveniences and change our routine to a certain extent, but it was all insignificant compared to what others were undergoing. At Hillandale we supplemented our meat rations by raising chickens, pigs and a couple of steers. I didn't want to get acquainted with the animals because I couldn't bear it when they were slaughtered. The butcher worked in one of the empty stables, carving the various cuts of meat and making several types of sausage. It was a luxury at the time to have such variety, but I could never get used to the thought of eating an animal I knew. Arthur captured my feelings precisely in his story about his lunch with Winston Churchill. They were served lamb, and Mr. Churchill asked his daughter, Sarah, "Is this one of our lambs?"

"I assure you, Father," she answered, "it is not one with whom you are personally acquainted."

One of our frequent weekend guests during the war was Wendell Willkie. He often brought along his wife and his son, Philip. Wendell was an attractive and lovable man, and our family became devoted to him. He delighted in telling us that the pigs we were raising were improperly common. "I'm going to send you some pedigreed pigs," he'd say, but he never did.

The children had never heard of Wendell Willkie until I took them to the 1940 Republican Convention in Philadelphia. It was the usual whirlwind affair, and the children, much to their surprise, had the time of their lives. Since I was backing Mr. Willkie (as was the *Times*), they became instant Willkie supporters.

We became acquainted with the Willkies after he lost the election. As I came to know him better, I realized that the defeat followed the pattern of his career. He never seemed to win anything. When he was a lawyer, his biggest case came when he represented the private power companies against the TVA. His presentation was outstanding and won him a reputation as a national figure, but he lost the case. As a Presidential candidate, he won the overwhelming support of the Republican Party but lost the election. Even when the stakes were small, poor Wendell couldn't seem to win.

At Hillandale we used to play a lot of parlor games—Chinese checkers, backgammon, gin rummy. Wendell would play all day long and lose every time. He always made some silly mistake. But he never got discouraged, and the bleary-eyed soul who had played with him all afternoon or evening would at last have to quit. Wendell would never quit first. He would just cry, "I'll win the next time!" I got to the point of cheating to let him win.

Another houseguest I remember with affection was Jan Masaryk. His father, Thomas Masaryk, the first President of Czechoslovakia, had been my father's friend back in the days when my parents vacationed in Karlsbad, and in 1937, Jan, now famous in his own right, spent a weekend with us at Hillandale. His lively spirit and natural gaiety infatuated us all. How the children shrieked with delight when, dressed in his cape, he'd chase them up and down the stairs and all through the house, pretending he was Batman! Those were such happy-go-lucky days. The picture sticks in my mind of Jan sitting at lunch with a sausage in one hand and a roll in the other and a bright grin on his face, saying, "Thank God I can relax here. Every meal I attend I have to make a speech. It's wonderful not to have to work!"

In 1945, Jan returned to the States to represent Czechoslovakia at the San Francisco conference at which the United Nations was founded. On the way back he spent a weekend with us at Hillandale. The Jan Masaryk who walked through our front door in 1945 was a changed man. The spark was gone from his eyes, the smile from his face. The succession of tragedies that had afflicted Czechoslovakia—the Munich pact, the devastation of the war and now the Soviet hold on the country—had drained him of all joy. He told me there was little to hope for. At the conference, he said, the Soviet Foreign Minister, Vyacheslav Molotov, had treated him, Czechoslovakia's Foreign Minister, like a lackey.

Jan's depression seemed to ease after a day or so at Hillandale, and in a light moment reminiscent of the 1930's he told us about his afternoon excursion with Mr. Molotov. They were making a tour of San Francisco, and the Soviet leader was astounded to see hundreds of cars parked outside a factory. He couldn't believe that the cars belonged to the workers inside the plant. They had then stopped at a restaurant for tea. The woman who owned the place recognized the Russian from his picture in the papers, threw her arms around him and planted a big kiss on each cheek with the words "My, you're even cuter than I thought!" Mr. Molotov went absolutely rigid. The incident, said Jan, smiling, was not exactly in keeping with Soviet protocol.

Less than three years later, the teletype machines at the *Times* brought us word that Jan's worst forebodings had come true. With the Communist coup of February 1948, the last democratic institutions in Czechoslovakia were snuffed out. We then learned that Jan Masaryk had died. The official Soviet report was that Jan committed suicide by leaping from a window, but, soon, the widely accepted belief was that Jan had been pushed to his death by the Russians. It was a tragic ending to the life of a brave man and a desperate hour for the people of that beleaguered land.

26

In the summer of 1944, the *New York Times* brought off one of
the scoops of the decade. The story created an international uproar.
The Russians accused the Americans of sabotage. The Americans
accused the British Embassy of leaking information. The State Department charged that the *Times* had jeopardized world peace.
The other papers were in a state, demanding to know why news
of such importance had been channeled only to the *Times*. Arthur
refused to reveal the source of the information, and the F.B.I. was
ordered to investigate. I don't know whether I should be proud of
it, but I was indirectly responsible for the entire affair.

The story, which appeared in the *Times* on August 23, gave
the substance of secret documents pertaining to negotiations among
the Big Four—the United States, the Soviet Union, Britain and
China—on the structure of the proposed international organization
to be called the United Nations. The documents revealed the

organization's outline for world peace and the concept of veto power in the Security Council. The story was written by Scotty Reston, who ascribed his information to an unimpeachable source.

Because Scotty had close ties with Anthony Eden, and Arthur and I had many British friends, the F.B.I. was inclined to blame the British delegates to the Dumbarton Oaks conference in Washington, where the plans for the United Nations had been drafted. No outsider could have penetrated the security measures at the secluded Dumbarton Oaks estate.

I've always had great respect for the investigative powers of the F.B.I., but their theory about the British was wrong and their interrogation of the Russian and American delegates was a waste of time. From what I could gather, the F.B.I. never came close to finding out that the informant was a member of the Chinese delegation, a man by the name of Chen.

To explain why Mr. Chen divulged such vital information, I must go back to one morning in the fall of 1912, when I entered a classroom at the Columbia School of Journalism to begin a course in modern European literature. I took a chair next to the best-looking man in the room, a young Chinese. In those days, a young lady didn't initiate a conversation until she had been formally introduced, so I would only glance at the handsome student out of the corner of my eye. Soon I discovered that he was peeking at me. After two or three classes, he mustered up the courage to ask if I would like to read an article he had published. I was complimented, but the article was a little disconcerting. It was a discussion of the Chinese custom of revenging oneself on an enemy by committing suicide on his doorstep, so that one's ghost would haunt him. Nonetheless, the young man and I became great friends. His name was Hollington Tong. I asked him how he got his first name, and he said that he had anglicized his name after meeting his compatriot Wellington Koo.

Both men went on to become important figures in the Chinese Nationalist Government. Wellington Koo became a distinguished diplomat. Holly, as I called him, rose from publisher of a leading Shanghai newspaper to Vice Minister of Information and, eventually, to Ambassador to the United States.

In the early 1940's, Holly accompanied Madame Chiang Kai-shek on one of her fund-raising tours around the United States. When he arrived in New York he gave a delightful Chinese dinner for our family. At the party, Marian and Orvil struck up a friendship with Holly's daughter and son-in-law, Mr. and Mrs. Chen. A few years later, Mr. Chen was a delegate to the Dumbarton Oaks conference, and Orvil introduced him to Scotty, who was assigned to cover the meetings.

The Chinese Government must have wanted to publicize the secret plans for the world organization, or even a reporter like Scotty could not have obtained the documents. And so, because I had made eyes at a handsome young man in journalism school, the *Times* got a major world beat and Scotty Reston won a Pulitzer prize.

Historians have not been very kind to my friend Holly. In a number of historical accounts he is accused, along with some other Chinese officials, of using his government position to make money. Undoubtedly there was a lot of corruption in the Chiang regime but I am certain that Holly was not among the offenders. He lived very modestly, and after retiring he and his wife shared an apartment in an unpretentious New York hotel with one of his daughters. None of this would seem to bear out the allegations of financial impropriety.

Holly came to a sad end. He had a stroke from which he never fully recovered. The family moved to California, and Holly died a few years later.

I daresay I'm the only person in the world outside the Tong family who cares what the history books say about Holly, but that hasn't stopped me from voicing my opinion. On reading Barbara Tuchman's book *Stilwell and the American Experience in China*, I was deeply troubled to see Holly portrayed in a most unflattering light. General Stilwell had apparently taken an intense dislike to Hollington, and would refer to him as sneaky and use other pejorative terms.

I wrote a letter to Barbara Tuchman saying I thought her book had done an injustice to Hollington Tong. Barbara's mother was a childhood friend; her grandparents, the Henry Morgenthau, Srs., had been my parents' friends; and I admired Barbara, an exceptionally talented writer on historical themes and delightfully modest about her capabilities.

I also raised the question with my friend Ambassador Chester Ronning, a former Canadian diplomat in China who had been acquainted with Holly, General Stilwell and Chiang Kai-shek. Chester agreed with me about Holly's honesty; he said Holly was perhaps the most honest man in the Nationalist Government.

As for Barbara, she wrote me a very nice note admitting that her portrayal of Holly had been influenced by Stilwell's views. Little could be done about a book already in print, but I felt a little better, knowing that Holly would be remembered by at least a few for the honorable man he was.

It was through Holly that I met Madame Chiang. One day I came home to find my Irish maid in a state of excitement. "Madam, the Queen of China telephoned," she announced breathlessly. "You're to call her back at the Waldorf-Astoria." I realized, of course, whom she meant; I had seen Holly a few days earlier and he said he would arrange an introduction. I returned the call, and Madame Chiang invited me to tea.

In the hour we spent together, Madame Chiang fulfilled many of my expectations. In American eyes she was a heroine—New Yorkers in particular had taken a shine to her—and after meeting her I could see why. She was highly intelligent and attractive, and she could charm the birds off the trees. Talking with her, I found it hard to believe the allegations that, behind her engaging personality, she was a selfish and ruthless woman. Even at the height of her popularity there were rumors that she was buying mink coats and other luxuries with the money she raised for the Chinese poor. It was also spread about that she was so pampered she would sleep only on silk sheets, and had brought her own with her to the White House. What the gossips never bothered to find out was that Madame Chiang had a skin ailment and could not sleep on cotton or linen. She was treated for this ailment at Presbyterian Hospital in New York. Her entourage took over an entire floor of Harkness Pavilion, and Secret Service men were stationed all over the hospital.

Shortly after her treatment, Madame Chiang came to dinner

at our house. The conversation turned to her talent for painting. Arthur mentioned the lovely picture she had given Wendell Willkie, and asked if he might have one. "I gave Mr. Willkie one of my paintings because he visited us in China," Madame Chiang said. "If you come to China, I will give you one, too."

It wasn't until 1957 that we were able to accept her offer. By then the Nationalist Government had been driven to Taiwan. The Generalissimo and his wife, who lived an hour's drive from Taipei, invited us to dinner. It was one of the highlights of our Far Eastern tour. I had the privilege of sitting next to the Generalissimo, and through an interpreter we spoke of the situation in mainland China. With his stubborn refusal to give up his dream of final victory, he made a date with me for dinner in Peking.

Arthur took the liberty of reminding Madame Chiang of her promise to him, and after dinner she brought out several of her hand-painted scrolls. "I told you I would give you one," she said. "Now you may have your choice." Arthur selected a work done in black and white. It hangs today in my New York apartment.

I thought her work showed a great deal of sensitivity, and I was particularly enthusiastic about a scroll painted with pink peonies. When Madame Chiang next came to New York, she presented me with a gift—that same scroll. It adorns my bedroom at Hillandale.

The Dumbarton Oaks case was far behind us and the F.B.I. had ceased to be a part of our lives when, one morning, an F.B.I. agent called on me at home. I couldn't believe they wanted to interrogate me after all this time, and I must have shown my qualm, for the agent said, "Oh, don't be upset. You're not directly involved. I've come to talk with you about the Charlie Chaplin paternity case."

I couldn't begin to guess why.

The agent reminded me of a dinner Arthur and I had had a year previously with Mr. and Mrs. Samuel Goldwyn at the "21" Club. "Charlie Chaplin is said to have come over to your table with a young lady."

I was able to confirm that: I remembered because it was the only time I'd ever met the actor.

"What I want to know," the agent said, "is: Did he introduce the woman as Mrs. Chaplin?"

"I haven't the foggiest notion what name he gave," I answered. "But I'm sure that if it had been Mrs. Chaplin, I would have remembered."

The agent seemed satisfied and left.

I had heard that Charlie Chaplin was being accused of taking young women across state lines, and of other immoral actions, but I hadn't realized how vigorously the Government was investigating the charges. I talked to Sam Goldwyn about it, and he said that while neither he nor his wife had been questioned about the "21" Club dinner, he knew the F.B.I. was set on making life difficult for Mr. Chaplin.

Among the most damaging accusations against the actor was that he was a Communist.

"It's a totally unfounded slander," Sam said. Like many Hollywood figures, he explained, Mr. Chaplin had performed in war-relief programs, and some of his material included Russian themes. But that, Sam said, had not been unusual during the war. He himself had been requested by the Government to make a film called *Song of Russia*. It was a foolish picture, he said. "The Russians were made to look like angels. The Government asked us to make that movie, and now they accuse Chaplin of being a Communist because he raised money for Russian war relief! It's absurd."

This anti-Communist hysteria, while in many ways understandable in the light of Stalin's behavior, was aggravated by the wild charges of Senator Joseph McCarthy, until it grew to such proportions that it became a national disgrace.

There was one night during the war when I thought I was involved in international espionage. It was fairly late when the phone rang, and a young lady from the British Embassy said she had some very important papers to deliver to Arthur immediately. When I told her he was away, she said she had to bring them over anyway. Affected by her conspiratorial manner, I told her not to ring the bell, as that would wake up the house: I would be looking out the window.

Time seemed to drag. At last a taxi pulled up and a young woman stepped out. I rushed downstairs and softly opened the front door. She handed me a big envelope bearing the legend "On His Majesty's Service."

"What's in it?" I asked, knowing I shouldn't.

"I think it's a speech by Noel Hall."

Noel Hall was a British economics professor active in the economic-warfare program, and a good friend of ours.

"Is that all?" I said. "Then why are you delivering it so late at night?"

"Oh, I have to catch a train, and I told Mr. Hall I would drop it off."

All my fancies of entering the world of Mata Hari burst like a bubble. So much for my brush with foreign intrigue.

The way the war affected one's behavior was never made clearer to me than by a word of advice one day from a New York taxi driver. There were not many cabs in circulation during the war, and to get a taxi usually required a good eye and a fast sprint. I was standing on the corner of Fiftieth Street and Fifth Avenue when I saw two passengers getting out of a taxi half a block away. I dashed over, jumped in and slammed the door.

"Well, wouldn't that jar you?" I heard someone say.

I looked out the window and saw a couple standing on the curb. Evidently they had been waiting politely for the previous passengers to get out. The taxi pulled away before I could think of what to do.

When I caught my breath, I said to the driver, "I feel terrible. I wouldn't have done that if I'd seen those people were waiting."

"Just relax, missus," he said. "The war'll be over soon and there'll be plenty of taxis again—then you can go back to being a lady."

27

When the advancing Allied armies came upon the grisly sight of the Nazi extermination camps, General Eisenhower decided that the full horror of what had been perpetrated should be shown to representatives of the Allied press, since the reports submitted to him by his officers seemed beyond belief. Arthur selected Julius Adler to represent the *New York Times* on the inspection group. When Julius returned, he said to us, "I realize that you want to know what I saw, and I'm going to tell you, but I don't ever want to talk about it again. I want to forget."

I shall not attempt to repeat here all that Julius reported to us. Every story ended in death and ashes. The fears and prophecies of my father and father-in-law had come true in a ghastlier fashion than either of them could have imagined. But there was one story that particularly struck me.

The journalists had been inspecting one of the concentration camps, and Julius and Norman Chandler of the *Los Angeles Times* went inside a barracks where a number of prisoners clung to the last thread of life. They were scarcely more than skeletons, beyond medical help, and most of them would be dead by the following day. As the two Americans entered this antechamber of death, the prisoners somehow realized that deliverance had come, and they raised a feeble, hardly audible cheer. For some, it was their last breath. Julius and Norman were in tears.

In 1947, Arthur and I were invited to see for ourselves what had happened in Germany. We traveled first to Munich, where we were guests in the home of George Shuster, commissioner of Bavaria in the American occupation regime, whom we had known when he was president of Hunter College. Entire sections of Munich lay in ruins. For some reason, I thought of the buildings as innocent victims, in contrast to the guilt of the German people, and I was sorrier for the heaps of rubble than for their homeless owners. I knew that the nation as a whole had not participated directly in Hitler's atrocities, but it must have known about them, and every face I looked at, everyone I spoke to, aroused my suspicion.

After Munich, we went to Bonn and Berlin. Berlin was by then a divided city. We stayed at the home of the United States High Commissioner for Germany, John McCloy. At a dinner given by Mr. McCloy and his wife, Ellen, I met a young German diplomat who six years earlier had been in the first wave of the German invasion of the Ukraine.

"It was a remarkable experience," he said. "Instead of regarding us as the enemy, the Ukrainians saw us as liberators. There was no resistance as we marched through the rich farm country. Everywhere we were greeted enthusiastically. The people were desperate for a savior."

Stalin had bled the countryside white with his collectivization drive. Thousands had died in man-made famines; many others had been sent off to Siberian prison camps. "Overnight they would have become faithful allies of Germany," the young man said, "but

Hitler didn't give them half a chance. He was so obsessed with his ideas of racial superiority that he despised all Slavs and ordered his troops to enforce his brutal policies. In time, the Ukrainians fought back."

At the invitation of a group of German industrialists, we next visited Düsseldorf and were taken on a tour of a steel mill that had survived the bombing. After that, we attended a dinner party given by the head of the plant. He was a most charming and cultivated man, and the part of the mill he lived in (his house had been bombed) was very tastefully furnished. He had a superb collection of Dresden china figurines, although the greater part of his collection had been destroyed, he said, when his estate in what was now East Germany was destroyed by the Russians.

About twenty leading West German businessmen had been invited to the dinner; I was the only woman present. If I had been directing a movie, I couldn't have done a better type-casting job. Except for our host, they were an arrogant, disagreeable-looking lot. I had a chance to talk with only a few of them, but I made a point of letting them all know I was Jewish. I wanted them to be uncomfortable, but I fear nothing could have done that. I knew that each one of them had grown prosperous on slave labor, and in a reckless moment I brought up the subject. The reaction was a blank stare. They knew nothing about that, they said.

But slave labor was a historical fact. More than seven million non-German civilians and two million prisoners of war had been made to work like animals on the farms and in the mills and mines. It was said that the first time a worker fell down on the job, he would be picked up; the second time, he would be shot. It was hard to imagine our attractive host as a part of this diabolical system. I tried not to think about it as I talked to him.

The most courageous non-Jewish Germans I knew were Hanna and Otto Kiep. During the Weimar Republic, Otto was German Consul General in New York, and he and his beautiful wife became our good friends. After Hitler became Chancellor, the Kieps were faced with a critical choice.

One evening, they telephoned us to ask if they could come over. It took them only a few minutes to walk from their home on

East Seventy-sixth Street, and Arthur and I took them up to the library.

Otto began pacing the floor. Hanna said, "We don't know what to do," and burst into tears.

Otto said, "I've been in the foreign service all my life, and Germany is my country. I'm from an old Prussian family, but I can't see my way clear to working for this Hitler and his Nazis. I just can't. His attitude toward the Jews is incredibly horrifying. I don't know whether to leave the foreign service or what."

He wanted our advice. Arthur and I felt helpless. We understood and sympathized, but being Americans we were unable to put ourselves in his position. "This is something you and Hanna will have to decide," Arthur said.

Otto nodded. "I just wanted to talk to people who would understand."

The Kieps returned to Germany. Otto resigned, and they moved to England so that their son and two daughters would not have to join the Hitler Youth.

In 1934, Otto and Hanna made a fateful decision. Germany, they reasoned, would never be cleansed of Nazism if anti-Nazis like themselves retreated from the struggle. They returned to their homeland and Otto re-entered the foreign service with the objective of undermining Nazi rule.

For a while, I had little communication with the Kieps. I was afraid to write, since a letter from an American Jew in our position might cause them harm. In 1935, Hanna somehow learned of my father's death and wrote me a beautiful letter of sympathy. It was very brave of her, and I acknowledged it with a note I tried to keep as innocuous as possible.

It wasn't until after the war that I heard from her again. She was living in Berlin. Otto, she wrote me, had become involved in a resistance movement against Hitler while still in the foreign service. A Swiss who was in on the conspiracy turned out to be a double agent, and Otto and the other plotters were arrested. Otto was tortured and hanged.

The Kieps' son was dead too. The German naval vessel on which he served vanished in action. The fate of the crew was never learned.

The only way I could think of to help Hanna was to arrange for an education for her college-age daughter Hildegard. I managed to get her a scholarship at Barnard, and soon afterward Hildegard arrived, looking nervous and exhausted.

It was understandable. She was entering a country she had left as a small child; she had not seen us in years; she was not fluent in English. It wasn't long, however, before she adjusted to her new surroundings and made new friends. She was a perfect darling. In so many ways she reminded us of her parents. Like them, she was very good-looking, a great big tall, beautiful girl, a young Valkyrie. Hildegard stayed in the States for two years before returning to Germany to marry her boyfriend, today a prominent physician in Munich.

The West German Government tried to make amends to Hanna by giving her a job at its Washington Embassy. Her assignment, she told me when she arrived, was to establish contact with American women—a difficult task, since she was unsure of the welcome she would receive from her old friends.

I suggested that I give a tea at which she could meet the presidents of some of the more important New York women's clubs, particularly the Jewish ones, whom I had come to know through my promotional work at the *Times*. Hanna was delighted.

"The tea," I said in my invitations, "is in honor of an old German friend of mine—a gentile—who was as much a victim of Hitler as any Jew." Everyone I invited came. It was quite a lively afternoon. Every imaginable question was put to Hanna. What was the German underground like? Had any German really been bold enough to make an attempt on Hitler's life?

Hanna told about many conspiracies, including the one in which her husband perished. She told of how she, too, had been involved in anti-Nazi activities and had been arrested, but had managed to regain her freedom by persuading the authorities that she was just an ignorant hausfrau.

That tea was the beginning of a long and productive career with the German Embassy, where she stayed until retirement age. Hanna then returned to Germany. Today she lives near her daughter Hildegard on the outskirts of Munich. Her second daughter, also named Hanna, married an American, Bruce Clement. He is a college professor and a writer of children's books. They live, with their four children, in Willimantic, Connecticut.

With the end of the war in Europe, the paper concentrated on covering the fighting in the Pacific. And the eventual victory in that theater was linked with the history of the *New York Times*.

In April 1945, William L. Laurence, the paper's science reporter, quietly took a leave of absence to join a top-secret government project. Arthur and Edwin James agreed to release Bill without inquiring into the nature of his assignment. Since the Government would be paying Mr. Laurence less than his *Times* salary, Arthur said he would make up the difference. He told me when it was all over that he and Mr. James had an idea that Bill Laurence was being recruited to record what would be the story of the century, and he was proud that a *Times* man had been selected for the task. "We didn't know any details," Arthur said, "but the government official who swore us to secrecy was Major General Leslie R. Groves."

General Groves, of course, became known subsequently as the man who had headed the project to make an atomic bomb.

Arthur heard virtually nothing from Bill Laurence for four months. Mr. James received one letter, saying cryptically that the world would not be the same after the day of the "big event."

That same summer, Arthur and I were invited by David Lilienthal, the chairman of the Tennessee Valley Authority, to inspect some dams under construction in Tennessee and Kentucky. We flew in a small plane over the Fontana Dam project. From the air, the workers constructing the dam looked like flies on a wall. To keep them happy on the job, popular and classical music was played alternately over loudspeakers. The work went on around the clock. It was essential, we were told, that the dam be completed soon, since power was needed at Oak Ridge.

I didn't know where Oak Ridge was, and asked Mr. Lilienthal about it.

"It's nothing we can talk about," he said.

It was not long before the name Oak Ridge became known to the whole world as one of the secret plants where the atomic bomb was developed. It was here, we were to learn, that William Laurence had been brought to write the story of the creation of the atomic bomb—an account that would be released at the right time to the newspapers. As its way of thanking us for Mr. Laurence, the Government would alert the *New York Times* first.

The alert came on August 2. As acting managing editor (Edwin James was on vacation), Turner Catledge got a call from Washington asking the *Times* to send a man to a certain address in the capital. Turner was mystified and called Arthur, who sensed what was up and told Turner to go himself. The rendezvous was with General Groves. The general told Mr. Catledge that a very important event was about to take place and that the *Times* should have someone near at hand, ready to receive the story at any hour of the day or night. Mr. Catledge decided on Sidney Shalett, who covered the War Department for the *Times*.

Arthur and I were entertaining a few guests for lunch at Hillandale when Mr. Catledge returned. He took Arthur aside. All that weekend, Arthur was fidgety and nervous. "What's the matter with you?" I kept asking him. "What's happened?" He said it was nothing personal, nothing to worry about.

On Monday, August 6, came a news flash: An atomic bomb had been dropped on Hiroshima. The awesome truth was out at last. Living with the secret, Arthur told me, had been one of the grimmest experiences of his life. "I was terrified," he said.

The *Times* of August 7 told the full story—ten pages of coverage, mostly from the account written by William Laurence. Bill had not witnessed the Hiroshima explosion, but he was on the plane that three days later dropped the second atomic bomb, on Nagasaki. The B-26 bomber barely escaped the blast. When I later told him how much I admired his courage, he said he had been too wrought up to feel afraid.

It is estimated that over a hundred thousand people died in the atomic devastation of Hiroshima and Nagasaki. As terrible as the statistics are, the alternative would have been an invasion of Japan, an action that would probably have cost the lives of half a million Americans and untold numbers of Japanese. The atomic bomb was the lesser of two evils, I thought then, and still think now.

The end was not far off. On September 2, President Truman

told Arthur he was waiting to hear the great news. At seven o'clock that evening, it came on the electric news sign girdling the Times Tower: "Official . . . Truman Announces Japanese Surrender." The crowds on Times Square went wild. Strangers embraced each other. The moment for which so many had fought and died was here. The war was over.

28

Arthur and I had always been against Zionism. But after the Second World War, when the D.P. camps began to overflow with survivors of the Holocaust, I had a change of heart. After the hell through which they had gone, the Jews of Europe were in need of a homeland in which to rebuild their broken lives. I began to contribute to the cause of establishing a State of Israel.

Arthur, however, held on to his anti-Zionist position. He did not believe in the concept of a Jewish nation. The Jews, he reasoned, were bound together by religion, not nationhood, and trying to turn back the clock two thousand years by re-establishing a Jewish state was, in his view, a piece of dangerous sentimentality. The wiser course, he thought, was to help the refugees find new homes in countries where they would be welcome.

Arthur contributed to an organization dedicated to resettling Jews in northern Australia. The region was a rugged wilderness not unlike Palestine, and seemed to lend itself to the system of kibbutzim pioneered by the Jewish settlers of the Holy Land. In time, it was thought, the Jews could convert the area into a self-supporting, productive colony.

At first the Australians were all for the idea. But the more they thought about it, the more doubts they had. Concerned that the newcomers might come to expect some kind of autonomy, or even independence, they began to back away from the commitment, saying they preferred to accept Jews individually rather than in groups.

When the Australian plan collapsed, Arthur gave some financial support to the Dominican dictator, General Rafael Trujillo, who had opened his country to European Jews. Some refugees ventured into the Dominican Republic but found life there so unpleasant that they left as soon as they could save enough money to do so.

Arthur continued to back all sorts of resettlement schemes. His attempts were continually frustrated. Many of the Jewish refugees were apprehensive about a future in some land where, in language and background, they would be utter strangers. Besides, few countries were ready to accept them. This lack of charity was appalling; no nation wanted to be burdened with large numbers of half-starved, sickly aliens. Where there should have been compassion, there were closed doors. As it was candidly put by one young American soldier who had been sent to Germany for occupation duty, "We found the refugees an unhealthy, dirty, miserable lot. We didn't like them. The Germans, on the other hand, were attractive, clean and friendly."

Arthur and I were not alone in our disagreement: Zionism was a heavily debated issue among American Jews. On one occasion, I remember, Arthur even came over to my side.

In the late 1940's we were vacationing in Tucson, Arizona, and Lord Astor and his American-born wife, Nancy, invited us to their house for dinner. Waldorf, Lord Astor, had been ill and had come to Arizona to recuperate. Nancy I had known for years: She was a native Virginian and a great admirer of my father; my parents had often visited Cliveden, the Astor country estate in England. When my father died, Nancy transferred her affections to Arthur and me. I found her amusing and liked her, although I considered her something of a lightweight.

That evening in Tucson, Nancy started sounding off—as she frequently did about many things—on Zionism. She made such outrageous statements that Arthur and I both found ourselves arguing like militant supporters of Israel. It was exhausting and frustrating, and when the evening was over, Arthur said to me, "I don't know why I always let that woman make me so mad that I say all those things I don't believe in."

Nancy was an opinionated woman who had always enjoyed the intellectual and political world, and at Cliveden she presided over a salon. My daughter Ruth had been to some of these gatherings during the war when she was stationed in England with the Red Cross; she became friends with Nancy and visited her frequently after that. Her clearest recollection of Nancy in those days was of a handsome woman hanging over a banister, chewing gum and spouting reasons why Ruth should become a Christian Scientist.

Nancy's strong-mindedness and flair had made her a figure in the Conservative Party and the first woman to hold a seat in Parliament, but it also carried her into the right-wing extremism fashionable in some British circles at the time, and there was a period before the war when she sided with the rising Nazi movement. I am convinced that it was basically a political affectation on her part, a terrible mistake she herself regretted in due course.

The day after our argument about Zionism, Waldorf phoned to say that Nancy had so enjoyed our discussion that she wanted to join us for lunch. He wouldn't be able to keep us company, as he had to stay home and rest. Before I could think of some excuse, the arrangements were made. Arthur was furious with me. We were in for another round.

Lunch was a buffet around a swimming pool at the Arizona Inn. The menu that day boasted homemade Southern fried chicken; Nancy asked the chef where he came from. He said Brooklyn.

"You learned to fry chicken like that in Brooklyn?" she asked disbelievingly.

"No, ma'am," he answered. "I'm originally from Virginia."

At that, Nancy launched into a speech. That a fellow Virginian would say he was from Brooklyn made her fly into a temper. A line of guests was backed up, waiting for their turn at the buffet table, as she proceeded to tell the bewildered chef what she thought of him. Arthur and I crept away, pretending we had never before set eyes on the woman.

At length, she ran out of breath—she never ran out of words—and moved on. She was so worked up over the renegade Virginian that she forgot all about the Jews, and we got through lunch and the rest of the afternoon without any further altercations.

The Zionist idea gained adherents rapidly in this country after the war, but many people, even strong supporters of Israel, hoped for a state in Palestine that would include all religious groups. One of these people was Judah Magnes, an old friend of the family. Judah had been a student of my grandfather's at Hebrew Union College in Cincinnati, and later a rabbi at Temple Emanu-El. His pro-Zionist leanings did not go over well with his congregation, and he left Emanu-El to go to Palestine. He founded the Hebrew University in Jerusalem and became friends with George Antonious, a Christian Arab. Together they worked to establish a Moslem-Jewish-Christian state, but the currents and crosscurrents among the three religions and cultures were too strongly at odds with this concept. The two leaders, hard as they tried, could establish no meeting ground. Both of them were to die deeply disappointed men.

Arthur and I were not strangers to Palestine. We had made a trip there in 1937, accompanied by Roger Williams Straus, Sr., and his wife, Gladys. Roger was president of Temple Emanu-El, co-founder of the National Conference of Christians and Jews, and a pro-Zionist. From New York, we took a vacation cruise aboard an Italian liner to Lebanon, then a French protectorate. From Beirut, we went by car to Damascus, and on to Palestine, then under British mandate.

In Jerusalem, we visited Judah Magnes and his family, and there, at his house, we met George Antonious. Mr. Antonious asked me how I liked Palestine. I said, "I know what I'm about to say is rude, this being your country, but I've never been any place

I disliked so much. Of course, it's the first place I've ever been where everybody hated each other."

He replied, "I don't know what you expected, but don't you realize that this isn't the land of philosophers? This is the land of prophets."

I was struck by the profundity of the remark. A philosopher is disposed to reason, to give-and-take, but a prophet thinks he has all the answers handed down to him by the Almighty. Considering the number of prophets of different religions all living in this tiny country, no wonder harmony had been unattainable.

We spent a week in Palestine. The country was in turmoil because of the influx of thousands of European Jews. The English were trying to limit this immigration by a strict quota system, the Jews were smuggling in new settlers, and the Arabs were afraid of being eventually outnumbered and ruled by hordes of newcomers. They were bitter, too, because the Jews would not employ Arab labor on collective farms established on land bought from Arab landowners. Because of the volatile situation, the British authorities assigned us a military escort, Group Captain Buss of the R.A.F. We later learned that he was with British intelligence.

At the invitation of a Jewish touring agency, we spent a day visiting several long-established and prosperous kibbutzim. The farmers we met had formerly been city dwellers. They had had to learn from scratch how to cultivate crops and raise livestock, and they had done a remarkable job of making the barren land fertile and productive. Their green fields contrasted sharply with the surrounding Arab land, which was brown and drab and strewn with rocks, its vegetation (except for a few scattered olive trees) largely consumed by herds of goats.

The kibbutzim we visited varied in the degree of private ownership permitted. In one kibbutz, no one owned anything, not even clothes. All the clothing went into a central laundry and was distributed at random. The effect of this "absolute equality" was that everyone wore ill-fitting clothes.

Another excursion was to the Sea of Galilee. On the way we stopped at a Paulist shrine on the site of a synagogue where Jesus is said to have prayed. We met a Paulist father who had once served in New York—at a church at Fifty-ninth Street and Columbus Avenue; after that he was stationed in China. He told us he much preferred China to Palestine, because it was so much easier to convert the Chinese to Christianity. "Here," he complained, "every Moslem expects four beautiful houris to care for him when he dies —so what have we to offer him?" He sighed. "The women are the only ones we can possibly convert, and the men will not let us talk to them."

In Jerusalem itself, I went on a tour of the Old City. I was on my own that day: Arthur and Roger were seeing some British officials, Group Captain Buss was accompanying them and I wasn't interested in joining Gladys on an inspection of the local hospitals— I hate hospitals. I was placed in the care of a strapping Arab guide. In my hand I carried some mother-of-pearl crucifixes I had bought at the Church of the Nativity in Bethlehem as gifts for Catholic friends at home; I wanted to have them blessed in the Church of the Holy Sepulchre.

Our first stop was at the ruins of Pontius Pilate's palace. In a dirty, dungeonlike room, we came upon a group of French pilgrims. Their guide pointed to a spot on the floor and said that that was where Jesus had stood, whereupon one of the women fell on her knees and kissed the designated spot.

From the palace, we proceeded to the Via Dolorosa to join a holy procession. Monks and nuns in their vestments led groups of pilgrims and tourists down the sacred road to the Church of the Holy Sepulchre. At each Station of the Cross, the worshippers stopped and chanted prayers. I made my way through the crowd until I was just behind the monks and nuns, feeling as though I was back with the Crusaders.

The church, built on the supposed site of Jesus's tomb, had five chapels—Coptic, Greek Orthodox, Armenian, Russian Orthodox and Roman Catholic. Since disputes among these sects were not uncommon, Arab soldiers were stationed outside to keep the peace.

Inside, it was dark and dingy, and I stuck close to my guide as we went from one chapel to another. At each altar, a priest took my crucifixes and blessed them. The gloomy chapels with their flickering candlelight made for an ominous atmosphere. My imagination began acting up; I saw myself being hauled off and burned at the stake as an infidel.

When we got to the Roman Catholic altar, I felt a little more at home. The crucifixes received their final blessing, I was handed a certificate of proof and—as in all the other chapels—I was urged to make a contribution. I must say I felt a great sense of relief when we stepped out of that church.

We had several interesting dinner engagements that week. One evening we dined with General Sir John Dill, commander of the British forces in Palestine. (During the Second World War, he was to serve as British representative with the Joint Chiefs of Staff in Washington.) Another evening we were guests at dinner at Government House. That evening stands out in my mind mainly for the seriousness with which a young British aide-de-camp took his job of keeping the guests circulating after dinner. Instead of moving the gentlemen around the room, he moved the ladies. Every time I got into a conversation with someone and was onto some interesting topic, the aide-de-camp in his Scottish kilts would reappear and ask if I would please come and meet someone else.

At last he maneuvered me toward the guest of honor, the Lord Chief Justice. As we came up to him, the Lord Chief Justice heaved himself halfway out of his chair and greeted me by saying, "I have had a very hard day." He then sank back into his chair. In a matter of minutes, he was asleep.

I didn't quite know what to do. The aide-de-camp was gone. But soon he was back, and announced: "Your Honor, I have at last caught your wife's eye, and she is preparing to leave."

At that, His Lordship sprang to his feet, exclaiming, "Thank God!" And without so much as a glance in my direction, he walked briskly off.

The aide-de-camp looked so pathetic that I had to assure him I was not a bit put out, only amused.

Our next destination was Transjordan, the emirate established by the British across the Jordan River, where we were to have lunch with the Emir, Abdullah (grandfather of the present monarch of Jordan, King Hussein). The British provided us with a car for the trip. In the front seat, his two pistols drawn at all times, sat our escort, Captain Orde Wingate; during the Second World War, he was to win fame as a British general in Burma. His charming wife was also with us. Captain Wingate was strongly pro-Zionist. He believed that the Jews' return to Palestine would bring about the Second Coming of Christ.

The Emir's palace was a large house on a barren hill overlooking the city of Amman. An aide welcomed us and showed us into the living room, whose only furniture was a row of straight-backed chairs lining the walls and some beautiful carpets on the floor. We asked if we could freshen up, and Gladys, Mrs. Wingate and I were shown to a washroom that obviously hadn't been used in years. It had one dirty towel, and the toilet paper was covered with cobwebs. We began to worry about the kitchen. It appeared that the Emir preferred to live in tents and used the palace only for special occasions. I understood why. It looked like a third-rate Hollywood movie set.

The lunch, despite our apprehensions, turned out to be excellent. The Emir was a jolly and friendly man. We sat at a large table in the palace dining room and were served exotic and tasty dishes by Nubian servants dressed in long white robes with red sashes and wearing red fezes. It was just as I would have imagined a lunch with a desert sheik, even if it took place in Western-style surroundings.

But our most curious experience during the trip occurred earlier that day, on our way from Jerusalem. Crossing the Jordan, we stopped on the bridge and got out for a better look at the river. As we stood there, along came a strikingly handsome Arab in a long green silk robe, carrying a small basket of oranges. He, too, stopped and offered us some of his oranges as a token of welcome to his country. He spoke English, and told us he had walked over one hundred and fifty miles, from Dan to Beersheba, with an American scholar. He showed us the American's photograph and asked if, by chance, we knew him.

The coincidence was uncanny. His companion had been none other than our friend John Finley, whom Arthur had only recently named editor of the *New York Times* editorial page.

Mr. Finley was an extraordinary man. Starting out as a rural schoolteacher in Illinois, he went on to become president of Knox College in Galesburg, Illinois, then Commissioner of Education for New York State and finally president of the City College of New York. Then, when already in his early sixties, he joined the *Times*.

All the while, he found time for his favorite pastime, walking. He became famous for his marathon treks. Once a year, he would walk the perimeter of Manhattan. Even in freezing weather, he never wore an overcoat or hat, only a Scottish scarf around his neck. In recognition of his yearly exploit, a footpath along the East River Drive was named the John Finley Walk, and a small bronze statue of Mr. Finley was put up alongside the path.

Mr. Finley's energy seemed boundless. I believe he was in his sixties when, after completing a lecture at Princeton University, he walked the fifty-five miles back to New York. I imagine that, tall and athletic though he was, our Arab of the Jordan River bridge had found it no easy task to keep pace with his American companion.

Mr. Finley's ambition on the *Times* was to head the editorial page. He finally got what he wanted. By then he was seventy-three. It was an act of consideration on Arthur's part. The quid pro quo was that the new editorial-page editor retire when he was seventy-five.

Mr. Finley was a charming and lovable man who delighted in a kind of playful evocation of imaginary things—of little people, of fairies and elves. One day this fancy created an embarrassing situation for the paper.

Mr. Finley wrote an editorial in praise of a woman educator he had known and admired for her work in establishing ungraded classes for handicapped children. He concluded by calling her a "truly grown-up, ungraded fairy."

When that line was set in lead type, it must have contained a spelling mistake, because it was pulled out to be reset. To mark the proper place, the faulty line was turned upside down and used as a space marker. When it was replaced by the reset line, it found its way—right side up—into a story about a society wedding. After speaking of the bride—what she wore and who her attendants were—the story gave a short biography of the bridegroom, saying that he had graduated from Groton and Princeton and was a "truly grown-up, ungraded fairy."

A correction in the next edition saying that the groom wasn't really a "grown-up, ungraded fairy" would only have made matters worse.

The two families were understandably upset. Fortunately, they knew the *Times* business manager, Louis Wiley, and all they asked was that he inquire into the circumstances surrounding the gratuitous insult.

The episode had two consequences. The printers were told to stop using discarded lines of type as space slugs. And someone sat down with John Finley and asked him, for safety's sake, to keep his fairies out of his editorials.

29

After the war, many Americans did volunteer work in veterans' hospitals, helping with rehabilitation and therapy programs, or providing the wounded with companionship, or seeing if they could line up jobs. Arthur and I would invite groups of veterans to Hillandale for a home-cooked meal and a day in the country. Once a week, Red Cross volunteers would bring the young men up from a veterans' hospital in the Bronx.

The men would arrive on stretchers, on crutches and in wheelchairs. Some were blind; others were recovering from amputations. My daughters and their friends would help us out on those days. The servicemen seemed to enjoy themselves, for the same ones would come back week after week. They took a particular liking to Marian and Orvil's two young children, Jacqueline and Robert. We had worried about how the children would be affected by the sight of crippled people; we needn't have. Jackie and Bobby did not even seem to notice the veterans' disabilities and thought that riding around on wheelchairs, on the men's laps, was wonderful sport. Little Jackie took a great fancy to a blind man named Jack. When he arrived she would run over, throw her arms around him and cry, "My Jack!" It was quite a love affair. In their innocence, the children handled the veterans much better than the grownups. Their exuberance and affection were exactly what the men needed.

Hillandale was ideal for entertaining large groups of people. The playroom was spacious, so that parties could be carried on indoors if it rained. In 1938, a year after my mother died and we inherited the estate, we began giving our Associated Press parties.

That year, Arthur was elected to the A.P. board of directors, and we decided to give a Sunday luncheon as a way of kicking off a board meeting that was to start the following day. The lunch became an annual event. Except for a couple of years during the war when there were gasoline shortages and we substituted with cocktails at our home in the city, we had a party at Hillandale every April. The A.P. meetings were always held during the last week of April, a time when the weather was most unpredictable, but we were lucky and held all our parties outdoors. On the average we'd have a hundred and fifty guests. In addition to the A.P. directors, we invited journalists and personal friends we thought the directors would enjoy meeting. We employed Sherry's, the catering service my parents had so often used, to handle the food and refreshments.

I shall never forget the last party we held there, in 1949. A couple of weeks before the party, Arthur received a letter from one of the invited guests, Colonel Robert McCormick, the publisher of the *Chicago Tribune*. The Colonel said he had acquired a helicopter, a great novelty in those days, and asked if there was a good area for him to land. Arthur sent him an aerial photograph of Hillandale, with instructions for landing in an area marked "C." It was a big field, where the children used to play baseball. To avoid confusion, Arthur marked the car-parking area "A" and the lawn-party area "B."

On the day of the party, the parking area filled up, the lawn was alive with people having cocktails, when suddenly there was a roar from the sky. Guests scattered in all directions and a bright red helicopter descended on the lawn. Written on it in bright gold letters was the legend "The Chicago Tribune, America's Greatest Newspaper."

Oblivious of the commotion, the Colonel stepped out, as cool as though he owned the place. Next thing we knew, he was offering people rides and the helicopter was taking off and landing, creating so much noise and confusion that Arthur had to ask him to take the helicopter down to the playing field, where he should have landed in the first place, and to leave it there. Mr. McCormick gave the instructions to his pilot without a word of apology for his mistake or for disrupting our party. He was an extraordinarily self-centered character. Since the helicopter had room for only one passenger, his wife had to come by car.

Upon his retirement from the A.P. board, the Colonel gave a dinner party of his own. When the toasts were offered, the compliments flew so thick and fast that the Colonel was moved to tears. He got up to respond, but was so choked up he had to sit down again. After a few minutes he collected himself and sprang to his feet, saying, "I can speak now." He went on to say that belonging to the A.P. board of directors had been a most meaningful association for him, because it was the only time in his life he had had the opportunity to serve with his peers. Apparently he regarded his associates at the *Tribune* as mere employees. He presented each board member with a gold key ring, engraved with the recipient's initials and his own.

Colonel McCormick was frightfully anti-British. He told me that as a small boy he had once gone to school in England and had been treated as an American roughneck. When his family moved back to America, he was sent to Groton and didn't like their English traditions any better. The result was lifelong rancor against England and against the Eastern establishments he associated with English ways. Whenever there was something the Colonel didn't like, it seemed the *Chicago Tribune* came out with an editorial blaming England.

*   *   *

Not long after the party at Hillandale at which Colonel Mc-Cormick made his sensational appearance, we began to pack our belongings to move to a smaller house we had bought in Connecticut. The decision was one we had debated for a long time.

When we first inherited Hillandale twelve years earlier, we thought it would be too expensive to maintain. My parents had also left us Abenia at Lake George, and the combined upkeep was so high that Arthur and I put both estates on the market. To sell properties like that in the Depression year of 1937 was very difficult, however, and we gave up trying to find a buyer for Hillandale.

I was just as glad. As the years went by, Hillandale turned out to be a wonderful country home for us. Arthur still thought it would be best to sell the estate because it was too big, and we would argue about it from time to time. We were having one of these arguments one weekend when David Bowes-Lyon, the brother of Elizabeth, Queen of England, was a guest at Hillandale, and David broke in to say, "Don't let Arthur make you sell your beautiful home, it's so cozy." I guess cozy is what it was—compared to Buckingham Palace.

With Abenia, however, it was different. We were in accord about having to sell that estate, and after almost eighteen months without a single offer we turned to Joseph Day, a New York real estate auctioneer with the reputation of being able to sell anything. At the auction, a friend of my parents who had no intention of buying Abenia made the opening bid just to get things started, but no one raised him and he found himself the owner of the Lake George estate. He had, as it happened, made an excellent investment. For only $35,000—Arthur and I had hoped to get a much better price—he got a huge house and three hundred acres of land. On the property were the farmer's and gardener's cottages, a garage with an apartment above it, another house with a laundry and extra maid's rooms, a guest house where my father's secretary had lived, yet another two-story guest house where my mother's sisters stayed when they came to visit and a bathhouse by the lake.

Out of all this, there was one thing Arthur wanted to keep. A year previously, in 1938, a committee representing the 1939 World's Fair, which was to be held on Long Island, asked us to sell them some of the willow trees at Hillandale for the fairgrounds. Arthur said he would give them the willows—we had a tremendous number of the fast-growing trees—if they would move this one particular item down to us from Abenia.

It was the spruce tree under which Arthur had proposed to me. The deal was made, and one day a tree arrived. We took one look at it and realized it wasn't the right tree.

Our tree, we were told, had suffered damage in a storm. The trunk was split and couldn't be moved. So they had brought a similar spruce instead. I suppose it was a bit of sentimental foolishness in the first place, but Arthur and I couldn't help feeling sad.

Hillandale served us well. But after my children were married and had homes of their own, even I had to agree that there was no longer any need for such a large house. In 1949, it was time to leave.

This time we had no difficulty selling the estate. It was bought by a Syrian couple who had made their fortune in Central America and, having nine children, found the place a comfortable size. They lived there six or seven years, then sold the estate to a developer, who sold it to the Board of Education of White Plains.

A few years ago, I went back to see Old Hillandale, as we had come to call it, having given the same name to our new Connecticut home. From the outside the house looked much like it used to. Inside, everything was different. The large living room and dining room were subdivided. The bedrooms were offices. But my father's old paneled library, now the office of the Superintendent of Schools, seemed little changed, and on the wallpaper of the rooms we had kept for our grandchildren I could see the faded marks of the children's scrawls.

The new Hillandale proved to be an equally wonderful home for Arthur and me. When we acquired the property, there were few trees near the house, and the main road ran directly before the front door. Arthur was a born landscape architect, and with the professional help of Alfred Geiffert he transformed the grounds. The road was rebuilt for privacy, a swimming pool was added and roads were cut through the woods. We gradually added to the fifteen acres we purchased with the house, and now own three hundred acres, most of it forestland. Except for landscaping around the house, most of the property was left in its natural state so that we could enjoy taking walks and drives.

When Arthur fell ill in 1957, the woods were his diversion. He would have new roads built, some areas cleared out and other areas planted. He would have road signs made naming each of the dirt roads—Carthage Hill, for instance, or Chattanooga Drive—and other signs put up near a commanding boulder or some particularly beautiful tree, naming the points of interest after each of our thirteen grandchildren.

The house is New England style, built of white shingles. It stands on a hill, with a view of other wooded hills from the back, overlooking a small lake we named Lake Susan, after Marian and Orvil's third child. Here, year after year, our large and ever-increasing family would gather for family celebrations and on Christmas and Thanksgiving. During the summer months and on weekends year round, friends and relatives would visit. On occasion we would have the opportunity to entertain delegates to the United Nations and visiting foreign leaders. One of our most distinguished guests was the Chancellor of West Germany, Konrad Adenauer.

We first met Dr. Adenauer at a Harvard University commencement when the university awarded honorary degrees to the Chancellor and to Arthur. The Chancellor could not accept an invitation to lunch at the *Times*, since he was not going to New York, but he did plan to visit a friend in Greenwich, Connecticut, and he promised to visit us at Hillandale if his schedule permitted.

Before starting back for Hillandale the following morning, Arthur called the *Times* to ask if there was anything new.

"There certainly is," exclaimed his secretary. "Tomorrow, Chancellor Adenauer, his Foreign Minister, the German Ambassador to Washington, the German observer at the U.N. and an interpreter who doesn't eat are coming to Hillandale for breakfast at eight-thirty in the morning."

I immediately telephoned my Hungarian cook, who assured me

that she knew what Germans liked to eat and would begin preparations.

The Chancellor and his entourage, escorted by police in cars and on motorcycles, arrived the next morning at eight-thirty sharp. It was a glorious summer day, so we were able to have breakfast on the back terrace, overlooking the woods. Everyone relaxed and seemed to enjoy the food thoroughly—all except the interpreter. As we had been forewarned, he wouldn't take a bite. It worried me to see this bright young man working so hard and not eating anything. I suppose he felt that to do his job efficiently he had to eat ahead of time.

The Chancellor must have enjoyed the visit, for when Arthur invited him again the following year, he readily accepted. This time he brought his son and daughter-in-law, and we invited our children. With the German party was the same nice young interpreter, who still refused to eat. After breakfast we sat talking in the library, and Buttons, our boxer, took a terrific shine to the Chancellor. She laid her head on his knee and rubbed herself against him. The Chancellor was charmed with her, but when he got up to leave his suit was covered with dog hair. It took us quite some time to brush him off.

Mr. Adenauer accepted yet another invitation to Hillandale, but President Eisenhower then invited all of us to the White House for the same day, so our invitation had to be dropped. The Chancellor told me that he was sorry he would not have the opportunity to have breakfast at Hillandale again and renew his acquaintance with Buttons.

Among the world leaders Arthur and I were hosts to during the 1950's were the Shah of Iran, Riza Pahlevi, and his Empress, Farah. They were our lunch guests at the *Times*. The conversation turned to the pressure the Russians were putting on Iran, and I said, "Excuse me, Your Highness, but hasn't Russia been trying to elbow its way into your country for over a century now?"

"Yes, that's quite true," the Shah exclaimed, clearly astonished, "but most Americans I've met don't know anything about Persian history. You're the best-informed American I've ever met."

I didn't want to disappoint the Shah by telling him that what

I knew of Persian history had been told to me by my governess, Miss MacDonnell, when I was a little girl. Miss MacDonnell's tales of her experiences in Persia—of the Shah and his ninety wives; of how in the summer the diplomats and nobility of Teheran would ride wild horses up into the mountains and live in luxurious tents until the heat had passed; of the political intrigue between the British and the Russians, and of how the Russians were trying to get control of Persia—had made a vivid impression on me. It was thanks to Miss MacDonnell and my good memory that the Shah thought me an expert on his country. He was so impressed with my knowledge that he sent me a signed photograph of himself, in a beautiful frame.

Another royal couple to attend a *Times* lunch was King Paul and Queen Frederika of Greece. All through lunch the poor King couldn't get a word in edgewise. Every time he opened his mouth to say something, the Queen would interrupt and speak for him, beginning by saying "he thinks" or "he says." The editors gave up trying to converse with the King; when lunch was over, they crowded around Queen Frederika. King Paul was left standing alone, gazing dejectedly out the window. I went up to him and asked his opinion about something. I'll never forget the smile of relief that spread across his face; I'd never seen anybody look so grateful. When the editors noticed that I had managed to get the King talking, a few of them came over and began asking him questions. I moved over to talk to the Queen.

Frederika, granddaughter of Kaiser William II, was a small, attractive woman with large hands, rather like a peasant's. When we had a moment alone, she told me an amusing story about her son.

When the boy was about eighteen, his father decided he should learn the duties of King. He was put in charge of some Cabinet meetings and assigned certain responsibilities. One night at about 2 a.m., when she and her husband were sound asleep, their son came rushing into their bedroom.

"A terrible crisis has occurred!" he said breathlessly. "I don't know what to do!" When he realized he had awakened his parents, he said, "Oh, do you want to go back to sleep and let me tell you the problem tomorrow?"

Queen Frederika laughed as she recounted the story. This was the young man who in 1973 lost the Greek throne to the Colonels' Revolt.

When Pierre Mendès-France, then Premier of France, came to New York in 1954 to attend a United Nations meeting, the French Ambassador and his wife gave a dinner in his honor. Arthur was unable to attend, and I went alone. When the meal was over and coffee and cordials were being served, I found myself in conversation with a young French journalist and the famous, or infamous, Andrei Vyshinsky, the Soviet representative at the U.N. I felt a little strange standing next to the chief prosecutor of the 1936–38 Moscow purge trials, at which so many people were sentenced to life imprisonment and death. Not having the nerve to broach that subject, I asked Mr. Vyshinsky, who had been conversing with the journalist in fluent if heavily accented French, how he had come to learn that language.

He replied that he had taught himself, to help pass the time when the Czarist Government sentenced him to five years in a Siberian prison camp for revolutionary activities. Unfortunately, he said, he had had no way of checking his pronunciation.

As he spoke of life in the Siberian camp, Jules Moch, a member of the French Cabinet, came over and joined the conversation. He said he, too, knew about prison life at first hand: The Nazis had imprisoned him during the German occupation. He and Mr. Vyshinsky were comparing notes on their prison experiences when someone came over and told Mr. Moch he was wanted by the Premier.

After the Frenchman excused himself, Mr. Vyshinsky said, "You know, Moch had a much worse experience than I did. When I was in prison I knew I would be there for five years and then get out, but when the Nazis jailed him he didn't know from minute to minute whether he'd be taken out and shot. That must have been very harrowing."

It was a startling remark coming from a man who had been implicated in so many deaths, and I wondered if he realized the irony of what he had said.

The following morning I picked up the newspaper to learn that Mr. Vyshinsky had died of a heart attack during the night. When Arthur saw the news he said, "You killed him. It was your conversation with him. It must have been the first time he realized what he had done."

Though Arthur was, of course, being facetious, I thought Mr. Vyshinsky may indeed have had a gleam of self-revelation that evening.

I happened to mention this one day to the United Nations Secretary-General, Dag Hammarskjöld, and he said he had come to know Andrei Vyshinsky quite well and had found him an extraordinarily complex man. On one level, he said, the veteran revolutionary was a devoted husband who adored his wife: She was an aristocrat, and Mr. Vyshinsky was protective toward her. On another level, he was a ruthless man filled with blind ambition who faithfully followed Stalin's brutal policies. "It was as if he had a split personality," Mr. Hammarskjöld said.

Of the many foreign leaders I met over the years, the one person I had special admiration for was Anthony Eden—both for his courage in resigning as Foreign Secretary in 1938 in protest against British appeasement of Hitler and for the high principles he continued to follow in his subsequent career. I had the pleasure of meeting him a number of times during his visits to the United States, and I saw him again in 1969, when he was Lord Avon and retired from public life.

Arthur had died and I was vacationing in Barbados when I received a luncheon invitation from the former Prime Minister and his wife, who were staying at their Caribbean holiday home. The invitation came about because Drew Middleton, former chief of the *Times*'s London and Paris bureaus, was a good friend of the Avons and had written to them of my stay in Barbados.

The Avons' chauffeur picked me up at my hotel and drove me into the mountains, to their beautiful old plantation home. I found I was the only guest. Lord Avon had not been well, and the doctor advised against too much entertaining. The lunch conversation turned to Israel, and I told them of my visit there the year before, and of having had coffee with Prime Minister Golda Meir. Lord

Avon said, "From my point of view, Golda Meir was my pinup girl."

I was highly entertained by his remark, and when I went to Israel the following spring, I passed it on to Mrs. Meir. She was not in the least amused. All she said was "Oh," and changed the subject.

30

In 1948, the *New York Times* endorsed Thomas E. Dewey for President. The paper believed, as did many people around the country, that after so many years of Democratic rule it was time for a change to a Republican Administration. The polls indicated that the nation had not been too impressed with Harry S. Truman during his three years in the White House, and that Mr. Dewey was a shoo-in.

The customary election-night party in the boardroom on the fourteenth floor of the *Times* was canceled. "I don't see any point in it," Arthur said. "There's no race." I agreed. I was voting for Mr. Dewey.

On Election Day, I left by overnight train for a Hebrew Union College board meeting in Cincinnati, without a thought to the voting results and not bothering to buy a newspaper at any of the station stops. At breakfast in the dining car the next morning, the steward handed me a paper. The headline said: "Truman elected!"

I gasped. "My, isn't that astonishing!"

The steward said, "I don't know why you should be so surprised, madam. Don't you know the pollsters never consult the poor people, and there are more poor than rich people in this country?"

I must confess that I didn't give full due to Mr. Truman's qualities as President—his plainspokenness and decisiveness—until late in his term, when he courageously dismissed General Douglas MacArthur for flouting the principle of civilian control over the military.

The dismissal, at the height of the Korean War, put an end to a career full of brilliant achievement not only in the military but in the political sphere. One of the most difficult problems faced by General MacArthur when he became head of the Allied occupation of Japan stemmed from popular American feelings about Emperor Hirohito. Many Americans argued that if democracy was to be implanted in Japan, the man regarded as a god by many of his subjects had to go. Other Americans, including General MacArthur and President Truman, felt that deposing the Emperor— who, in any case, was only a figurehead—would cause potentially explosive distress among the Japanese people. The General's solution was one I heard from Virginia Gildersleeve, the dean of Barnard, who was in Japan at the time, helping to reorganize the Japanese educational system, and who got the story from General MacArthur himself.

One day, she related, General MacArthur called on the Emperor and asked him if, for the benefit of American public opinion, he would issue a statement to the effect that he was a human being and not a god.

The Emperor replied, "I couldn't do that. I'd feel like such a fool! Of course everybody knows I'm not divine."

MacArthur persisted, and the Emperor finally agreed. The statement had a strong impact in the United States and the issue was dropped.

Prior to the Presidential campaign of 1952, the *Times* said it was prepared to endorse a Republican nominee of suitable qualifications and international outlook. Arthur still thought the country needed a change after so many years of Democratic control, and the paper's announcement—unprecedented in the *Times*'s history—was intended to help persuade the Republicans to choose an internationalist for their standard bearer. The leading Republican candidate, Robert A. Taft, had isolationist views. A Taft Presidency augured a repetition of the disastrous policies adopted after the First World War. When the Republicans nominated General Dwight D. Eisenhower, whose career had proved him to be a capable leader oriented to world affairs, the *Times* endorsed him for President.

Arthur had met the General when he was Supreme Allied Commander in Europe and had grown to like and admire him. I agreed with Arthur's preconvention reasoning, and I had no doubt that General Eisenhower was a fine commander, but the several times I met him before his nomination were rather disillusioning for me.

Our first meeting was in 1948, when the General, having retired from the Army, took over as president of Columbia University.

There was considerable excitement at the university over his appointment. Columbia had been in trouble for a long time. Its former president, Nicholas Murray Butler, was a fine educator who had built up a superb faculty, but he had been in office since 1902, and as he got on in years his effectiveness suffered. Yet he would not retire. This told on the school, which was mired in financial difficulties ever since the Depression. Finally, when he was eighty-three, Mr. Butler agreed to step down.

The university was in desperate need of vigorous new leadership. Installing a temporary successor, the trustees looked about for a man of required stature. The search lasted three years. Then Thomas Watson, one of the trustees and the head of I.B.M., came up with the idea of asking Dwight Eisenhower, arguing that the General would make a great administrator and fund raiser.

General Eisenhower had just taken over the office when I made an appointment to see him on behalf of the Federation of Jewish Philanthropies. I had been selected by my fellow members to ask the new president to make an address at our annual fund-raising dinner. It was thought that I would have some influence with him—

what with Arthur being friendly with the General and both of us being university trustees, I of Barnard and Arthur of Columbia.

General Eisenhower agreed to make the speech, but said that, not being a native New Yorker, he didn't know a thing about the federation and would need some background information. He added that since he was "not a reading man," he would like to have someone brief him.

The federation board members were very excited. The popular war hero would be a wonderful drawing card. This would be his first public appearance in New York, and a full house was assured.

I arranged for the federation's executive director, Joseph Willen, to brief the General, and the two of us went together to his office. But before either of us could get in a word about the federation, General Eisenhower launched into a soliloquy that lasted twenty minutes.

He began by saying, "I just want you to know that I have no prejudice against the Jews." He went on to inform us that he had no prejudice against the Catholics, either. In fact, he said, he had only recently learned that his chief aide, General Gunther, was a Catholic. Next, he told us all about his mother's religious convictions, and how she had raised her sons to be good churchgoers, taught them all the virtues, and so forth and so on.

Joe and I sat there listening politely when his secretary came in and said, "General Eisenhower, your next appointment is here."

Joe said, "Thank you very much—it was a pleasure seeing you," and we left.

When we got outside, Joe said, "I can't thank you enough for inviting me. It was fascinating, but it doesn't seem the General has learned much about the federation."

We didn't hear from General Eisenhower until two days or so before the dinner, when his office informed us that he had come down with the flu and could not attend. By then every seat at the dinner had been sold. We had to get a pinch hitter, Herbert Lehman, who spoke that evening and obviously did very well—no one asked for his money back.

The next time I met the General was shortly before the Republican Convention. Arthur invited him and his wife for a Sunday lunch in White Plains. Though now a civilian, the Republican candidate came with an aide-de-camp, Colonel Robert Schultz. Poor Colonel Schultz was treated like a flunky by Mamie. She was constantly sending him on errands: First she wanted her purse, then a handkerchief, then another drink. I found the whole display unnecessary and disconcerting and thought less of the General for it.

My reservations about Mr. Eisenhower increased during the campaign. There was one incident I found particularly distressing.

One morning after his nomination, the General asked Arthur to his home at 60 Morningside Drive to discuss the problem of Senator Joseph R. McCarthy. Mr. Eisenhower confided that while he would rather have skipped the senator's home state of Wisconsin, his campaign managers wouldn't let him do it. So now he was in a dilemma: "I know McCarthy will be on the platform with me, and I despise him and everything he stands for. But I can't criticize him if he's sitting right there. Yet saying nothing might be interpreted as an endorsement. I don't know how to handle it. Have you any suggestions?"

Arthur thought for a moment and replied, "Yes, I have."

Joe McCarthy, he pointed out, had just accused General George C. Marshall of being "soft on Communism" and a traitor. The former Army Chief of Staff had been General Eisenhower's superior officer during the war.

"I know you're devoted to him," Arthur said, "so why don't you use your speech to pay a tribute to General Marshall?" That would be an effective reply to Senator McCarthy.

The suggestion delighted Mr. Eisenhower. "That's brilliant," he said. "That's exactly what I'm going to do."

The day the General was to speak in Milwaukee, Arthur received a call from the *Times* campaign reporter, William Laurence (known at the office as "Political Bill," to differentiate him from "Atomic Bill" Laurence). The message was: "The General wants you to listen to his speech. He says you'll hear something you like."

Arthur and I watched the appearance on television. The crowds applauded as Mr. Eisenhower rose to deliver his speech. Sitting on the podium, as expected, was Senator McCarthy.

The address was long. Each time Mr. Eisenhower paused,

Arthur and I thought he would speak of General Marshall. But each time he turned to some other issue.

We waited and waited for the big moment. It never came. The speech ended; people applauded; the General smiled and gave a farewell wave.

It seems that at the last minute his political advisers had dissuaded him from bringing up General Marshall. Arthur was disappointed, but didn't take it too seriously; I suppose he was more realistic about politics than I was. To me, General Eisenhower's decision to remain silent betrayed a grave lack of character.

I remember walking to the polls with Arthur on Election Day and saying, "I've committed myself to voting for Eisenhower and I will, but I want you to know it's against all my instincts. It's only out of love for you and loyalty to the *Times* that I'm going to pull that Eisenhower lever."

I have always been sorry that Dwight Eisenhower defeated Adlai Stevenson that year. I didn't know Mr. Stevenson then, but I thought his campaign was brilliant. His sister, Elizabeth Ives, was an old friend, and I remember writing her to explain why the *Times* felt it could not endorse her brother. She replied that she did not fully comprehend the paper's reasoning but respected our decision.

In hindsight, I feel certain that if Adlai Stevenson had been elected in 1952, the country's course in foreign affairs would have been entirely different. I think that if John Foster Dulles had not been Secretary of State, the Middle East would not be in the mess it is in today. Mr. Dulles's policies ruined our relations abroad. Perhaps his worst mistake was when he lost his temper over the Aswan Dam and, in effect, gave the project to the Russians. In the process he forfeited our chance for maintaining a strong influence in the Arab world.

I knew Mr. Dulles fairly well. He was intelligent, friendly and pleasant personally, and he and his wife were always kind to me; I just didn't care for his politics. After Mr. Eisenhower was elected, Anne McCormick said, "I hope he doesn't make Dulles Secretary of State. I've watched Dulles's performance at a number of international conferences, and in my opinion he's demonstrated a complete lack of sensitivity and understanding."

Anne expressed my feelings precisely. As courteous as Mr.

Dulles was in his personal relations, he was narrow and self-righteous in his political attitudes.

When Mr. Stevenson and Mr. Eisenhower were in contention for the Presidency again in 1956, I told Arthur that this time I would vote for Mr. Stevenson. The *Times* was endorsing President Eisenhower for a second term, but I felt I had discharged my obligation to the paper four years earlier. When Arthur tried to change my mind, I said, "Nothing doing. Maybe you still believe in the General, but I don't!"

Perhaps what I held most against General Eisenhower was his affiliation with Richard M. Nixon. I had always regarded Mr. Nixon as an evil man. From the time he ran a smear campaign against Helen Gahagan Douglas in California, I never had any use for him. I didn't like the way he rode to fame on the Alger Hiss case or the way he played along with the McCarthy hysteria. I met him one day when he was Vice President. He came to the *Times* for lunch, and I was placed next to him. He was polite and interesting enough, but there was something about his personality I just didn't like. Nothing could have induced me to vote for Mr. Nixon when he declared his candidacy in 1960, with President Eisenhower's full support. I was for John F. Kennedy right from the start.

Arthur, of course, was much more judicious than I in deciding whom to support in the 1960 election. He had the responsibility of committing the *New York Times* to one or the other candidate, and he watched the performance of both men and discussed the issues at length with both the Democrats and the Republicans. Finally, after much deliberation, he said, "Iphigene, we're coming out for Kennedy." I was greatly relieved.

Only on one occasion did Mr. Nixon make a good impression on me. It was in December 1968. Arthur died, and Mr. Nixon, then President-elect, attended the memorial service at Temple Emanu-El. The *Times* had not supported him in the November election; still, on that awful day, he came through the snow and sleet. After the service, he walked up to me to express his condolences. I thanked him, and replied that Arthur had always liked and respected him.

Arthur, in fact, *had* found some positive attributes in Richard

Nixon. He thought that one's impression of Mr. Nixon improved on closer acquaintance.

General Eisenhower never did rise in my esteem. When he was still President and Arthur's associates at the *Times* were planning to celebrate his twentieth anniversary as publisher, Mr. Eisenhower, among others, was asked to make a few personal remarks, to be recorded and played for Arthur on the evening of the party at the "21" Club. Instead of taking a few minutes to make a recording, the President had his press secretary, Jim Hagerty, issue a statement on his behalf. The message was perfectly acceptable, but I thought he might have taken the trouble to deliver it himself.

Mr. Stevenson, on the other hand, recorded a lovely tribute, saying he felt the *Times* had always been fair to him, even though he had "tripped over it on the way to the White House." Some time later, he sent me his photograph, signing it: "To Iphigene Ochs Sulzberger from a great admirer." When a friend asked me how I rated such an inscription, I said, "Mr. Stevenson knew that when the *Times* endorsed Eisenhower, I voted for him nonetheless. He evidently realized I was a woman of judgment."

Such was the wisdom of Adlai Stevenson. After the election, we got to know him well. He became an especially good friend of Marian's.

I had long wanted to give Arthur something special for his twentieth anniversary as publisher. He had once told me he would love to own a painting by Winston Churchill. Arthur knew the former Prime Minister well, and he also knew that this was one amateur artist whose work was unobtainable. Only two people were known to have owned a Churchill painting—Lewis Douglas, the American Ambassador to Great Britain, and Bernard Baruch, who was Mr. Churchill's close friend. I resolved that Arthur would be the third.

The anniversary was only a few months away and I had still not figured out how I was going to get a Churchill painting. Arthur and I were on a European tour, and one evening, while having dinner at the British Embassy in Paris, I mentioned my problem to the Ambassador, Gladwyn Jebb, making sure Arthur was out of earshot. Gladwyn was an old friend from the days when he represented Britain at the United Nations and he and his wife were frequent guests at Hillandale.

Gladwyn considered the problem for a few minutes and asked if I knew Mr. Churchill's daughter Mary and her husband, Christopher Soames. I said I had met them several times.

"Good," he said. "Christopher is your best bet."

I wrote Christopher the following day, saying we would be in London soon and asking if he could help. Shortly after our arrival in London, he telephoned.

"I got your letter," he said, "and I know how fond my father-in-law is of Arthur. But you know, he'd rather part with one of his children than with one of his paintings."

"Well, Christopher," I replied, "would you please tell the Prime Minister that if he doesn't want to give up a painting, we'll settle for you or Mary."

The next thing I knew, the painting was on its way. It was a landscape drawn at a little coastal village outside Venice. And it arrived in time for me to give it to Arthur on the day of his celebration.

Winston Churchill also contributed a personal tribute for the anniversary dinner. He recorded a little speech, telling of his affection for Arthur and for the *Times*, and mentioning that his grandfather, Leonard Walter Jerome, had once owned a substantial number of shares in the paper before the days of Adolph Ochs.

Arthur liked the painting so much that a few years later he got the notion of having an American exhibit of Winston Churchill's work. He was on the board of trustees of the Metropolitan Museum, and he suggested an exhibit in commemoration of D Day.

The idea was not well received. The museum said it would be lowering its standards by presenting an amateur's work. Arthur heartily disagreed. He argued that Mr. Churchill's amateur status was beside the point—he was a good painter and a colorful world figure. After considerable lobbying Arthur got the idea approved.

The exhibit was a huge success. Mr. Churchill shipped over many of his works; Arthur's Venetian landscape was there too, and it stood out as one of the better paintings.

I had met the Prime Minister only twice. The first time was when Arthur and I were invited for lunch at Chartwell, Mr. Churchill's estate. After the meal, when Arthur and the British statesman adjourned to discuss business, I accompanied Mrs. Churchill on a walk around the grounds.

It had been raining, and when we returned to the vestibule of the house I noticed that my shoes were covered with mud. Mrs. Churchill handed me some tissue to wipe them off. I began to clean them very carefully, so as not to get mud on the floor, when I realized that Mrs. Churchill was growing impatient with my slowness. At last she could restrain herself no longer and said, "My, you're making a miserable job of that! Put your foot on this stool."

I raised my foot, and she began vigorously wiping off my shoe, letting the mud fly in all directions. I must be the only woman who has ever had the wife of a British Prime Minister clean her shoes. I guess that makes me some kind of historical character.

On our second visit to Chartwell, Arthur and I took a walk around the estate with the Prime Minister. Mr. Churchill took some bread crumbs with him to feed the fish in the pond. He said he talked to the fish and they would come up to be fed.

When we reached the pond, he started chuckling and tossing the bread crumbs. "See," he said, "the fish are coming up because they hear me." I wasn't sure whether he was pulling our leg or just fooling himself.

Mr. Churchill would say some of the most extraordinary things. Robert Menzies, when he was Prime Minister of Australia, told me of an incident that occurred at a Commonwealth Conference in London:

All the Commonwealth Prime Ministers were invited to dinner at Buckingham Palace. After dinner, as Queen Elizabeth II and Prince Philip mingled among the guests, Mr. Churchill got tired of standing and sat down on a nearby sofa. The Prime Minister of Pakistan, Khawaja Nazimuddin, was standing next to him, and Sir Winston invited him to sit down too. Poor Mr. Nazimuddin didn't know whether to stand in the presence of the Queen or sit with the British Prime Minister, so he compromised by balancing himself on the very edge of the sofa.

A butler came by with a tray of brandy cordials. Mr. Churchill took a glass and offered one to Mr. Nazimuddin.

"No, thank you, I don't drink," said the Pakistani.

"What did you say?" asked Mr. Churchill, who was going deaf.

"I said I don't drink," Mr. Nazimuddin said loudly.

"You *what?*"

"I'm a *teetotaler*—I don't *drink*," Mr. Nazimuddin shouted, at which Sir Winston gasped, "Jesus! I mean, God! I mean, Allah!"

Mr. Churchill also had some rather peculiar habits. My cousin Julius Adler used to tell us stories about the time in the 1940's when Mr. Churchill was writing his memoirs. Julie saw quite a bit of him then, because he had been assigned to negotiate the first-publication rights: The *Times* and *Life* were together paying over a million dollars for the Prime Minister's personal account of the Second World War.

Julie said Mr. Churchill had an erratic schedule. He kept secretaries on duty around the clock. He might wake up in the middle of the night and dictate something; he usually dictated the first draft and refined it in the writing.

One evening, Julie called on Mr. Churchill and found him sitting up in bed, working. Oddly enough, though all the electric lights were on, a candle was burning on the night table. Julie's curiosity was getting the better of him when the Prime Minister's cigar went out and he leaned over and relit it from the candle flame.

Julie was accompanied on some of these visits by Andrew Heiskell, who was then representing *Life*, and Louis Loeb, the *Times* lawyer. Mr. Churchill hated lawyers and had refused to invite Louis to Chartwell for the earlier negotiations. Louis naturally resented this, having made the trip abroad to be in on the discussions. Arthur took corrective action. When Mr. Churchill came to New York for the next phase of the negotiations, he had him over for lunch at the *Times* and introduced him to Louis—with no mention of Louis's being a lawyer. Thus, Louis was able to take part in the subsequent talks.

The last time Arthur saw Mr. Churchill was when Sir Winston was staying in New York with Bernard Baruch. Conversation was just about impossible. Mr. Churchill's health had deteriorated badly, and he was practically deaf. Mr. Baruch, who wore a hearing aid, tried to persuade Mr. Churchill to use one too, but to no avail.

I can understand Mr. Churchill's aversion to the instrument, especially in those days, when hearing aids were pretty cumbersome affairs. I've had to use one for the past six years and it's a constant bother. I'm always having to adjust the volume if the person I'm listening to has a very soft or very strong voice. Sometimes, when I'm wearing it, people think I'm stone deaf and speak so loudly that the feedback practically blows me to the ceiling.

I know there's at least one good reason for not wearing a hearing aid. I learned it back in 1929 from Thomas Edison, who was quite an old man then, and very deaf.

I had come down with a bad case of whooping cough, which I had given to all my four children, and went to Miami Beach, then a lovely place, for a couple of weeks' rest. My father accompanied me; it was his seventy-first birthday, and he felt he deserved a week off. During the vacation, we received an invitation from Mr. Edison, who was a friend of my father, to have lunch with him at his home in Fort Myers.

Mr. Edison at the time was working on a way to develop rubber from goldenrod. He took us on a tour of his greenhouse and told us that while his experiment had been successful, it took great quantities of goldenrod to yield a small amount of rubber and the process was therefore impractical.

At the lunch table, Mrs. Edison handed each of us a pad and pencil and said, "My husband can't hear, so if there's anything you want to say, just write it down."

It was a frustrating experience. Even when there was something I wanted to say, the conversation had moved on to another subject by the time I finished writing it.

My father was seated next to Mr. Edison, and throughout the lunch kept bellowing in his ear. Mr. Edison replied very softly, and to hear him my father had to put his ear practically into Mr. Edison's mouth.

At last my father asked, "Mr. Edison, with all your genius for inventing, why haven't you perfected a hearing aid for yourself?"

Thomas Edison beamed and said, "What most people have to say isn't worth hearing."

31

In 1954, Arthur and I went to India in the company of our long-time friends George Woods and his wife, Louise (known affectionately as Louie). George, who was then president of the First Boston Corporation, later headed the World Bank; today, he is one of the three trustees of the Ochs estate. We made the crossing on a British airlines Comet, then the newest of the passenger jets. Not long after they were introduced, several Comets blew up in midair and the plane was taken out of operation. The problem was apparently metal fatigue. Fortunately, the metal didn't get tired while we were aboard, but *we* were exhausted. The Comet had to refuel frequently, and each time we landed we had to disembark and show our passports and health certificates.

We traveled as guests of the Indian and Pakistani governments, and our first stop on the subcontinent was Bombay. There we stayed at Government House, a magnificent complex built for the

British Viceroy that now served as a guest house for officials of the Indian Government. The grounds had glorious gardens, then in full bloom, and a museum.

Besides taking in the regular tourist sights, we visited several universities in both India and Pakistan. Arthur was chairman of a bicentennial committee organizing a program to mark the founding of Columbia University in 1754, and he was getting a number of Indian universities to participate in what would be an international celebration, the theme of which was "man's right to knowledge and the free use thereof."

The high point of our stay in New Delhi was having lunch in the garden of Jawaharlal Nehru's home. The setting was beautiful and in the garden Mr. Nehru kept a caged giant panda that had been given to him by the Chinese. The Prime Minister was charming, as was his daughter, Indira, who acted as hostess. At lunch Louie and I were seated on either side of Mr. Nehru and he offered us some of the beautiful fruit from the bowl on the table, asking us if we had sampled the delicious fruits of India. We said we hadn't (not adding that we had been warned not to eat uncooked food), whereupon the Prime Minister peeled a fruit and handed us each a slice. Louie and I exchanged glances of fond farewell and ate. We needn't have worried, there were no ill effects.

Near New Delhi we visited some villages with a team from Point Four, a technical assistance program proposed by President Truman that worked to improve living conditions on farms and in villages. Our first stop was a village that had not received assistance from Point Four. It consisted of mud huts plastered on the outside with drying cow dung, which was to be used as fuel, and clay streets that became mud in the rainy season. There was one communal fresh-water well for drinking water, bathing, laundering and watering cattle, and one well for the lowest caste—the untouchables (Gandhi renamed the caste Children of God in an effort to abolish untouchability).

We were then shown a village where the Point Four team had been at work. Villagers were paving the streets, they were cooking on solar-heated outdoor stoves and had a three-tier fresh-water fountain: the highest level was for drinking water, the second for bathing and laundering and the third had been made into troughs for the animals. In contrast to the other village, there was an atmosphere of hope.

However, substantial improvement to the thousands of villages in India seemed remote. The problems were devastating. I had thought that poverty, disease and starvation could not have been worse than what I had seen in Egypt in 1937. But the slums we saw in India, especially in contrast to our luxurious accommodations, were shocking.

From New Delhi we proceeded to Jaipur, the first planned city in the world; then to Agra, the site of the Taj Mahal; and on to Benares, the holiest city to the Hindus. Our official guide in Benares was the vice mayor of the city, who accompanied us everywhere, including to a tea with the Maharajah. When in conversation I mentioned having known the leader of the untouchables, Dr. Bhimrao R. Ambedkar (we met back in my college days when he was a student at Columbia University), the vice mayor said that he too was an untouchable and was one of the fortunate to have made a successful career.

While walking down the streets of Benares we saw men carrying to the Ganges River a litter covered with flowers on which lay a dead cow. The cow, being sacred, was going to be thrown into the same waters where masses of pilgrims were bathing and drinking the so-called holy waters. To me, worship of the cow is a most self-destructive religious tradition. The animal is neither killed nor cared for and as a result India has one of the world's largest cow populations and is one of the lowest milk producers.

We went on to Calcutta. At the Calcutta railroad station we saw refugee families from East Pakistan (now Bangladesh) who had been camping in the station for several years. Some families had no shelters and lived on the streets. I saw a bundle of what looked like old, dirty sheets, which was a man lying asleep. Many women working on construction jobs carried heavy burdens on their heads and babies on their backs or at their breasts. The sad, fatigued faces of these women haunted me.

From Calcutta we proceeded north to Katmandu, holy to the Hindus and the Buddhists alike; there, in the distance, we could see Mount Everest. We were, I believe, among the first fifty people of European origin to visit the Nepalese capital, and we were quite the attraction. Crowds would gather around us clapping and laughing.

We then continued to Pakistan where we were guests at Government House in Karachi, and dined one evening with Prime Minister Nazimuddin (the teetotaler). In Karachi we were introduced to a group of educated women who had organized vocational programs and schooling for refugees during Pakistan's transition to nationhood. These ladies had come out of purda to help with the enormous problems the new nation faced. As one said: "How could we succeed if half the educated class—the women—remained in seclusion?" The ladies gave us a tour of a refugee camp which, though lacking in many facilities, was a vast improvement on the villages we'd seen in India. We also visited a hospital staffed by women doctors, all of whom, I think, had received their medical training in England.

We continued on to Peshawar and drove through the Khyber Pass, where we saw the regimental names carved into the rock by the British troops of an earlier era. Pakistan and Afghanistan were not on speaking terms, and when we came to the border we were not permitted to set foot on the Afghan soil. Arthur took a step toward the border checkpoint, but the Afghan sentries raised their rifles and he thought better of it. There was a camel train wending its way through the pass and in my mind's eye I saw Alexander the Great with his Greek army marching to the Indus River.

We continued with our itinerary in Pakistan and went to Swat, where we dined with the Wali. After the introductions were performed, the Wali asked me what I would like to drink. "What do you have?" I asked.

"Oh," he said, "ginger ale, orange crush, soda pop."

The Wali was a Pathan and a strict Moslem, and Louie and I were the only women at the dinner table. I sat between the Wali and General Ayub Khan, then commander-in-chief of the Pakistani Army (and later Prime Minister). The Wali began holding forth about Israel, a subject which I had not been warned was an obsession of his.

"Israel is not a nation," he affirmed. "It is merely the figment of the imagination of one man—Weizmann." Before I realized it, I found myself saying, "And how does that differ from Pakistan?"

For, of course, no nation is more indebted for its creation to the will and energy of one man than Pakistan is indebted to Mohammed Ali Jinnah.

The Wali gave me an enraged look, and I imagined him about to shout "Off with her head" when Ayub Khan came to my rescue.

"She's got you," he said, laughing, to the Wali. "The two countries are, of course, identical."

The Wali kept spluttering, and I fear we might have had a difficult time getting out of Swat if Ayub Khan hadn't offered us a lift back to Karachi in his plane. From there we headed back home.

Three years later, in 1957, we invited the Woodses to join us again, this time on a trip around the world. George was busy, but Louie came along. However, she was suffering from ulcers and faced the possibility of an operation, so it was decided that she would go only as far as Japan, the Philippines, Taiwan and Hong Kong, where there would be Western-trained doctors to treat her. Also in our party were Arthur's nephew Cyrus Sulzberger and his wife, Marina, who was Greek, and charming, intelligent and lovable. They lived in Paris, so we joined them in Tokyo, our first stop.

I remember telling Arthur before we left that he looked tired, but he assured me he felt fine. He'd had no serious health problem since that incident of heart strain in the 1930's, and I saw no cause for worry.

From the moment we touched down in Tokyo, it seemed we were guests of honor in Japan. We found ourselves in a round of dinners and luncheons and at countless cocktail parties, where we had to stand for long hours and shake hands with government officials, diplomats, journalists, leading citizens—innumerable people who were never going to remember us or we them. I tried to dissuade Arthur from attending some of these functions, but he said he felt fine.

One evening, the publisher of the Tokyo *Mainichi* gave a big party for us at his home. I was surprised to see that only the room set aside for the traditional tea ceremony had Japanese decor; the rest of the house was furnished in Western style. I thought this very sensible; it can't be too comfortable to sit and sleep on the floor.

Another day Arthur and I were received by Emperor Hirohito and Empress Nagako. They occupied temporary living quarters in an office building on the Imperial grounds, since the repairs undertaken after the wartime bombing of the Imperial Palace were still going on. We were ushered into a living room tastefully decorated with French antiques—and, after a few moments, into another room, where the royal couple awaited us.

For the next half hour Arthur spoke with the Emperor and I with the Empress. Each had an interpreter. My conversation was something of a trial because I kept forgetting Arthur's instructions not to look at the interpreter when my words were rendered into Japanese but to keep my eyes on the Empress. We talked about our children and my impression of Japan.

While in Tokyo, we visited our Japanese friends the Kasés. We had come to know them quite well when Mr. Kasé served as the Japanese observer at the United Nations (before Japan had become a U.N. member). Mrs. Kasé welcomed us to Tokyo with a delightful ladies' luncheon for Louie, Marina and me. It was in the old-fashioned Japanese style, and the women we met could not have been more charming or interesting. Among the guests was the mother-in-law of the Emperor's brother.

The Kasés' daughter, Reiko, an unusually intelligent and attractive girl, had been accepted into the junior class at Barnard when the family lived in New York. I believe she was the first Japanese student enrolled at that college after the war. Mrs. Kasé was under the impression that I was responsible for Reiko's admission, and I could never convince her that her daughter had been accepted solely on her merits.

Reiko excelled at Barnard. In her senior year, she shared the first prize with another student for the best original English composition. When I heard that, my newspaper instincts were aroused and I phoned Turner Catledge, then managing editor of the *Times*, and told him I thought it would make a wonderful human-interest story. Shortly afterward, a piece about the award, with a photograph of Reiko dressed in a kimono, appeared in the *Times* and attracted a great deal of attention. Reiko was asked by magazines all over the country to write something for them. She decided that since she was an amateur writer, the only magazine she was qualified to submit articles to was *Seventeen*. The other offers she turned down, saying she was inexperienced and needed time to develop her writing skills.

I saw Reiko again on a trip to the Far East in 1973. She told me she had been translating American books into Japanese. One she liked in particular was by Harrison Salisbury of the *New York Times*. She said she didn't have much time for creative writing, being a doctor's wife and the mother of four children, but she was active in a group devoted to furthering the emancipation of Japanese women. "It isn't a radical movement, like in the United States," she said. "Here, when we do things, it is in the traditional, refined Japanese manner."

From Tokyo we traveled to the beautiful ancient capital of Kyoto, and then to Nara and Osaka, going part of the way by railroad. I found myself wishing we had trains that good in the United States. But the high point of our visit to Japan, at least for me, was when we were shown around the Mikimoto pearl fisheries near Osaka.

From Japan we flew to Taipei. The Chinese and American officials in Taiwan outdid themselves in hospitality, providing such a whirl of entertainment that we nearly collapsed from all the parties and feasts. Arthur, in particular, was exhausted. He realized that he had better slow down, and declined an invitation for a day's flying trip to Quemoy and Matsu, the two small Nationalist-held islands just off the Chinese mainland.

But we could not dissuade Cyrus, always the eager journalist, from going. Cyrus returned pale and shaken. The day, he said, had been dark and stormy, and the plane had to fly at a low altitude to avoid radar detection. Cyrus was airsick, and swore he would never fly below the clouds in bad weather again.

As for the danger, that hadn't bothered him in the least. Nothing could deter Cyrus when a news story was involved.

This was the visit during which we had our memorable dinner

with Generalissimo and Madame Chiang Kai-shek. After that we flew on to Manila.

We made the usual tourist excursions to Corregidor Island and Bataan, where General Wainwright and his men had held out so doggedly against the Japanese before making their historic Death March. We visited our friend Carlos P. Romulo, the former Philippine delegate to the United Nations and Ambassador to the United States. General Romulo had had a heart attack and was recuperating at home. We dined at the American Embassy with Ambassador Charles Bohlen. Chip Bohlen was a good friend of Marina and Cy. After long and distinguished service as a specialist on the Soviet Union and Ambassador to Moscow, he had been assigned to the comparatively minor Manila post because Secretary of State Dulles wanted him out of the way. In my opinion it was a grievous waste of much-needed Soviet expertise.

From Manila we proceeded to Hong Kong, where we spent a delightful first evening with the British Governor and his wife, Sir Alexander and Lady Maurine Grantham. They couldn't have been more charming, but I must say they were an odd-looking couple; he was over six feet tall and she couldn't have been more than four feet ten.

Hong Kong was overflowing with refugees from Chinese Communist rule. These poor people lived in tin shacks in the hills, or literally on the sidewalks. It occurred to me that if China's Maoist society was half as good as Peking claimed, there would not be so many escapees, many of whom had fled by swimming through shark-infested waters to what they must have known would be a life of poverty.

Louie bade us farewell in Hong Kong, and the rest of us continued to Southeast Asia. In Bangkok we were met by Bernard Kalb, an outstanding *Times* correspondent who, unfortunately for the *Times*, left the paper a few years later for CBS News. From Bangkok we made a one-day excursion to Cambodia, to see the temples of Angkor Wat. This required filling out a lengthy questionnaire. Not only did we have to state our nationalities and occupations but we had to give our parents' and grandparents' names. In any event, we were cleared, and early one morning, picnic lunches in hand, we boarded a plane.

The day turned scorchingly hot, and after seeing the temples we went to freshen up at a hotel. To get back into Thailand that evening we had to fill out another set of long and detailed forms. One of the questions was "How much money do you have with you?" Bernie, fed up with all the red tape, wrote, "1,000,000 dollars —in cash." The authorities didn't even question him.

From Bangkok we flew to Rangoon. Our first night there we had dinner at the American Embassy with Ambassador and Mrs. Walter McConaughy. It was a very enjoyable evening. We left early for our hotel to get a good night's rest.

The next morning, Arthur said his left side was numb and he couldn't move. "Iphigene," he said, "I think I've had a stroke."

I rushed off to find Cy and Marina. With the Embassy's help, they located a Dr. Suvi, an Indian who had received his medical education in Edinburgh. By the time the doctor arrived, Arthur's left side was completely paralyzed.

Arthur was taken by ambulance to a British nursing home where Dr. Suvi had his own clinic. The doctor brought in a heart specialist, a former British Army physician. Together they prescribed a course of treatment. Thanks to Cy, Marina and Bernie, and the excellent care provided by the doctors, I felt reassured.

The Ambassador and his wife, who couldn't have been kinder or more helpful, told me that Dr. Suvi was the leading physician in Rangoon and that the heart specialist was first-rate. The staff at the clinic also seemed eminently professional, and the nurses were most attentive and competent.

After two weeks, Dr. Suvi said Arthur was well enough to travel. He advised against our staying any longer, as the climate was not good for Arthur's condition, and said the best thing would be to get him home as soon as possible. I telephoned Marian in New York—she had offered to come out to Rangoon, as had Arthur's physician, Howard Rusk—and told her we were on our way home.

Cyrus and Marina insisted on making the long journey with us. It would have been grim without them, and I was grateful for their company.

Dr. Suvi saw us out to the airport. In the years to follow, we kept in touch. His life was soon to undergo a drastic change. In

1959, the new Burmese regime of Ne Win threw out the Indians and Chinese as undesirable aliens, and Dr. Suvi was among those expelled. They gave him less than twelve hours' notice, confiscated his clinic, forbade him to take any of his possessions with him and put him on a plane to India. He wrote me from Calcutta. Calcutta, he said, was short of doctors, and he would have no trouble starting a new practice.

We flew from Rangoon to Manila on a Swedish airline. We had been assured that the stewardesses had medical training and that it would not be necessary to hire a nurse. The stewardesses proved to be kind but not very competent, and I resolved to find a nurse for the rest of the journey.

In Manila, we were met by an ambulance from the Seventh Day Adventist Hospital and a doctor from a nearby American air base. Our children had arranged everything from New York, including our hotel rooms and round-the-clock nurses for Arthur. One of the nurses was a lovely Filipino woman trained in the States. Her name was Juliana Balthazar, and I asked her if she would make the rest of the trip with us and stay on as Arthur's nurse. She agreed, and for the next year and a half Juliana proved to be a wonderful nurse and a lovely person—we still keep in touch.

We stayed in Manila two days before boarding a Pan Am flight for Hawaii. Those were the days before jet travel, when Pacific crossings took twenty-four hours and planes had sleeping berths for passengers. The berths were all upper bunks, but Pan Am removed four passenger seats and installed a comfortable bed for Arthur. In Hawaii, our good friend Henry Kaiser, of Kaiser Aluminum, met us at the airport and got us settled into a hotel. We stayed two nights before making the trip to San Francisco, where Marian met us and accompanied us on the final lap.

Back in New York, Dr. Rusk supervised Arthur's therapy. Within six months Arthur was able to walk with no difficulty. He made a good recovery. Yet this was to be the beginning of the most difficult years of our lives. Over the next eleven years, my husband's health would slowly and irreversibly deteriorate.

32

In 1960, while we were vacationing in northern Italy, Arthur had a second stroke.

It had been a restful three weeks. Arthur took the therapeutic radium baths at the health resort of Abano, and we enjoyed sightseeing in the nearby towns of Padua, Vicenza and Verona. Then, early one morning, we left for Venice to spend the day with George and Louie Woods. Sometime during the trip, Arthur began to feel the numbness returning.

We had been with the Woodses an hour or so when he told George about it. Then he told me. We returned to Abano as quickly as possible. By the time we reached our hotel, Arthur was sure he had had a minor stroke.

I phoned the hotel doctor. He hadn't heard of anything but mud baths. The next day we left for London to get the proper medical attention.

I had notified the family, and when we arrived in London, Ruth was there to meet us. The doctors said Arthur's condition wasn't serious but he needed complete rest. We decided it would be less strenuous to go home by ship. As it happened, Turner Catledge and his wife, Abby, were returning to New York aboard the same liner.

I was able to relax with Ruth during the ocean voyage, and Arthur for the most part stayed in bed. Back home, he once again made a good comeback and was able to return to work.

In 1961, in recognition of his excellent recovery, he was given an award by the American Heart Association. Each year the association makes a presentation to a prominent citizen who has had heart trouble, so as to encourage heart patients to return to active lives. The previous year the award had been given to Lyndon Johnson; as the former recipient, he was to make the presentation to Arthur. This came to the attention of President Kennedy, who, seeing a good opportunity to promote the work of the American Heart Association, arranged for the award to be made at a small, informal ceremony in the Oval Office. He invited Arthur and me and Dr. Howard Rusk (who was very active in the association) to lunch beforehand.

When we arrived at the White House, we were ushered into the Red Room and greeted by Jacqueline Kennedy. Vice President Johnson entered and a marshal announced: "The President of the United States."

In walked a handsome man who looked young enough to be my son. The six of us adjourned to the dining room. I found myself seated between the President and the Vice President of the United States. Mighty few women, I imagine, have been in that position.

Mr. Johnson expressed his regrets that Lady Bird had been unable to attend, then went on to tell me about a problem he was having. He said he wanted to put a qualified Negro on his staff but couldn't find the right man; still, he would persevere in the search. He added that he had great faith in the blacks.

I don't remember my conversation with President Kennedy, but I know I found him utterly charming and felt completely at ease. Mrs. Kennedy also impressed me. She was attractive and intelligent.

After the lunch, when we had coffee together, she told me what she was doing to redecorate the White House.

After the renovation done during the Truman years, the President and Mrs. Truman had called in a New York firm to do the decorating, and their work, Mrs. Kennedy said, had not been too imaginative. Her own objective, she said, was to find furnishings belonging to the period when the White House was built, and in the right style for each of the different rooms. She told me she had discovered high-quality pieces in the White House storerooms, and had formed a decorating committee headed by the American-antiques expert Pierre Dupont to help with the project. The committee not only acted as consultants but solicited contributions from private collectors.

By all accounts, Mrs. Kennedy was doing a magnificent job. As a gesture of my enthusiasm, I sent her a Lowestoft plate I had found in a New York antique store. It was about the size of a dessert plate and it bore the coat of arms of the United States. The committee wrote me a nice thank-you letter, and I received word from Martha Bartlett, a friend of mine who was close to the First Family, that Mrs. Kennedy was delighted with the gift. Sometime later, Mrs. Kennedy gave a televised tour of the White House, and our maid, who was watching the broadcast, came rushing to me in a state of great excitement. She said that sitting on one of the tables was my plate.

On the day of the award presentation, Mrs. Kennedy and I rejoined the men in the Oval Office after coffee. The ceremony was attended by reporters and officials of the heart association. Photographs were taken, there was handshaking, thank-you's were exchanged, and we began to take our leave. I was standing near the President when he looked at a large pile of inauguration ceremony programs on his desk and said to me, "You weren't at the inauguration. Would you like a program for a souvenir?"

I thanked him very kindly and started to leave when he said, "Wait a minute, give that back to me. I want to write something on it."

He wrote: "To Mrs. Arthur Hays Sulzberger, who helped make these festivities possible."

Evidently he had heard that I had been a Kennedy supporter

long before the *Times* had endorsed him, and he was giving me the credit for influencing the paper's decision. As we left his office, the President said to me, "I know I got my job through the *New York Times*."

The following year, Arthur's health deteriorated rapidly. He had another minor stroke that made walking very difficult. Our family doctor, George Carden, made the sad but accurate prediction that Arthur would soon be confined to a wheelchair. He suggested we get a full-time nurse.

Marian knew a pretty English nurse whom Arthur liked, and she wound up staying with us for several years. I would be hiring other nurses after that. I soon learned that practical nurses are much better than registered nurses, who stand on their dignity and expect to be waited on.

The years of Arthur's illness were naturally a strain on me, but Arthur was very considerate and uncomplaining and, when I got nervous, was all for my getting away, taking a trip with a friend to relax. There was only one time he objected to my leaving. That was in 1966 when Harold Hochschild invited me on a month's trip to Africa with his niece Blakie and her husband, Robert Worth. Knowing that I would probably never have such an opportunity again, I went.

During those difficult times, the sustaining love of my family and friends was a blessing. People were very sympathetic, though I'd tell them I was in fine health and it was Arthur who needed their sympathy. One exceptionally thoughtful gesture was a call from Mrs. Kennedy's secretary, telling me that Arthur and I would be receiving an invitation to dinner at the White House. "The President and Mrs. Kennedy realize your husband is in poor health and possibly cannot attend," she said, "and they wanted you to know they'd be delighted if you would come by yourself."

Arthur was all for my going, and I accepted. Ruth and her husband, Ben, were also invited, and we arranged to stay together while in Washington.

The dinner was in honor of Grand Duchess Charlotte of Luxembourg and her son and heir, Prince Jean, who is now the Grand

Duke. Ruth, Ben and I were ushered into the East Room, where all the guests were lined up in alphabetical order to be presented. I was delighted to discover that the "S" just ahead of "Sulzberger" was "Steinbeck"—John Steinbeck. In the few minutes I had with the author, I told him how much I enjoyed his latest book, *Travels with Charlie*, and asked him how the dog was doing.

"I'm very sad," he said. "Charlie has just died."

The next morning, when I visited the *Times*'s Washington Bureau, the staff eagerly asked if I'd picked up any news tips at the dinner. "Only that Charlie Steinbeck is dead," I said.

The following day the news was written up in the column "Washington Notes." That's how Charlie Steinbeck got his obit in the *Times*.

Much to my surprise, I was seated at that dinner between Prince Jean and Pierre Dupont; the Prince was on Mrs. Kennedy's right. The Kennedys had not adhered to the usual protocol: Instead of seating guests according to rank at a long table, which would have put me down somewhere below the salt, they had small round tables that seated ten or twelve each. The Prince and I discussed child-rearing. He had, I think, six children, and he said he found it difficult to keep them from being spoiled; instead of having them tutored privately, he sent them to school. He seemed a very nice young man, and I thought it was unfair to him to have been placed next to some old, undistinguished lady. I am sure it wasn't for fear of competition that Mrs. Kennedy had selected me.

Lyndon Johnson was there and he was kind enough to come across the room and ask about Arthur. When the evening drew to an end and I was preparing to leave with Ruth and Ben, the President came over and asked if we had seen the Rose Garden. We hadn't, and he invited us to come back in the morning and have a look. The next day he gave us a private tour.

As President, Jack Kennedy made some serious mistakes—the Bay of Pigs and Vietnam were two of them—and I don't think he worked with Congress as well as he could have. Despite these shortcomings, he succeeded in arousing the country in a positive way. The people of America were behind him. In fact, most of the world was behind him. He and his wife brought charm and culture to the White House, and it was a tragedy for mankind when he was murdered.

After the assassination, I wanted to do something for Jacqueline Kennedy, and I thought of inviting her to a dinner party. When Marian learned of my plans, she said, "Don't. She's a young woman, and she goes with a different crowd. It's nothing personal, Mother, but I think she'd be bored to tears."

I took Marian's advice. A year or so later, I ran into Mrs. Kennedy in the lobby of the Carlyle Hotel. She was with some friends, and I went over and said, "I'm so glad to see you again."

She smiled politely, but it was obvious that she didn't remember me. I said, "Perhaps you don't remember me. I'm Iphigene Sulzberger."

The name meant absolutely nothing to her. She courteously said hello and left.

I realized then that Marian had been right. My feelings weren't hurt; in fact, the episode gave me a better understanding of the enormous strain of being First Lady. That poor woman must have had to meet thousands of people.

Arthur was in reasonably good health when he decided in early 1961 to go into semi-retirement and to turn his job over to a younger man. He wanted to make the transition slowly, so that he could, if necessary, act as adviser to the new publisher. The choice of his successor was not a difficult one.

Orvil Dryfoos had been with the *Times* since 1942, and Arthur had given him more and more responsibility over the years, finally naming him president of the company. Arthur liked Orv's patient and sensitive manner. Like Arthur, Orv would examine an issue in all its aspects before, quietly but firmly, arriving at a decision. While he would work to expand the *Times* still further, he was clearly committed to doing so without violating any of my father's journalistic principles. He was not the driving executive type but had an easy and affable personality that made him very popular with the staff, from executives and reporters to office boys and mail clerks. Though he had established himself as a reliable and resourceful leader in his own right, he shared Arthur's unassuming ways, and when asked about his rise in the company he'd quip, like Arthur, "I got there by marrying the boss's daughter."

In November 1961, Arthur became chairman of the board and Orv, then forty-eight, was named publisher.

That same year, Charlie Merz retired after twenty-three years as editor of the editorial page, and it was up to Orv to select a successor. On Charlie's and many other people's recommendation, he named my cousin John Oakes.

John had outstanding credentials. He had graduated from Princeton magna cum laude, having made Phi Beta Kappa in his junior year, and went on to become a Rhodes Scholar. Joining the *Times* in the 1940's, he spent three years working on the News of the Week in Review section before being picked by Charlie Merz for the editorial board. Now John was to head the board, a job he would have for the next fifteen years.

Though we knew Orv had a defective heart, it had never given him any trouble, and we fully expected him to remain at the helm until retirement age. Arthur and I hoped that by that time Punch, who was thirteen years younger than Orv, would have accumulated enough experience to take over. It was not to work out that way.

In December 1962, the printers' union went on strike against the *Times* and seven other New York dailies. The dispute developed into the worst newspaper strike in the city's history, lasting 114 days. The frustrating and wearisome negotiations were charged with hostility. Bertram A. Powers, head of New York Typographical Union No. 6, and Amory Bradford, the *Times*'s general manager and chief spokesman for the Publishers Association, proved bitter antagonists. Both became increasingly chilly and arrogant, making conciliation all but impossible. Several times the negotiations were on the verge of collapse, and each time Orv stepped in and persuaded the chief negotiators to calm down and resume their talks.

The strain on Orv was enormous. When the strike was finally settled in the spring, he and Marian left for a badly needed vacation in Puerto Rico. They had been there just a few days when Orvil had a heart attack.

He was admitted to a hospital in San Juan; when his condition stabilized, he and Marian flew back to New York. From the airport, Orv was taken by ambulance to the Harkness Pavilion at Columbia Presbyterian Hospital. Orv never left that hospital. He died on May 25, 1963, of a heart attack. He was only fifty. There is little doubt that the unrelenting tensions of the long strike had cost him his life.

Orvil's death was a heavy blow to the *Times* and, of course, a horrible shock to our family. Orv was much beloved by so many people. To me he was like a son. We shared a common love for the outdoors and used to take long walks through the woods at Hillandale. We'd talk about business and politics, and a lot about our family (Orv had a very strong sense of family), and I remember how his eyes would twinkle under his bushy eyebrows and a broad smile would light up his handsome face.

We asked Scotty Reston to deliver the eulogy. Scotty is like family to us, and he has a way with words, a way of making people understand and giving them reason for hope. In many ways Scotty reminds me of my father. Like my father, he came from a pious and poor family, and through tremendous energy and ambition worked his way up to become a leading figure in the journalistic world. And, like my father, he never forgot his impoverished past and the people who helped him along the way. I've always felt that Scotty and my father shared many of the same principles. For one thing, they were both great believers in America. The eulogy Scotty delivered at Temple Emanu-El that May morning expressed beautifully what I and so many others felt about Orv:

"The death of Orvil Dryfoos was blamed on 'heart failure,' but that obviously could not have been the reason. Orv Dryfoos' heart never failed him or anybody else—ask the reporters on the *Times*. It was as steady as the stars—ask anybody in this company of friends. It was as faithful as the tides—ask his beloved wife and family. No matter what the doctors say, they cannot blame his heart."

In this numbingly sad time in our lives, Arthur and I had to decide who would take over as publisher. The decision weighed heavily on me, as Arthur had not been at all well.

In the last two years he had grown weaker and weaker. As the doctor explained, it was a gradual deterioration, accompanied perhaps by mild strokes that did not paralyze him but left him feeling worse each time. By 1963, as Dr. Carden had predicted, he had lost the use of his legs and was confined to a wheelchair.

There are times, however, when circumstances stimulate a patient's last reserves of strength, and this was what happened now. Arthur became as alert as in the days before his illness, and with his customary rational approach to serious matters he took on the responsibility of choosing a successor.

Amory Bradford, who was capable of handling the job, was very quickly ruled out. He had shown himself during the strike to be an arrogant man who didn't get along with people. Many staff members made no secret of their view that Amory's unapproachable and superior airs made candid discussion difficult.

For three weeks we carefully considered the alternatives. We wanted to keep the *Times* a family enterprise, if possible. After much deliberation, we decided to take something of a gamble and name our son as the new publisher.

Punch was young—only thirty-seven—and still learning the newspaper business, but we believed he had definite potentialities as publisher and would grow quickly with the job in the face of new responsibilities. On June 20, when we made the announcement, Amory Bradford resigned.

It was remarkable how quickly Punch began to demonstrate initiative and decisiveness. In his first year as publisher, he began to prepare the company for the introduction of computer technology. In a move to phase out the anachronism of the Sunday department's virtual independence of the rest of the paper—an arrangement that had suited the pioneering Sunday editor, Lester Markel—Punch created a new position of executive editor, with responsibility over both the Sunday and daily staffs. For this job he chose Turner Catledge, who had been managing editor since 1951. Clifton Daniel became the new managing editor.

Punch's resourcefulness and the manner in which he conducted himself were a source of great pride to Arthur and me. Sudden promotion can often bring on a swelled head; there was no danger of that with Punch. He had grown up within the *Times* and was neither awed by the great editors he had met there nor overwhelmed by a sense of his own importance. Early in life he had developed a sunny disposition; he was quick to make friends; these were qualities that served him well as publisher. He realized his need to learn, and his modest, forthright personality invited communication with the staff. It wasn't long before Arthur and I were satisfied that we could not have made a wiser decision when we selected Punch to be the fourth publisher of the *New York Times*.

Arthur continued going to the office, even though his health was declining. He'd arrive in a wheelchair pushed by a nurse. Our two papillon dogs would be sitting in his lap. For a couple of years he was able to keep up with business transactions and give his son helpful advice, but as time wore on his vision was affected, his memory began to fail and he became just too tired to cope. He stopped going to the office. It was an awful thing for a man with such energy and gusto to become slowly and irreversibly crippled. Through it all, he was remarkably brave.

On December 12, 1968, Arthur died peacefully in his sleep. He was seventy-seven years old, the age at which my father died.

The memorial service was held at Temple Emanu-El. In accordance with Arthur's instructions, there were no flowers—and, of course, no Mozart. The service was attended by many of the nation's political and business leaders, and I received cables of condolence from every part of the world. We had asked Arthur's close friend Charlie Merz to speak, but Charlie, having just written a tribute for the editorial page, acknowledged that he was just too emotionally exhausted. Scotty Reston delivered the eulogy, as he had done for Orvil five years earlier. He said:

"Shortly after Arthur Hays Sulzberger joined the *Times*—almost fifty years ago—Alfred North Whitehead wrote a little book called *Symbolism* in which he said something which, for me, describes with remarkable precision Arthur Hays Sulzberger's problems and achievements on the *Times*.

" 'It is the first step in wisdom,' Whitehead wrote, 'to recognize that the major advances in civilization are processes which all but wreck the society in which they occur. . . . The art of free society consists, first, in the maintenance of the symbolic code, and secondly, in fearlessness of revision. . . . Those societies which cannot combine reverence to their symbols with freedom of revision must ultimately decay from anarchy or from . . . slow atrophy. . . .'

"This may help us understand. Newspapering is a savagely competitive business. You have to make major advances or die. The graveyard of great newspapers, alas, is very wide and deep, but Arthur Sulzberger risked the changes and made the advances.

"He combined reverence to the symbol and tradition of the *Times*—and reverence is the right word—with fearlessness of revision. This is no time or place for comparisons, but in most newspapers the owners tend to consolidate and the managers to innovate.

"Maybe because Arthur Sulzberger thought of himself in terms of stewardship rather than ownership, he managed to strike this difficult balance between the two, and my own experience with him was that he was more fearless in revision than most of us.

"What is particularly interesting is how he did it. He didn't have the particular swing or melody of our craft when he joined the *Times* at twenty-seven.

"He never even learned how to run a typewriter. He was not a specialist in gathering news or advertising. He was not a prophet of the coming age.

"He was not full of self-confidence when he took over and he didn't even begin with the confidence of his associates, but by any standards of excellence or commerce or ethics, he was a remarkable success.

"The explanation, I believe, was simple integrity. He combined a general ease and charm in personal relations with good judgment, a belief in young men like Orvil Dryfoos and Arthur Ochs Sulzberger, and a true and natural morality of action.

"He was not a moralizer, but he preserved the vanishing gift of actually listening to what other people said and then thinking about it before he answered.

"The result was that men went away from him feeling that they had been heard out to the end and that they were treated fairly, for he had the gift of reminding us, by his gusto and his example, of the decencies of life."

33

When you lose someone you love as much as I loved Arthur, there will always be moments of feeling painfully alone, but being a widow does not have to mean a lonely life. Shortly after Arthur died, I pulled myself together, reminding myself that I was blessed with good health, a devoted family and the financial freedom to do just about anything I pleased. I was seventy-six, an age when the years become very precious, and I was determined to make the most of my life.

During the two years preceding Arthur's death I'd been pretty much a recluse, and it was time to get back in circulation. Soon my engagement book was filling up with luncheon and dinner appointments; I began getting involved again in projects with Barnard, the Parks Department and the Girl Scouts, and I started traveling. With one of my children, grandchildren or friends as a companion, I made trips to Europe, the Soviet Union and Israel.

My life became so busy that my family, not to mention my doctor, was always telling me to slow down. But my philosophy is "What I don't do today I might not be able to do tomorrow," so I keep going.

At the age of eighty-one I had one of the most memorable experiences of my life. It began on September 1, 1973, in the British colony of Hong Kong, when I left the customs house in the border town of Lo Wu and walked across the covered railroad tracks to Shumchun in the People's Republic of China. China! Never in my wildest imaginings did I expect to be one of the first Americans to rediscover this fascinating country whose doors had been virtually closed to the West for a quarter-century. Now I was setting out on a three-week tour of five cities.

The visit had come about as a result of a dinner conversation at the home of Audrey and Seymour Topping. Top, as Seymour is known to his friends, was then assistant managing editor of the *Times*. (He is now managing editor.) Among the guests that evening was Audrey's father, Chester Ronning, a tall, handsome man with a vibrant personality who, at the age of seventy-eight, seemed to have unflagging energy. Audrey had talked to me about her father but this was the first time I had met him, and I was very much taken with him.

Mr. Ronning was born in Fancheng, a town three hundred miles up the Han River from Hankow, where his Norwegian parents were missionaries. When Chester was thirteen, his mother died and he and his elder brother were sent to live with an aunt in Iowa. About a year later they joined their father and five younger brothers and sisters in Camrose, a small town in Alberta, Canada, which was to be their permanent home. In 1945, after fifteen years as head of the Camrose Lutheran College, Mr. Ronning was appointed First Secretary at the Canadian Embassy in the Chinese Nationalists' wartime capital of Chungking, which moved to Nanking at the end of the war. He remained with the Embassy, rising to become Chargé d'Affaires until the Nationalist Government fled the mainland to Taiwan. He subsequently served as Ambassador to Norway, Ambassador to Iceland and Canada's High Commissioner to India.

At the Toppings' dinner, Mr. Ronning gave an account of his

most recent excursion to China with Audrey and Top. The stories were enthralling, and so was the storyteller. As he spoke, he'd make sweeping gestures with his arms, and his eyes were by turns intent and dancing with delight. I had never met anyone quite so captivated by a subject as Mr. Ronning was by China. During a pause between stories, I said I was keen to visit China and asked him how I should go about getting a visa. He sat back in his chair, smiled and said, "Do nothing. Just leave it to me."

A month or so passed. Then, one day in June, he phoned me at Hillandale and proposed that I join Audrey, her daughter Susan and his friend Dr. Herman Tarnower on a trip to China that August. He had arranged for the necessary visas, and said I could take a companion along. I was terrifically excited, and when I asked my granddaughter Susan Dryfoos if she would like to accompany me, she was thrilled.

Three days after setting off—we spent a night in Vancouver and another night and day in Hong Kong to adjust to the jet lag—we stood on the Chinese border. On the other side we were met by Li En-chu, vice chairman of the People's Association for Friendship with Foreign Countries, which acts as host for travelers with friendly links with China and for tourists involved in cultural exchanges. Mr. Li was an old friend of Chester's, and he helped us through the formalities. With his tanned, craggy face and wispy goatee, he looked as if he'd been cut out of an old Chinese scroll.

No one asked to see the lengthy documents we had filled out, declaring our money and other valuables, nor was our luggage examined. The only thing we had to do was surrender our passports; we were told they would be returned to us when we left the country. That made me a little nervous, but, of course, I had no choice. Not until later in the trip, when I had learned more about the Chinese system, did I realize that everything about our tour had been "taken care of," right down to the most minute details.

From the border town of Shumchun we proceeded by train to Canton. There we were met by three interpreters, who accompanied us on the entire tour. The interpreter assigned to Susan and me was a very pleasant middle-aged woman named Mrs. Li, who was quick to inform me that she was a secretary by profession and was filling in because the Friendship Association was short of interpreters. Her English was weak, but it wasn't long before we got to understand each other well and became very friendly. Like our other Chinese escorts, she seemed untiring and ever-ready with a winning smile.

Occasionally she'd say revealing things to me, and I was flattered by her trust. For instance, she admitted that she had liked to dress up in long skirts in the prerevolutionary days, and had stored her old clothes in a trunk at home and sometimes tried them on. Like the men, the women of the China of 1973 made a virtual uniform of baggy trousers and overshirts in subdued browns, greens and blues. The women wore no makeup and had their hair cut short or pulled back into a bun.

The tourists, too, were casually dressed in shirts and slacks. I don't like slacks; I find them uncomfortable, and unsuitable for a woman of my age, so I wore dresses. I think I must have been the only woman in the entire country wearing a dress.

From what I observed, most people we would call "blue-collar workers" had two sets of clothes—a patched-up outfit for working and a newer set for holidays. About the only way you could distinguish a "white-collar worker" was by the better quality and cut of his trousers and shirt. (Another measure of success was ownership of a manual sewing machine or bicycle or transistor radio.)

In contrast to the drab attire of their elders, the young children were colorfully dressed in mix-matched plaids and striped shirts and slacks. The little girls usually had bright red ribbons in their hair. I imagine that the parents, having such a dull wardrobe themselves, took pleasure in outfitting their young ones.

The hotel accommodations took a bit of getting used to. When I lay down on my bed that first night in Canton, it felt like lying on the floor. There was only a thin, hard mattress placed on top of an unyielding wooden frame. A straw mat served as a bottom sheet and a great big Turkish towel, woven with a pink, blue and white design, as a top sheet. The same was true of the hotel in Kweilin, where we spent the next four days. I couldn't understand why the Chinese, who had been so inventive in other ways, had never thought of a more comfortable sleeping arrangement. After one night I was black and blue. Fortunately, Audrey got the hotel manager in Kweilin to find us some thicker mattresses. Mine sagged in the middle, but at least I didn't get any more bruises.

As it turned out, our hosts did provide Western-style mattresses in the hotel rooms reserved for us in Hangchow, Nanking, Shanghai and Peking. The decor of these better hotels, however, was more in keeping with the 1900's than the 1970's. Cavernous, dimly lit hallways led into high-ceilinged rooms. The furnishings were simple and usually bland: There were always the overstuffed chairs with antimacassars and, on the night tables, thermos bottles of hot water painted with brightly colored flowers. Next to the thermos would be a teacup and a dish of tea leaves. As soon as I got into my room I'd pour some of the hot water into a drinking cup; when it cooled, I could use it for drinking and brushing my teeth.

I had been told by previous visitors to China not to use the tap water. I could see why. It was often rust-colored (when it was there at all). As Chinese food always made me thirsty, I usually wound up drinking lukewarm water; I just couldn't wait for it to cool.

The food was more than ample (it was like living on quantities of hors d'oeuvres), but the truth is, I really didn't like it that much, and I lost weight while I was there. Part of the problem was that I was so damn clumsy with the chopsticks I couldn't get the food to my mouth. It wasn't long before I decided to capitalize on my old age and ask for a fork. I said I was just too old to learn. Furthermore, I was always wondering what the different dishes were, and if, after six courses, the meal was just starting or about to end. About the only thing I recognized was scrambled eggs. Luckily, breakfasts were Western-style, so at least I got off to a good start every day.

In every city we visited a banquet was thrown in our honor—sometimes two. A Chinese banquet, incidentally, means there are a lot of courses, not necessarily that there's a large group of people. For instance, one night in Hangchow, Susan, Dr. Tarnower and I were given a banquet. Aside from our two interpreters, there were just four city officials at the table.

The Chinese like to offer toasts during these parties. During our first banquet in Canton, I innocently raised my glass of *mao-tai* in response to a toast and took a sufficiently large swallow. It nearly blew my head off. *Mao-tai* is, I believe, pure alcohol or close to it. The Chinese very proudly claim it's more potent than vodka, and I believe them. After that first swallow I developed a violent case of the hiccups. Fortunately, in China, if you're of an advanced age, such indiscretions are politely overlooked. After that I learned to sip the firewater gingerly or, if possible, not at all. The Chinese would serve a sweet wine in addition to the *mao-tai*, and I would take a sip of that. Apparently the Chinese have quite a sweet tooth, because the only soft drink they served was a very sweet orange pop. I found the taste disagreeable, and preferred their tea and beer. The Chinese beer was excellent, and not bubbly, so I didn't get the hiccups.

From the moment we set foot in China, we were given the V.I.P. treatment. There was always someone at our side to help us with posting a letter, shopping or cashing traveler's checks. We had chauffeur-driven Russian Volgas, Japanese Toyotas and Chinese sedans at our disposal. Every several days we were briefed on the activities ahead. We were taken to schools, communes, factories, theatrical productions, museums—whatever showed the positive aspects of the Chinese Communist society. At each place of interest we would be taken to a conference room, served tea and briefed on what we were about to see. The official in charge would lecture at great length, then the translator would translate at great length, and my mind would begin to wander, so that when the briefing was over I hadn't a clue to what we were in for.

Nothing I saw in China impressed me more than the countryside around the city of Kweilin, in the south. In art books and museums I had seen the ancient Chinese scrolls depicting fantastic landscapes of moss-green mountains soaring from the banks of gentle rivers, but I had thought them to be abstractions in the artists' minds. Not at all. Now, it was as if we were stepping into one of those extraordinary scenes.

On the morning of September 5, along with our interpreters and picnic lunches, we boarded a houseboat for a day's excursion down the Li River. For the next six hours we sat at a table on the upper deck, trying to absorb the beauty around us. In addition to our party, there was a very pleasant Canadian couple, accompanied by their interpreter. On the deck below were Chinese passengers on their way to Yangso, our destination.

There was an almost sacred peacefulness as we glided down that fifty-mile stretch of river. We were towed by a launch, so we did not even hear the motor. The landscape seemed as strange and unearthly as the craters of the moon. From the edge of the river, the mountains rose almost vertically for hundreds of feet. They were covered by some kind of low vegetation, and their unusual contours, we were told, had inspired Chinese folklore for thousands of years. As we floated down the river, the guides narrated legends about the peaks. We heard of dragons and giants and evil demons. I tried to envision these beings, as suggested by the unusual rock formations, but soon gave up. The stories were too long-winded, and I preferred to appreciate the landscape as a natural wonder.

The river offered many other sights. There were little villages with graceful bridges, a colorful pagoda nestled in the hillside. On the river's edge we saw water buffalo. We passed an old man in a dugout canoe fishing with a cormorant, a family in a houseboat poling their way upstream. Other boats carried cargo. Some were hauled by men and women harnessed to ropes on the river's bank; others were towed by tugboats.

Twilight was gathering when we docked in Yangso. It took us two hours to make the return trip to Kweilin by car. There was little conversation on the way back. The day had been so spectacular that each of us was immersed in his own thoughts.

Situated upstream, between dramatic mountains and lakes, Kweilin is used as a vacation resort by the Chinese upper crust. In addition to the beauty of its countryside, Kweilin is noted for its network of caves and grottoes, which have such lovely names as "Folding Silk Cave." The way it was explained to us, the area was under water two million years ago and the soft limestone of the mountains was eroded into a maze of underground passages, stalactites and stalagmites.

Our group was to make a two-hour tour of one of these caves, but it was decided with due respect for my age that I should have a private one-hour tour. This was fine with me, because I wasn't all that keen on being underground. Accompanying me on this excursion was my interpreter, a guide and two young Chinese women who insisted on supporting me as I walked (which was a terrible nuisance), as well as a man who walked ahead of me with a folding chair in case I grew weak or tired. They sometimes over-did the "Venerable One" act!

After four days in Kweilin, Chester, Audrey and Susan Topping left on a trip through the Yangtse River gorges, while Dr. Tarnower, my granddaughter and I took a train to Hangchow; the plan was to join up again in Peking.

The train trip took twenty-six hours. It was fiendishly hot, and the fan in the compartment shared by Susan and me gave us no relief. The tap water in the washroom was so dirty we couldn't even cool our faces with it. Luckily, I had a package of Wash 'n Dri in my hand luggage, and the weather cooled off a bit at night. The berths at least were comfortable, which was a relief after the sagging mattress in Kweilin.

What impressed me immediately about Hangchow (as later in Nanking) was the clean streets and the way the city had been laid out. There were wide boulevards and many beautifully land-scaped public parks. There were man-made lakes where people enjoyed rowboating, and gardens planted with flowers.

The main form of transportation was the bicycle; bicycle traffic was so heavy that there were frequent collisions.

"Everything is so disciplined here," I said to one of our Chinese hosts. "Why haven't the bicycle riders been taught to drive safely?" He said nothing could be done to correct the cyclists' dangerous habits. It was one of the few things on which Chairman Mao evi-dently hadn't laid down the law.

In every other aspect of life, his precepts prevailed. His picture was everywhere—on streets, in public buildings, in restaurants, in private homes. "To serve the people by furthering the revolu-tion" was a phrase we heard countless times. It was then the central theme in art, literature, the theater, the schools—even in the songs the little children sang.

Aside from Mao, the Communist deities were Marx, Engels, Lenin and Stalin. I couldn't understand why Stalin was in. Not only had he treated his own people barbarically but he had thrown his weight on Chiang Kai-shek's side during some key periods of the Communist-Nationalist struggle and had stripped Manchuria of heavy industry right after the Second World War. When I asked our hosts about this, I was told, "Everybody makes mistakes. Stalin did, too."

The Chinese were quick to inform us that their Communism is very different from that of their bitter enemies, the present-day Soviet leaders. From outward appearances at least, the Chinese didn't seem oppressed. Unlike the Russians, who had struck me as a rather dour lot when I visited the Soviet Union, the Chinese we saw did a great deal of laughing and joshing. Ambassador Ronning, who spoke fluent Chinese, had a grand time singing songs and enjoying light moments with his Chinese friends. But from what I've read in the history books, the "liberation" hadn't been a bed of roses. It was accompanied by widespread persecution, including mass trials and executions of many landlords.

One of our guided tours in Hangchow was to a tea plantation. At the customary briefing, I noticed some fine pieces of furniture in the room and asked about the history of the house. When told it had belonged to a landlord, I asked what had happened to him. "Oh, he's living very happily in a peasant's house," the guide said. At least, I thought, he's happy because he's alive.

After seeing how tea was picked and processed, we visited a "typical peasant family" in their home. I think they must have been rather well-to-do peasants, because the house was two stories high and had several large rooms. One of the bedrooms had a very handsome antique bed. Our hostess, an affable elderly woman, said she had been born in the house. I asked if the bed was a family heirloom.

"No," she replied. "When the landlord's furniture was divided up, this bed was given to my daughter-in-law." I wondered what kind of bed the happy landlord was sleeping on.

Our hostess's adorable grandson entertained us with a dance, and we were about to leave when we were asked if we wouldn't like to see their two pigs, which were penned in a shed just off the living room. Every family, we were told, could buy two baby pigs each year. One they were allowed to eat on New Year's Day, and the other was to be sold to the state. The animals and their stall were remarkably clean, and I asked if they had just been washed. I was assured that they were always this clean, but I had my doubts.

I must say, though, that, by and large, the animals I did see looked well cared for. The water buffalo were plump, and the donkeys and horses well filled out. I saw only three dogs. I assume the Government discourages keeping animals except for food or labor.

For the most part, the labor we saw was done by manpower. There is some modern equipment, such as tractors and trucks, but not much. Human labor on a mass scale is the backbone of the economy. Everyone works in China.

Most students go to work after "middle school"—what we would call junior high. We visited a middle school in Nanking. Recess had been called just as we arrived, and the children came dashing out of their classes, shouting and carrying on much like children anywhere. They ran all over the playing field; the boys played with a ball and the girls skipped rope. Our guides and the school principal apologized for the children's behavior, saying we had arrived ahead of schedule, but to us their carryings-on were a welcome sight. After seeing so many youngsters perform dances and sing political songs, it was refreshing to have a glimpse of children behaving like ordinary children.

Besides such expected subjects as language, arithmetic and science, the curriculum included revolutionary politics, literature and art. There was also heavy emphasis on physical education, military training and productive labor. The school was equipped with a swimming pool and agricultural facilities. Since a student's performance in school would determine his future, studies were taken very seriously. In the English and physics classes we visited, the children were most attentive. I asked what happens if a pupil misbehaves, and was told that he is made to stand before the class and is criticized by his schoolmates. After disgracing him in this way, his peers will not talk to him until he mends his ways. I was assured that it was a very effective form of discipline. No child can stand to be ostracized by his friends for very long.

The same system of discipline is used in the communes and housing projects. When there is fighting or pilfering or a minor offense is committed, the accused is questioned before a jury of his friends and neighbors. If he is found guilty, the group rebukes him. That, we were told, is the only punishment. When I asked what was done in the case of more serious crimes, I was told they had no serious crimes.

"Hasn't a husband ever lost his temper and killed his wife?" I asked.

My hosts had a good laugh, then admitted that such serious things did occasionally happen and were handled by the courts.

After ten days during which we visited three cities—Hangchow, Shanghai and Nanking—we joined up with the Ronning contingent for our final week in Peking. It was a week filled with memories—dining with Vice Minister Ch'iao Wang-wa, walking through the Forbidden City, dancing on the Great Wall of China with Chester Ronning. One day I shall never forget was September 19, my eighty-first birthday.

We were touring the Summer Palace and had just seen Longevity Hill. It was about noon when we entered a quiet courtyard. We had paused for a few minutes when a door opened up on a pavilion, and there stood a large round dining table. A chorus of "Happy Birthdays" went up, and I was escorted by Chester to a chair. As soon as everyone was seated, Chester lifted his glass and said, "To the birthday child!"

With that began a feast of many courses. One of the dishes was noodles. A tradition in China is that the longer the noodle you swallow on your birthday, the longer your life will be. As I'm still quite well at eighty-eight, I guess it didn't matter too much that I couldn't get through one noodle without chewing it.

For dessert we had a Western-style birthday cake with an icing of roses that had been baked at the Peking Hotel. I said to my hosts, "You treat me so well that I'm coming back for my ninetieth birthday and settle here!"

There were so many memorable experiences, but the highlight came on the night before we were to leave Peking for our trip home. We left our hotel in chauffeured cars without being told where we were going. Our Chinese hosts had kept us in suspense since four o'clock that afternoon, telling us only that we would be meeting someone very important. The drive took about five minutes. We arrived at a building in the Square of Heavenly Peace and entered a doorway. An elevator took us up two floors, the door opened, and standing there was Premier Chou En-lai.

As the senior member of the group, I was the first to walk out and shake his hand. He gave a warm, friendly smile and greeted me through his interpreter.

We were in the Great Hall of the People, and the Prime Minister took us to the Hupeh Room, choosing it because Hupeh Province was where his old friend Chester Ronning had been born. Some photographs of the group were taken, and we were seated around a large dining table.

I was on the Prime Minister's left, the side for honored guests in China. On the table was an assortment of cold dishes. As the waiters began piling the hors d'oeuvres on our plates, I asked them to give me only one of each. I suspected there was a lot more food to come, and I was right. There was an abundance of courses, all elegantly prepared. We had wine from Chou En-lai's native province of Kiangsu, his favorite soup (made from ducks' feet) and, of course, plenty of *mao-tai*. I noticed that Mr. Chou avoided drinking the firewater. He'd raise his glass in a toast, but when he put it down it was still filled.

The Prime Minister was friendly and lighthearted, and I felt at ease immediately. We started talking, and I told him how envious my family was of our visit, particularly my son.

"Your son wants to have a *New York Times* correspondent in Peking?" he asked.

"Of course he does," I said. "He feels just the way you do, that it's very important for China and America to know each other better, to understand each other and be friends. What better way is there than to have someone here who can report the news and interpret it for the American public?"

"But these articles would be written from just one point of view," the Prime Minister said.

"We try to present many different opinions," I said, "so the reader can make up his own mind. We have a special page, just for articles that oppose the *Times*'s editorial policy."

"Ah," he said, "you would never publish something saying the United States ought to go Communist or pro-Communist."

"If you write a signed article saying the United States should go Communist, I guarantee it will get front-page coverage."

Chou En-lai laughed and said, "I don't want to be a columnist for the *New York Times*."

Several *Times* correspondents had visited the People's Republic, but the paper had had no success in opening a bureau, and hopes of making headway in that direction had been set back by an incident the previous May. Just as relations between the two countries were starting to warm up, the *Times* accepted an advertisement by the Chinese Nationalists that called the Taiwan regime the Republic of China. This displeased Peking, which protested officially to managing editor Abe Rosenthal. Abe, in good *Times* tradition, replied that there was nothing morally objectionable to the ad, and that what a foreign government chose to call itself was its own affair and not the *Times*'s. When the protesting Chinese Communist official said, "You want to get a correspondent in, don't you?" Abe said he was sorry but that was not the way the paper did business. A news story on the Peking Government's displeasure with the ad appeared in the paper, and that seemed only to aggravate the situation. Perhaps the incident could have been handled more tactfully, but the *Times* wanted to make clear that it couldn't be bribed.

I was the first *Times*-related person to be invited to China since this episode. My journey was not intended to patch things up, and though I did have a talk with Punch about this matter before leaving, neither of us thought I would have an opportunity to meet any important policy maker in China, much less Prime Minister Chou En-lai. Besides, one doesn't think of one's elderly mother as an emissary. The weekend before departure, I happened to be talking with Max Frankel, the Sunday editor, and he said, "If you can get in a good word, try." It was with this in mind that I continued my conversation with Chou En-lai.

I asked the Prime Minister why my nephew Cyrus Sulzberger's visa had been revoked. He said, "We don't like his point of view."

"I don't always agree with him either," I said, "but isn't it helpful to have different viewpoints?"

"Perhaps," he said, "but I don't like his viewpoint."

I don't know if this conversation had anything to do with it, but Cyrus's visa was reinstated, and he was able to enter China two days later.

The Prime Minister asked if I had approved of President Nixon's visit to China.

"I certainly did," I replied, "but I disapproved of the length of time it took him to get here. I believe in recognizing governments that hold effective power in their countries. When Chiang Kai-shek left, the United States should have recognized your regime immediately."

The Premier nodded. He said the *Times*'s editorials on this matter had been favorable.

He then asked who owned the *Times*, and I told him it was a public corporation in which anyone could buy shares. "Would you like to buy some stock?" I asked. "Perhaps even one share?"

The Prime Minister threw back his head and laughed. "You're a very good propagandist."

"I've been at it a long time."

"Then," he said, "you can tell your son he can come to China any time he wants next year."

After dinner, an official came to ask me when my son wanted to make his visit. I said I had no idea but would ask. "How should he go about making the arrangements?"

"Just tell him to apply, and he'll have no trouble."

Punch wasn't able to take up the offer until 1976. By then Chou En-lai was dead. Punch was able to enter with an Associated Press group.

After the dinner we adjourned to another area of the big state dining room and were seated in large overstuffed armchairs. Tea was served, and the Prime Minister himself distributed crimson packages of cigarettes among his guests. The playful pandas on the cigarette boxes reminded him that during the recent visit of Georges Pompidou, the French President had asked if he could take two of the animals home with him.

"I couldn't give him two pandas," Mr. Chou said. "The Shanghai zoo is worried I'm giving too many away. They're difficult to raise, and there are too many nations for a pair of pandas each."

The discussion then turned to more serious matters, about which our host spoke at length. He talked about his youth, which was interesting, but the interpreter wasn't too good and I couldn't follow everything. From there he went on about the continuing struggle to bring China out of its feudal ways. He talked on and on without interruption, and as time went by I began to feel very sleepy. I was sitting next to Chester Ronning, struggling mightily to keep my eyes open, when at last I thought I could stay awake no longer. When I thought no one was looking I gave Chester a poke in the ribs. He looked and, seeing that I was barely awake, said to the Prime Minister, "You must be exceedingly tired with all you've been through—President Pompidou's visit and your having to meet all your other obligations. It's late and I think we ought to be going."

"But I'm not at all tired," the Prime Minister protested, and talked on for another half hour. I think he would have gone on till dawn if Chester had not stood up and said, "I really think we must go. We've taken up too much of your time already."

With that the Prime Minister rose, and all the other Chinese leapt to their feet.

Mr. Li of the Friendship Committee came over to me and said, "You look awfully tired."

I admitted I was. "The Prime Minister must be exhausted, too." The session had lasted three hours.

"Oh no, he's just getting steamed up."

I imagine Mr. Li and the other officials, who undoubtedly knew everything Chou En-lai had said by heart, were grateful to this old lady who just couldn't stay up all night.

The clock was striking midnight as we said good-by. The next day, while the others in our party would be leaving for Tibet, Susan and I would be heading back to Canton to begin our trip home. There would be other trips to other places in the world, but none so grand as our visit to China.

34

My granddaughter Susan wrote something to me in September 1972 that I have always treasured. These were her words:

" 'God in his infinite wisdom has seen fit to bless us with success and good health; what more could we wish for?' Your father spoke those words on September 19, 1892, the day his 'precious lump of humanity'—you, Granny—were born. 'I realize I have prospered beyond my deserts and merits,' he said on that occasion, 'and can account for it only by my good luck.'

"It is that moment, when you came to life with black curly hair and the cutest of hands, and undoubtedly sneezing in a soundless funny way, that we, your grandchildren, celebrate today. And for us, the soft, handsome lady you are at this moment of becoming eighty years old brings the same feeling of preciousness your father expressed so beautifully.

"For us, that preciousness lies not so much in what you've been in the past but in what you are today, in the way you touch us now and will touch us tomorrow.

"You're a human *living*, not just a human being. You take us traveling abroad, and we buckle up with indigestion, cramps or old-fashioned fatigue, while you're full of energy, bringing us meals in bed, fluffing our pillows. We tour museums, historical sites; you question the guides with the curiosity of a child, relate unheard-of historical tidbits, and invite strangers to speak of their lives. We dine with dignitaries in chandeliered suites or lunch in self-service, fly-swatting cafés, and you're a classy lady and our best friend.

"You're involved in beautifying parks and streets, preserving wilderness and wildlife, restoring historical landmarks, supporting the creative skills of craftsmen, advising reporters and relatives on the welfare of the *New York Times*, providing relief to the Indians and to the poor in Harlem and in slums around the world, and yet you're never too busy to spend time with us. You come to graduation exercises, phone to invite us over, and write a postcard from abroad just to say hello.

"And when we're together, we're never generations apart. You're right there, listening with your heart, speaking of your confidence in our ability to grow, supporting our goodness, and asking only that we move toward the 'humanness' in being. With you we're not ashamed to flop, to launch unedited thoughts, and we feel safe, as though we were alone. With you we're never ashamed to ask for a book, a car, money or a hug. You invite us to be ourselves, to laugh at our silliness and confront our mistakes.

"You touch us and we touch ourselves. We take your gifts but never get around to saying how much they mean. They are very precious. We love you for all the meaning you give to our lives, for being our friend . . . for just being."

In my old age, I have never been more fully appreciated, more overestimated than in that tribute on my eightieth birthday—and I have received many wonderful tributes.

In 1975, the Parks Department awarded me a certificate for having "helped create many of the city's parks." In 1978, I was given an honorary degree by Bishop College in Texas for my contributions to the United Negro College Fund. That same year I was awarded a medal for outstanding service to Barnard College. All these honors have, I suppose, made my head spin a little faster. But I am proud of the things I have been able to accomplish.

Some of them have contributed a little to the look of the city that I have lived in for almost eighty years. When in 1948 New York City was planning a series of festivities to mark its fiftieth anniversary as Greater New York, I had the idea, enthusiastically endorsed by the Parks Association board, for a campaign slogan: "Give your city a birthday present, plant a tree or bush in Central Park or Prospect Park." We succeeded in raising $25,000. The largest donation was from Macy's, which gave $5,000, I think, for the cherry trees in Central Park. They still bloom profusely every spring.

Other efforts of mine have been directed at improving conditions for people. Particularly satisfying to me was my success in raising funds to build a library at Barnard; in initiating a vacation program for the elderly that now provides several thousand old and lonely people with a two-week summer holiday each year; and in expanding the city's sixty-five-year-old cooperative-education program so as to enable some thirty high-school students a year to learn gardening at the New York Botanical Garden. Just recently I received a certificate for being "an outstanding friend to cooperative education." Who am I to question the nice things people may wish to say about me? As my father-in-law used to say, "Flatter me—I can stand a lot."

When you're almost eighty-seven years old and haven't reached your dotage, people tend to think you're truly remarkable, which often makes me tempted to say I'm pushing ninety. Sometimes it seems to me that having lived as long as I have is my chief claim to fame: People often think that I must have reached some profound conclusions about life and that what I have to say is to be taken very seriously.

When I am expected to make some prophetic statement, I delight in showing off the coat of arms that Arthur designed for me back in the mid-twenties. It depicts a very female duckbill platypus perched on top of the world and supported on either side by lions. Aloft on wings in the heavens is a copy of the *New York Times*. From the newspaper emerges a hand clutching a pen, a symbol of the pen being mightier than the sword. To keep me from getting a swelled head, Arthur also threw in a bar sinister. On the bottom of the picture is the motto *"Rien n'est impossible."* The more one has seen and experienced in life, the more questions one raises, the more one realizes that, as my coat of arms says, nothing is impossible.

I haven't as yet reached any other profound conclusions about life—after all, I still have time. There's always tomorrow, and the next day, and the next. There are still more questions to ask, still more answers to reflect upon, still more places to see, still more people to meet. Maybe I'll finally get the chance to meet the Foreign Minister of Japan. I was supposed to meet him once at a *Times* luncheon, but he had to cancel. He sent me a beautiful coral necklace nonetheless. Perhaps next time he's in New York, we'll get together.

Who knows what next month may bring? My calendar looks pretty full. On the fifteenth I have an invitation to a party from a foreign ambassador, and on the twenty-fourth I've been invited on a private tour of the Metropolitan Museum. I see there's a *Times* board meeting coming up; that means I'll get a chance to see my children. My children are all so busy these days that it's difficult to keep up with them. As for my grandchildren, many of them have homes outside of New York, so it's hard for us to meet.

Maybe, soon, I'll go to Washington again. I've got a couple of great-grandchildren there I haven't seen in a while. This time I think I'll take the air shuttle, though the Amtrak is nice, especially on Sunday.

I remember one Sunday, when Arthur was alive, I was traveling by train from Washington back to New York. A man sitting across the table from me in the dining car announced that he hated being on the train because it was such a bore. When I said I didn't mind it in the least on Sunday, because it gave me a chance to read the paper, he said, "Oh, that's a waste of time. There's nothing in the paper, and if there was, it would all be a pack of lies."

At that, I went into my commercial: If he read the paper I was reading, he would find it quite satisfactory.

He replied, "You know, it *was* a very good paper, but it's been sold recently, and it's very rapidly falling to pieces."

"I think you're mistaken," I said. "I've never heard of it being sold."

"Oh, yes," he assured me. "It's been sold."

"Well," I said, "it so happens that my husband works on the *New York Times*, and he tells me it's been in the same family for over seventy years."

The man shook his head and said, "You people at the bottom of the ladder never know what's going on at the top."

Index

Aaron, Blanche, 16
Abano, 266
Abdullah, the Emir, 230
Abenia, 83-85, 95, 171, 178, 236-37
Abt, Elizabeth, 193
Adenauer, Konrad, 238-39
Adler, Ada Ochs, 5, 13, 18, 59, 60, 170
Adler, Cyrus, 107
Adler, Harry, 18, 60, 97, 122, 170
Adler, Julius, 74, 78-80, 125; childhood
  of, 18-19, 38, 59-62; Churchill and,
  254; concentration camps inspected
  by, 215-16; *New York Times* and, 148,
  169, 172-76, 178, 193
Afghanistan, 259
Africa, 197, 269
Agra, 258
Alaska, 64
Alberta, Canada, 278
Alexander Palace, 141-42
Alexander the Great, 259
Alexander III, 138
Alloway, Harry, 22-24
All Quiet on the Western Front, 75
"All the News That's Fit to Print," 46
Alms, Frederick, 18
Alms Hotel, 18
Ambedkar, Dr. Bhimrao, R., 258
American Civil War, 3-5, 173, 184
American Farm School, 83
American Heart Association, 267
American Hebrew magazine, 108
American Israelite, 11, 13
American Legion, 128, 188

American Museum of Natural History,
  116, 203
American Red Cross, 196-97, 199, 204,
  225, 233
Ames, Elizabeth, 88
Amman, 230
Amstel Hotel, 76
Amsterdam, 75-76
Amtrak, 295
Anderson, Professor Benjamin, 68
Angell, Robert, 185
Angkor Wat, 263
Antonious, George, 226
Arabs, 227, 228, 230, 231, 249
Arequipa, 133
Argentina, 133
Arizona Inn, 225
Armonk, 115
Arnold, Susan (governess), 29
Arnold, Willie, 28
Arthur, President Chester Alan, 15
ASPCA, 160
Associated Press, 47, 121, 124, 131,
  290; Adolph Ochs and, 9, 22, 170,
  234-35
Astor Hotel, 201
Astor House, 28
Astor, Lord, 224-25
Astor, Nancy, 224-25
Aswan Dam, 249
Atahualpa, 132
Atlantic City, 38, 58-59, 61-62, 194
Atomic bomb, 220-22
Auer, Mischa, 84

Auer, Professor Leopold, 84, 113-14
Australia, 223-24, 253
Austria, 74, 95, 194
Austro-Hungarian Empire, 11
Avery, Milton, 88
Avon, Lord. *See also* Eden, Anthony

Bahia, 134
Balkans, the, 196
Balthazar, Judith, 265
Baltimore, 119, 125
Baltimore *News*, 124
Baltimore *Sun*, 46, 120, 124
Bangkok, 263-64
Bangladesh, 192, 258
Barbados, 242
Barnard College, 184, 245, 247, 277, 293-94; Hildegard Kiep at, 219; Iphigene Ochs a student at, 67-71, 77-78, 119; Reiko Kasés at, 261-62
Bartlett, Martha, 268
Baruch, Bernard, 94, 158-59, 251; Churchill and, 254-55
Basel, 111
Bass, Mayor E. A., 128
Bataan, 263
Bavaria, 216
Bay of Pigs, 270
Beauty and the Beast, 32
Beersheba, 230
Beirut, 226
Belgium, 38, 123
Belt Parkway, 163
Benares, 258
Bengalis, 192
Benjamin Dean School, 44
Bennett, James Gordon, 27, 47, 54
Bergstrom, Jim, 103
Berle, Mlle (governess), 42-43
Berlin, 136, 173, 216, 218
Bernheim, Alice, 63
Bernheim, Dr. Ruth, 168, 171
Bernstein, Leonard, 88
Bethlehem, 228
Bettman, Gilbert, 13
Bettman, Iphigene Maloney, 13, 152-53

Bible, the, 39, 110, 149
Bibliothèque Rose, 39
Billy (dog), 168
Biltmore Hotel, 123
Birchall, Frederick, 191
Bishop College, 293
Blaine, James, 23
Blanco, Dr., 134
Bliss, Robert Wood, 134
Bohemia, 11
Bohlen, Charles, 263
Bolivia, 133
Bombay, 256
Bondi, Mrs., 31, 39
Bonn, 216
Bourbon Tombs, France, 14
Bowes-Lyon, David, 236
Bradford, Amory, 272, 274
Brandeis, Louis, 94
Brazil, 134
Brearley School, 151, 199
Britain. *See* England
Brooklyn, 51, 160, 225-26
Bronx, the, 155, 160, 233
Browning School, 152
Brown, John (painting of), 32
Bryant Park, 29
Bryan, William Jennings, 25, 119-20
Buckingham Palace, 236, 253
Buddhists, 258
Buenos Aires, 133-35
Burma, 230, 265
Burundi, 192
Buss, Group Captain, 227-28
Butler, Nicholas Murray, 246
Buttons (dog), 239
Byrd, Richard, 91
Byrnes, Professor Eugene, 185

Calcutta, 258, 265
California, 152, 210, 250
Cambodia, 263
Camp Wadsworth, 79, 81
Camrose, 278
Camrose Lutheran College, 278
Canada, 101-104, 204, 211, 278

Canton, 279-81, 291
Capone, Al, 112
Carden, Dr. George, 269, 274
Carlyle Hotel, 271
Carnegie, Andrew, 35
Carnegie Hall, 34-35, 113
Carney, William, 189
Caruso, Enrico, 33, 93
Casino, the, 157
Catherine the Great, 138, 141
Catledge, Abby, 267
Catledge, Turner, 197-98, 221, 261,
    267, 274
CBS News, 263
CCC camps, 153
Cedar Knoll School, 149-50
Cedar Street house, 15, 16
Central Conference of American
    Rabbis, 11
Central Park, 34, 36, 148, 154, 155, 186,
    196, 294; Robert Moses and, 156-59,
    162-63; zoo in, 160
Chamberlain, Neville, 194
Chamonix, 63
Chandler, Julius and Norman, 216
Chaplin, Charlie, 212-13
Charles of London, 117-18
Charlotte, Grand Duchess of Luxem-
    bourg, 269
Chartwell, 253-54
Chattanooga, 35, 58-60, 78, 97, 122;
    Adolph Ochs' death in, 170; Adolph
    Ochs' early years in, 7-10, 15, 20-22,
    32, 53; Julius and Bertha Ochs bur-
    ied in, 4-5; Milton Ochs in, 129-31;
    Ochs' family life in, 17, 19; Ruth
    Sulzberger in, 199; tribute to
    Adolph Ochs in, 127-29
*Chattanooga City Directory and Business
    Gazetteer*, 8
Chattanooga Dispatch, 7-8
Chattanooga Symphony, 199
Chattanooga Times, 59, 170, 178; Adolph
    Ochs' early association with, 6, 8-10,
    20-22, 25, 45-46, 48; Adolph Ochs'
    fiftieth anniversary as publisher of,
    127-29; George and Milton Ochs

and, 97, 129; Harry Adler and, 122;
    Ruth Sulzberger and, 128, 199
Cheever, John, 88
Chen, Mr. and Mrs., 209-10
Chiang Kai-shek, Generalissimo, 210,
    211, 212, 263, 285, 290
Chiang Kai-shek, Madame, 209, 211-
    12, 263
Ch'iao Wang-wa, Vice Minister, 287
Chicago, 23
Chicago Times-Herald, 23
Chicago Tribune, 234-35
Child's History of England, 40
Chillicothe, Ohio, 81
China. *See* People's Republic of China
Chou En-lai, Premier, 288-91
Chungking, 278
Churchill, Clementine, 253
Churchill, Prime Minister Winston,
    205, 251-55
Churchill, Sarah, 205
Church of the Holy Sepulchre,
    228
Church of the Nativity, 228
Cincinnati, 3-4, 11, 12, 15, 18, 152, 226,
    244
City College of New York, 231
Clark, James Beauchamp, 119
Claudel, Paul, 114
Clement, Bruce, 219-20
Clement, Hanna Kiep, 219-20
Cleveland, President Grover, 23
Cliveden, 224-25
Cohen, Daniel Hays Rosenchein,
    199
Cohen, James Matthew Rosenchein,
    199
Cohen, Richard, 200
College of Physicians and Surgeons,
    199
Colorado, 64, 129
Columbia Presbyterian Hospital, 194,
    273
Columbia School of Journalism, 78,
    176, 209
Columbia, South Carolina, 81
Columbia Teachers College, 41, 150

Columbia University, 67, 200, 258; Arthur Sulzberger and, 109, 247, 257; Eisenhower and, 246
Combined New York Morning Newspapers, The, 102
Comet (jet), 256
Conant, James, 185
Coney Island, 31, 53, 71, 160
Conquest of Peru, 132
Consolidated Edison, 199
Coolidge, President Calvin and Mrs., 121-22, 129
Cooper-Hewitt Museum, 83
Cornell Medical College, 200
Cornell University, 185, 200
Corregidor Island, 263
Croce de Guerra, 173
Croix de Guerre, 173
Cuba, 47, 85, 270
Cunningham, S. A., 8
Current History, 98
Curtis, Cyrus, 97
Cuzco, 132
Czar of Bulgaria, 14
Czechoslovakia, 206-207

Damascus, 226
Dan, 230
Daniel, Clifton, 274
Darnton, Mrs. Eleanor, C., 200
Dartmouth Medical School, 199
Daughters of the American Revolution, 107, 188
Daughters of the Confederacy, 5, 61
Davis, Richard Harding, 47
Day, Joseph, 236
Dean, Mrs., 67
Delmonico's, 203
Democratic Conventions: 1912, 119-20, 122; 1924, 120-21
Denmark, 142
Depression. See Great Depression, the
Der Stürmer, 191
Deutschland, the, 62
Dewey, Thomas E., 244
Dickens, Charles, 40, 43

Dill, General Sir John, 229
Distinguished Service Cross, 173
Dominican Republic, 224
Douglas, Helen Gahagan, 250
Douglas, Lewis, 251
Dr. Sachs's School for Girls, 40-42
Dryfoos, Jacqueline Hays, 199, 233-34
Dryfoos, Orvil E., 198-99, 210, 233, 238, 271-73, 276
Dryfoos, Robert Ochs, 199, 233-34
Dryfoos, Susan Warms, 199, 238, 279-81, 284, 291, 292-93
Dulles, John Foster, 249-50, 263
Dumbarton Oaks Conference, 209-10, 212
Dupont, Pierre, 268, 270
Duranty, Walter, 137-38
Düsseldorf, 217
Dutchess County, 183
Duveen, Lord, 118
Dyslexia, 40, 67, 150, 152

East Germany, 217
East River Drive, 231
Eden, Anthony, 209, 242-43
Eden Musée waxworks, 33
Edinburgh, 264
Edison, Thomas, 255
Egypt, 197, 258
Einstein, Albert, 92
Eisenhower, Mamie, 248
Eisenhower, President Dwight D., 215, 239, 246-51
Eliot, George, 16
Elizabeth, Queen of England, 236, 253
Elman, Mischa, 84
Ely, Misses, 44
Empire State Building, 115
Engels, Friedrich, 284
England, 76, 142, 204, 208, 224, 227, 252, 253, 259; Persia and, 240; Robert McCormick and, 235; Ruth Sulzberger in, 119, 225; World War I and, 76; World War II and, 194, 196-97, 218, 242
English-Speaking Union, 203

Erfurt, 74
Ethiopia, 172

Fabergé Easter eggs, 138
Fancheng, 278
Federal Bureau of Investigation, 208-209, 212-13
Federation of Jewish Philanthropies, 246
Fifty Year Club of Chattanooga, 130-31
Fine, Benjamin, 188
Finland, 101, 144
Finley, John, 231-32
First Boston Corporation, 256
First National Bank of Chattanooga, 8
First Plattsburgh Businessman's Camp, 78, 79, 111
Flatiron Building, 51
Fleming, Mr., 18
Flint, Charles, 25-26
Flint's, 30
Floradora, 33
Fontana Dam project, 220
Fordham University, 184
Ford Motor Company, 199
Fort Jackson, 81-82
Fort Myers, 255
Fort Sill, Oklahoma, 81-82
"Foxy Grampa," 55
France, 194, 199
Franck, Ben, 28, 97
Franco, Francisco, 190
Frankel, Max, 289
Franklin, Benjamin, 70-72
Frederick the Great, 141
Frederika, Queen of Greece, 240-41
French Legion of Honor, 97, 173
Froebel League School, 151, 184
Furman, Carol Fox, 200
Fürst Bismarck, 63

Gaddis, Zulu, 31
Gandhi, 257
Gannon, Father Robert, 184
Gauss, Dian Christian, 92

Geiffert, Arthur, 237
Gerald, the (hotel), 28
Germany, 4, 124, 142, 224; Nazi, 169, 173, 190-94, 216-19; World War I and, 74-77
Gershwin, George, 114
Gilbert and Sullivan operettas, 61
Gilbert, Mrs. Margaret, 104, 128
Gildersleeve, Dean Virginia, 184-85, 245
Girl Scouts, 149-50, 277
Gish, Lillian, 61
Golden, Arthur Sulzberger, 199
Golden, Ben Hale, 199, 269-70
Golden, Lynn Iphigene, 199
Golden, Michael Davis, 199
Golden, Stephen Arthur Ochs, 199
Gold standard, 25
Goldwyn, Mr. and Mrs. Samuel, 212-13
Gordon, Dorothy, 88, 203
Göring, Hermann and Mrs., 124
Gorki, 139
Grace Church, 83
Grace Line, 131
Grand Canyon, 64
Grant, Barbara, 200
Grantham, Lady Maurine, 263
Grantham, Sir Alexander, 263
Grapes of Wrath, The, 152
Grasty, Charles, 120, 122, 124-26
Grayson, Mrs. Cary T., 125
Great Depression, the, 140, 146-49, 152-53, 169, 236; New York Times and, 146-48, 172, 179-80; Robert Moses and, 160-61, 163-64
Great Train Robbery, The, 62
Greece, 83, 142, 240-41
Greenbaum, Edward, 80, 156
Greenwich, Connecticut, 151, 238
Grimm, Brothers, 40
Gristede, Mrs., 162
Groton, 232, 235
Groves, Major General Leslie R., 220-21
Guggenheim, Daniel, 35
Gunther, General, 247

Hagerty, Jim, 251
Halifax, Nova Scotia, 64
Halley's comet, 56
Hall, Noel, 214
Hammarskjöld, Dag, 242
Hangchow, 281, 284-85, 287
Hankow, 278
Harding, President Warren, 120, 122
Harmon, Governor Judson, 120
Harmonie Club, 56
Harper's Weekly, 190
Harry Bassett (horse), 14-15
Harvard University, 185, 238
Harwich, England, 76
Hawaii, 265
Hawthorne, Nathaniel, 39
Hawthorne, New York, 149
Hayden's, 118
Hayes, Roland, 35
Hays, Rachel Peixotto. *See* Sulzberger, Rachel Peixotto Hays
Hearst, William Randolph, 27, 47, 54
Hebrew Union College, 11, 110, 226, 244
Hebrew University (Jerusalem), 226
Heckscher, August, 164
Heckscher Playground, 157
Hegi, Edward, 39
Hegi, Mademoiselle Christine (governess), 36, 38-39, 42, 63
Heidelberg, 4
Heifetz, Jascha, 84
Heiskell, Andrew, 199, 254
Heiskell, Marian. *See* Sulzberger, Marian Effie
Hélène (governess), 38
Helsinki, 144
Henriette, 74-76
Henry Hudson Parkway, 160
Henry Street Settlement, 71
Hermitage (Leningrad), 141
Hewitt, Mrs. Charles B., 83
Heyman, David, 80
Hillandale, 170, 171, 178, 202, 207, 212, 221, 252, 279; Adolph Ochs at, 166-69; Associated Press parties at, 234-36; the new, 237-39; Orvil Dryfoos at, 273; sale of old, 236-37;

veterans entertained at, 203, 233; Wendell Willkie at, 205-206
Hindus, 258
Hirohito, Emperor, 245, 261
Hiroshima, 221
Hiss, Alger, 250
Hitler, Adolf, 169, 172, 204, 218-19; appeasement of, 242; Franco backed by, 190-91; Poland and, 137; the Ukraine and, 217; underestimations of, 192, 194
Hochschild, Harold, 269
Holland, 74, 107, 199
Holmberg, A. William, 199
Holmberg, Ruth Rachel. *See* Sulzberger, Ruth Rachel
Homer, Louise, 84
Homer, Mrs. Sidney, Jr., 84
Homer, Sidney, 84
Hong Kong, 260, 263, 278-79
Hoover, President Herbert, 115, 123-24
Horace Mann High School, 109
Horowitz, Sadie, 71
Hortense, Mlle (governess), 38
Hotel Berlin, 137
House, Reverend John Henry, 83
Hoving, Thomas, 164
Hudson Bay Fur Company, 55
Hughes, Charles Evans, 108
Humane Society, 160
Hundred Neediest Cases, 100
Hunter College, 109, 216
Hunter Museum, 199
Huntington art collection, 32
Hupeh Province, 288
Hussein, King, 230
Hutman, Miss, 70
Hutton, Mrs., 117
Hutus, the, 192
Hyde Park, 182-83
Hylan, John, 154-55

I.B.M., 246
Iceland, 278
Illinois, 231
India, 256-58, 264, 265, 278
Indonesia, 192

Industrial Removal Office, 108
Ingals, Chella Otisa, 31
Inner-Ocean, 23
Iowa, 278
Iran, Shah of, 239-40
Ireland, 13
Ireland (butler), 168
IRT subway, 31
Isaacs, Marcel, 52-53
Israel, 223-24, 225, 242, 259, 277
Italy, 144, 162, 266
Ivan the Terrible, 142
Ives, Elizabeth, 249

Jack and Charlie's, 114-15
Jacob Riis Park, 160
Jaipur, 258
James, Edwin (Jimmy), 200-202, 220-21
James, Monique, 202
James, Simone, 202
Japan, 172, 260-61, 295; MacArthur
    and occupation of, 245; World War II
    and, 187, 195, 220-22
Jean, Prince of Luxembourg, 269-70
Jebb, Gladwyn, 251-52
Jerome, Leonard Walter, 252
Jerusalem, 226, 228, 230
Jesus, 227-28
Jewish Board of Guardians, 149
Jewish Encyclopedia, 108
Jewish Institute of Religion, 110
Jewish Theological Institute, 107
Jinnah, Mohammed Ali, 260
Johnson, Gerald, 92
Johnson, Lady Bird, 267
Johnson, Lyndon (Vice President), 267, 270
Johnson, President Andrew, 7
Jones, George, 22-23
Jordan, 230
Jordan River, 229-231

Kaiser Aluminum, 265
Kaiser, Henry, 265
Kalb, Bernard, 263-64
Kapuskasing, Ontario, 102-105, 204

Karachi, 259-60
Karlsbad, 14, 206
Kases, Reiko, 261-62
Kases, the, 261
Katmandu, 258
"Katzenjammer Kids," 55
Keller, Fritz, 39
Kennedy, Jacqueline, 267-71
Kennedy, President John F., 250, 267-71
Kennedy, Will, 8
Kentucky, 4, 220
Kern, Jerome, 114
Ketchikan, 64
Khan, General Ayub, 259-60
Khyber Pass, 259
Kiangsu, 288
Kiep, Hanna, 217-19
Kiep, Hildegard, 219
Kiep, Otto, 217-19
Kimberly-Clark Company, 102-104, 204
Kingsley, Darwin, 127
Knickerbocker Hotel, 93
Knox College, 231
Knoxville Chronicle, 6-7
Knoxville, Tennessee, 6-7, 9, 48
Knoxville *Tribune*, 7
Kohlsaat, Herman, 23-24
Koo, Wellington, 209
Kopay, Mr., 65
Korean War, 153, 245
Kremlin, 138, 142
Kropotkin, Prince, 141
Ku Klux Klan, 115, 120
Kweilin, 280, 281-84
Kyoto, 262

Ladies' Home Journal, 97
La Guardia, Fiorello, 155-56, 161-62, 170
Lake Champlain Hotel, 79
Lake George, 78, 81, 83, 86, 114, 171, 236
La Nación, 134
Landas, the, 18
Landau, Bavaria, 4

La Prensa, 134
"Last Token, The," 32
Latin American, 131-35
Laurence, William L. ("Atomic Bill"),
  220-21, 248
Laurence, William ("Political Bill"), 248
Lausanne, 38
Lawrence Smith School, 152
League of Nations, 93-94
Lebanon, 226
Leguía, Augusto, 132-33
Lehman, Herbert, 247
Lenhoff, Hannah, 204
Lenhoff, John, 204
Leningrad, 141, 144
Lenin, Nikolai, 284
Lenox School, 151
Levinson, Budd, 200
Levinson, Judith. *See* Sulzberger, Judith
  Peixotto
Levy, Bertha. *See* Ochs, Bertha Levy
Levy, Dr., 67
Levy, Dr. Robert, 171
Levy, Mayer, 4
Levy, Nelly, 31
Lewisohn, Adolph, 157-58
Li En-chu, 279, 291
Life magazine, 254
Lilienthal, David, 220
Lima, Peru, 131-33, 135
Li, Mrs., 279-80
Lincoln Center, 33
Lincoln School, 150
Lindberg, Charles, 91, 169
Lindsay, Mayor John, 164
Lippmann, Walter, 72-73, 190
Little Theater, 203
Loeb, Louis, 254
Lodge, Henry Cabot, 93
London, 252, 266-67
London *Times* bureau, 242
Longacre Square, 49
Longfellow (horse), 14-15
Lookout Mountain Hotel, 128-29
Loomis School, 152, 200
Los Angeles, 64
Los Angeles Times, 216
Louisville *Courier-Journal*, 7

Lo Wu, 278
Luce, Henry, 175
Luxembourg, 269

McAdoo, William Giggs, 120
McAneny, George, 100-101
MacArthur, General Douglas, 245
McCarthy, Senator Joseph R., 213, 248,
  250
McCloy, Ellen, 216
McCloy, John, 216
McConaughy, Ambassador and Mrs.
  Walter, 264
McCormick, Anne O'Hare, 162, 175,
  249
McCormick, Colonel Robert, 234-36
McCullers, Carson, 88
MacDonnell, Henrietta, 43-44, 52-53,
  72, 74, 76, 79-80, 110, 168, 240
McDowell, Ephraim, 130
MacGowan, Colonel John, 7-8
McKinley, President William, 25, 29
Macy's, 56-57, 113, 294
Madison Square Garden, 120
Magnes, Judah, 226
Maine, 64
Majestic Hotel, 29
Manchuria, 285
Manila, 265
Mao, Tse-tung, 284
Marconi, Guglielmo, 52-53
Marion, Ohio, 122
Markel, Lester, 175-76, 274
Markel, Meta, 113
Marshall, General George C., 248-49
Marx, Karl, 72, 284
Masaryk, Jan, 206-207
Masaryk, Thomas, 206
Massachusetts Institute of Technology,
  188
Matsu, 262
Matthews, Herbert, 189
Mattson, Walter, 104
Mayflower, 13
Mayer. *See* Levy, Mayer
Mayor's Council on the Environment,
  199

Medas, Thea, 193
Meir, Prime Minister Golda, 242-43
Mendès-France, Pierre, 241
Mendoza, 133
Menzies, Robert, 253
Merck & Co., Inc., 199
Mer de Glace, 63
Merz, Charles, 184, 190, 272, 275
Merz, Evelyn, 190
Metropolitan Museum of Art, 31-32, 252, 295
Metropolitan Opera, 33, 84
Meyer, Anne Nathan, 72
Miami Beach, 255
Micah (prophet), 110
Middle East, views on, 249
Middleton, Drew, 242
Mid-Week Pictorial, 98, 176
Mikimoto pearl fisheries, 262
Miller, Charles R., 69, 77, 97, 101, 174; Adolph Ochs and, 23-26, 49, 95-96, 99
Miller, Hoyt, 174
Milwaukee, 248
Mississippi, 130
Missouri, 119
Mizpah Cemetery, 5
Moch, Jules, 241
Molony, Helen Wise, 12-13
Molony, James, 13, 52
Molotov, Vyacheslav, 207
Montague, Theodore G., 8
Montevideo, 134
Moore, Ambassador Alexander, 132
Morgan, J. Pierpont, 26, 144
Morgenthau, Eleanor, 183
Morgenthau, Henry, Jr., 182-84
Morgenthau, Henry, Sr., 120, 182, 210
Moses, Robert, 156-65
Moses, Mrs. Robert, 157-58
Moscow, 137-38, 141, 196, 197, 241
Mount Everest, 258
Mount Hope, 170
Mount Morris Park, 109
Mount Vesuvius, 63
Mozart, Wolfgang Amadeus, 113, 275
Münchhausen, Baron von, 42-43
Munich, 74, 194, 207, 216, 219

Mussolini, Benito, 144, 162, 172, 190

Nagako, Empress, 261
Nagasaki, 221
Nanking, 278, 281, 284, 286, 287
Nara, 262
Nashville, 5
Nashville American, 21, 129
Natchez, Mississippi, 4-5
National Conference of Christians and Jews, 226
National Council of Jewish Women, 108
National Guard, 81, 173
Nazimuddin, Khawaja, 253-54, 259
NBC television, 203
Nehru, Indira, 257
Nehru, Jawaharlal, 257
N. Erlanger, Blumgart & Company, 107-108
Nepal, 258
New Amsterdam, 107
Newark, New Jersey, 202
New Delhi, 257-58
Newell Sanatorium, 170
New Guinea, 174
New Haven, Connecticut, 46
Newhouse, Mrs., 30
Ne Win, 265
New Jersey, 119
New Orleans, 78
Newport, Rhode Island, 107
New Republic, the, 72, 190
New School for Social Research, 69
News of the Week in Review, 175, 176, 272
Newspaper Guild, 177-78
Newspaper Row, 48
New York Botanical Garden, 294
New York Child Adoption League, 149
New York City, 28, 48, 51, 60, 108, 199, 247; Al Smith and, 115; Boss Tweed and, 22; fiftieth anniversary of, 294; parks of, 154-65. See also Central Park
New Yorker, the, 157
New York Globe, 119
New York Herald, 23, 47, 49, 55, 96
New York Herald Tribune, 157, 159, 183, 200, 205

New York *Journal*, 23, 47, 55
New York Life Insurance Company, 127
New York Public Library, 29
New York State, 108, 114, 188
New York Stock Exchange, 198
New York *Sun*, 46, 91
New York Times, 35, 39, 59, 69, 72, 85, 88, 89, 115, 122-23, 127, 136, 137, 152, 157-59, 162, 164, 169, 171, 173, 184, 188-190, 215, 231, 232, 238-40, 261-63, 269, 270, 278, 293-96; Adolph Ochs' acquisition of, 22-27; Adolph Ochs' early years at, 45-57; Arthur H. Sulzberger as publisher of, 172-83, 250-54, 275-76; Arthur H. Sulzberger's early years at, 100-105; Arthur (Punch) Sulzberger as publisher of, 274-275; atomic bomb and, 220-22; Churchill and, 252, 254; Chou En-lai and, 288-90; Democratic Convention (1912) and, 119-20; Depression and, 146-48, 172; Iphigene Sulzberger at, 200-203, 219; Latin American coverage developed by, 131-35; Orvil Dryfoos as publisher of, 271-73; Presidential elections (1948-60) and, 244-51; United Nations story in, 208-10; World War I years at, 77, 90-99; World War II years at, 191, 195-98, 204-207; WQXR and, 88, 113, 203
New York Times Company, 24-25, 179; Julius Adler and, 173-74; Spencer Trask and, 85
New York Typographical Union No. 6, 272
New York *World*, 23, 47, 55, 190
Nicholas II, 138, 142
Nixon, Richard, 250-51, 290
Nizhni Novgorod, 139, 141, 145
Normal College Training School, 109
Northcliffe, Lord, 77
Norway, 101, 278
Noyes, Alexander Dana, 146
Nuremberg, 191, 193

Oakes, George, Jr., 97-98, 104

Oakes, John B., 80, 97-98, 104, 164-65, 272
Oak Ridge, 220-21
Oberhof Resort, 74
Ochs, Ada. *See* Adler, Ada Ochs
Ochs, Adolph Shelby, 130, 170
Ochs, Adolph Simon, 61-74, 77, 83-85, 111, 113, 116, 119, 121, 124, 127-30, 147-48, 190-194; acquisition of *New York Times*, 22-27; Arthur Sulzberger and, 79-80, 100-105, 172-73, 175-76; early years at *New York Times*, 45-57; early years in Chattanooga, 5-10, 13-18, 20, 21; Edison and, 255; estate of, 178-79; family life in New York, 28-44; final years, 166-71; World War I and, 90-99
Ochs, Bertha Levy, 4-5, 15-17, 34, 58, 130, 166-70
Ochs, Bertie Gans, 97-98
Ochs, Frances Van Dyke, 129-31
Ochs, George, 4-5, 24-25, 97, 129
Ochs, Iphigene. *See* Sulzberger, Iphigene Ochs
Ochs, Iphigenia Miriam Wise, 12, 52, 54, 58, 59, 62-64, 111, 123, 128; at Hillandale, 166, 167, 170, 171, 178; courtship and early married life, 14-19; family life in New York, 28-44; in World War I, 74-76, 83
Ochs, Julius, 3-6, 9, 59, 173
Ochs, Louis, 5
Ochs, Mattie, 5, 13, 18, 59-60, 74
Ochs, Milton, 5-6, 129-31, 170, 173
Ochs, Nannie, 5, 33, 59-60, 98, 104, 167
Ochs, William Van Dyke, 130, 173
Odessa, 144
Ohio, 120
Ontario, 102-104
Orchard Beach, 155, 160
Osaka, 262
Oxford University, 184

Pabst Hotel, 49
Padua, 266
Pahlevi, Farah, 239

Pahlevi, Riza, Shah of Iran, 239-40
Pakistan, 253-54, 256-59
Palace of Rest and Culture, 143
Palestine, 111, 226-30
Palm Beach, Florida, 169
Palmer, Margaret Ochs, 130
Pan Am, 265
Panama Canal, 131
Pardee, Miss, 87
Paris, 97, 124, 251, 260
Paris *Times* bureau, 201-202, 242
Parks and Playgrounds Association, 155, 156
Parks Department, 277, 293-94
Parrott, Reverend Edward M., 83-84
Patton Hotel, 130
Paul, Franc M., 7
Paul, King of Greece, 240
Paz, Alberto Gainza, 134
Peabody Award, 85, 88
Peabody, George Foster, 83, 85, 87-89
Pearl Harbor, 187, 195-96, 198
Peking, 212, 281, 284, 287-89
Peking Hotel, 287
Pennsylvania Station, 170
People's Association for Friendship with Foreign Countries, 279
People's Republic of China, 32, 172, 228; Dumbarton Oaks case and, 208, 209-11; Hoover and, 123; travels in, 212, 278-91
Persia, 239-40
Peru, 131-35
Peshawar, 259
Peter and Paul Fortress, 141
Pfeifers, the, 78
Phi Beta Kappa, 272
Philadelphia, 60-61, 97-98, 106, 129; Republican Convention in (1940), 206
Philadelphia Public Ledger, 60, 97
Philadelphia Times, 97
Philippines, the, 260, 263
Philip, Prince of England, 253
Pierre Hotel, 60
Pilate, Pontius, 228
Pinehurst, North Carolina, 195
Pittsburgh Leader, 132

Pizarro's tomb, 132
Plattsburgh, New York, 78-79
Plaza Hotel, 176
Plum Street Synagogue, 15
Plymouth, England, 62
Point Four program, 257
Poland, 136-37, 194, 196
Pompidou, Georges, 290-91
Porter, Cole, 114, 194
Portland, 64
Potter, Bishop Henry, 49
Powers, Bertram A., 272
Prague, 204
Preface to Politics, A, 72
Princeton University, 92, 173, 185, 231-32, 272
Printer's Row, 48-49
Prohibition, 104, 112, 114-15, 128
Prospect Park, 159, 294
Providence, Rhode Island, 6
Prussia, 124, 218
Publishers Association, 272
Puerto Rico, 272
Pulitzer, Joseph, 27, 47, 54
Pulitzer prize, 188, 191, 210
Purple Heart, 173

Quemoy, 262

Rangoon, 264-65
Raymond, Henry J., 22
Read family, 29-31, 36-37
Read, Hermia, 30
Redfield, D. M., 46
Red Hook, Brooklyn, 163
Reform Judaism, 11, 12
Remarque, Erich Maria, 75
Republican Convention (1940), 206, 247
Reston, James (Scotty), 196-97, 209-10; Arthur Sulzberger eulogized by, 275-76; Orvil Dryfoos eulogized by, 273
Rhodes Scholar, 272
Rio de Janeiro, 134-35
Ritter, Victor, 161

Riverside Park, 160
Robinson, James Harvey, 69-70
Rockefeller Foundation, 185, 202
Rockefeller University, 199
Rodenberg, Gustav, 6
Rodgers, Richard, 114
Romulo, Carlos P., 263
Ronning, Ambassador Chester, 211, 278-79, 284-85, 287, 288, 291
"Roosevelt Bears, The," 55
Roosevelt, Eleanor, 16, 183-84, 186-88
Roosevelt, President Franklin Delano, 153, 179, 181-83, 186, 187, 196-97
Roosevelt, President Theodore, 35, 51-52
Roosevelt, Sara Delano, 183
Rosemary Hall School, 151
Rosenchein, Matthew, 199
Rosenthal, Abe, 289
Royal Air Force, 227
Royal Astronomical Society, 92
Rule, Captain William, 7-8, 21, 129
Rumania, 142, 201
Rusk, Dr. Howard, 264-65, 267
Russell, Lillian, 132
Russia. *See* Soviet Union

St. Bernard's School, 151
St. Petersburg, 84
Salisbury, Harrison, 262
Salt Lake City, 64
San Diego, 57
San Francisco, 64, 207, 265
Sanger, Elliot, 113
San Juan, 272
Sans Famille, 39
Santiago, 133, 135
Santos, 134
Saratoga, 84, 86-87, 114
Saturday Evening Post, 97
Savoy Hotel, 137
Schiff, Jacob, 35
Schultz, Colonel Robert, 248
Sea of Galilee, 227
Seattle, 64
Seebeck, Baron von, 78

Seixas, Benjamin Mendes, 107
Seligman, Eustace, 72
Sembrich, Madame Marcella, 84
Sensenbrenner, F. J., 102-104, 128
Sensenbrenner, Gertrude, 103-104, 128
Sephardic Jews, 107
Seventeen magazine, 262
Seventh Day Adventist Hospital (Manila), 265
Shalett, Sidney, 222
Shanghai, 209, 281, 287, 290
Sheeny, John, 154
Sheppard, Professor William, 69
Sherry's catering service, 52, 80, 234
Shumchun, 278-79
Shuster, George, 216
Siberian prison camps, 140, 142, 216, 241
Siegfried, 33
Silberman, Rabbi Joseph, 80
Silver Star, 173
Simkhovitch, Professor Vladimir, 70
Sisters of Notre Dame, 12
Slavin, Egypta Nila, 31
Sloan, Professor W. N., 77
Smith, Al, 114-16, 120, 123
Smith College, 184, 199
Soames, Christopher, 252
Soames, Mary Churchill, 252
Song of Russia, 213
Sons of the Revolution, 107
Sousa, John Philip, 61
South America, 131-35, 197
Soviet Union, 75, 77, 207-208, 239, 263; Aswan Dam project and, 249; China and, 285; in 1943, 196-97; Persia and, 240; travels in, 136-45, 277; Vyshinsky and, 241-42
Spain, 132, 142, 172
Spanish-American War, 47
Spanish Civil War, 189-92
Spanish Inquisition, 107
Spartanburgh, South Carolina, 79-81
Spencer Trask & Co., 85
Spruce Falls Power and Paper Company, 104
Squier, Dr. J. Bentley, 96, 125, 168

Squier, Leah, 125
Squier, Ursula, 80
Stalin, Joseph, 145, 213, 242, 284; Poland and, 137, 196; the Ukraine and, 216
Stark, Dr., 18
Staten Island, 155
Steinbeck, Charlie (dog), 270
Steinbeck, John 152, 270
Sterns, the, 35
Stevenson, Adlai, 249-51
Still, Clifford, 88
Stilwell and the American Experience in China, 210
Stilwell, General, 210-11
Straus, Gladys, 226, 228, 230
Straus, Isidor, 56
Straus, Nathan, Jr., 56-57, 113, 155-56
Straus, Nathan, Sr., 56-57, 113
Straus, Oscar, 56
Straus, Roger Williams, Sr., 226, 228
Strauss, Mrs. Samuel, 119-20
Strauss, Samuel, 119
Streicher, Julius, 191
Studebaker, Dr., 186-88
Stuyvesant, Peter, 107
Sulzberger, Anna, 108
Sulzberger, Arthur Hays, 75, 91, 94-95, 121, 123-24, 150-52, 162, 169, 170, 223-26, 295; as publisher of *New York Times*, 172-83, 189-98; courtship and early married life of, 78-82, 112-16; early years at *New York Times*, 100-105; family history of, 106-11; later years of, 266-76; travels of: Far East (1957), 260-65, Germany (1947), 216-22, India (1954), 256-60, Palestine (1937), 226-32, South America (1928), 131-35, Soviet Union (1929), 136-45; world leaders and, 231-43, 244-54
Sulzberger, Arthur Ochs, Jr., 200
Sulzberger, Arthur Ochs (Punch), 67, 104, 116, 151-52, 200, 272; as *New York Times* publisher, 274-76, 288-90
Sulzberger, Carol Fox, 200
Sulzberger, Cathy Jean Furman, 200

Sulzberger, Cynthia Fox, 200
Sulzberger, Cyrus, 80, 260, 262-63, 289-90
Sulzberger, Cyrus, Jr., 108
Sulzberger, Cyrus Lindauer, 106-11, 191
Sulzberger, David Hays, 80, 109, 111
Sulzberger, Iphigene Ochs, 85, 88, 119-24, 166-69, 174, 178, 182, 183, 292-96; childhood of, 18, 19, 26, 28-44, 48-73; courtship and early married life of, 78-82, 110-18; family history of, 3-18, 97, 98, 129-31; later married life of, 266-77; *New York Times* and, 89-99, 120, 172-74, 200-203, 208-10; public service by, 148-50, 154-65, 184-88; travels of: Far East (1957), 260-65, Germany (1947), 216-22, India (1954), 256-60, Palestine (1937), 226-32, People's Republic of China (1973), 278-91, South America (1928), 131-35, Soviet Union (1929), 136-54; world leaders and, 233-43, 244-55; World War I years and, 74-78, 93; World War II years and, 190-96, 211-14, 223-26
Sulzberger, Judith Peixotto (Mrs. Budd Levinson), 116, 151, 161, 199-200
Sulzberger, Karen Alden, 200
Sulzberger, Leo, 80, 108-109
Sulzberger, Louise, 111
Sulzberger, Marian Effie (Mrs. Andrew Heiskell), 82, 116, 170, 233, 238; adult life and work of, 198-99, 210, 233, 251, 264, 265, 269, 271-73; schooling of, 67, 150-51, 184
Sulzberger, Marina, 260-61, 263-65
Sulzberger, Meyer, 107
Sulzberger, Rachel Peixotto Hays, 107-109, 110, 111
Sulzberger, Ruth Rachel (Mrs. A. William Holmberg), 113, 116, 128; adult life and work of, 199, 225, 267, 269-70; schooling of, 150-51, 184
Suvi, Dr., 264
Swat, 259-60
Switzerland, 39, 192

Symbolism, 275

Taft, Hobart, 152
Taft, President William Howard, 52, 93, 152
Taft, Robert A., 246
Taipei, 212, 262
Taiwan, 212, 260, 262, 278, 289
Taj Mahal, 258
Talimer, Bernard, 60-61
Tanglewood Tales, 39
Tarnower, Dr. Herman, 279, 281, 284
Teheran, 197, 240
Temple Emanu-El, 80, 110, 170, 226; Arthur Sulzberger eulogized at, 250, 275-76; Orvil Dryfoos eulogized at, 273
Temple Israel, 109
Temple Israel Cemetery, 170-71
Tennessee, 26, 220
TennesseeValley Authority, 206, 220
Tennyson, Alfred, Lord, 16
Texas, 293
Thackery, William Makepeace, 43
Thailand, 263
Theatre Guild, 114
Third International Zionist Congress, 111
Thompson, Virgil, 88
Thuringen Forest, 74
Tibet, 291
Tidewater Paper Mill, 101
Tidings Brought to Mary, 114
Tilney, Dr. Frederick, 96, 99, 169
Time, Inc., 199
Time magazine, 175
Times Facsimile Corporation, 198
Times Hall, 203
Times of London, 77
Times Tower, 49, 90
Tokyo, 260-62
Tokyo *Mainichi*, 260
Tong, Hollington, 209-11
Topping, Audrey, 278-80, 284
Topping, Seymour, 278-79
Topping, Susan, 279, 284
Toronto, 204

Touro, 107
Transjordan, 229
Trask, Katrina, 85-87
Trask, Spencer, 25, 85-87
Travels with Charlie, 270
Triana, 86
Triborough Bridge and Tunnel Authority, 164
Trujillo, General Rafael, 224
Truman, President Harry, 221-22, 244-45, 257, 268
Tsarskoye Selo, 141
Tuchman, Barbara, 210-11
Tucson, Arizona, 224-25
Turkey, 75, 138
Tuskegee Institute, 35, 85
Twain, Mark, 35
Tweed William Marcy, 22
"21" Club, 114, 212-13, 251

Ukraine, 216-17
Uncle Tom's Cabin, 32
Union League Club, 96
Union of American Hebrew Congregations, 11, 109
United Nations, 241, 242, 261; delegates to, 238, 252, 263; secret Big Four plans for, 207, 208-10
United Negro College Fund, 293
United Neighborhood Houses, Inc., 108
United Press, 170
United States Atlantic Fleet, 201
United States Congress, 61
United States Marines, 152, 200
United States Supreme Court, 181
University of Chattanooga, 199
University of Prague, 204
Untermyer, Samuel, 54-55, 127-28, 178
Urban League of New York, 108
Uruguay, 134

Valparaiso, 133
Van Anda, Carr Vattel, 77, 91-93, 95-96, 97, 101, 104, 191
Vancouver, 279

Vanderbilt art collection, 32
Van Dyke, Henry, 87
Vassar College, 30
Venice, 252, 266
Verne, Jules, 39
Verona, 266
Versailles Treaty, 94, 192
Via Dolorosa, 228
Vicenza, 266
Vietnam War, 153, 270
Virginia, 224-26
Vyshinsky, Andrei, 138, 241-42

Wainwright, General, 263
Waldorf-Astoria, 211
Wali, the (of Swat), 259-60
Walker, Mayor Jimmy, 157
Walker, R. E., 170
Wallach, Leopold, 49
Walsh, Commissioner, 128
Walter Reed Hospital, 174
Wanamaker, John, 56
Wanamaker's, 56
Warsaw, 136-37
Washington, Booker T., 34-35
Washington, George, 107
Watson, Thomas, 246
Weimar Republic, 217
Weizmann, Chiam, 259
Westchester County, 107, 167
West Germany, 217, 219, 238
West Point, 173
Whalen, Grover, 128
Whitehead, Alfred North, 275
White Plains, 166-67, 237, 248
Wide World Photos, Inc., 198
Wiley, Louis, 54, 97, 104, 232
Willen, Joseph, 247
Williamsburg, Virginia, 185, 202
Williams, Roger, 107
William II, Kaiser, 240
Willimantic, Connecticut, 220
Willkie, Philip, 205
Willkie, Wendell, 183, 205-206, 212
Wilson, President Woodrow, 78, 81, 93-95, 119-22
Wingate, Captain Orde and Mrs., 230

Wisconsin, 102, 103, 128, 248
Wise, Elsa, 12
Wise, Emily, 12
Wise, Harry, 12, 17
Wise, Helen. *See* Molony, Helen Wise
Wise, Ida, 12
Wise, Iphigenia Miriam. *See* Ochs, Iphigenia Miriam Wise
Wise, Isaac, Jr., 12
Wise, Isadore, 12
Wise, Jonah, 12
Wise, Julius, 12
Wise, Leo, 12-13
Wise, Rabbi Isaac M., 11, 12, 62, 109
Wise, Regina, 12, 63
Wise, Selma Bondy, 12
Wise, Theresa Bloch, 12
WMCA, 113
Wolf's Pond Park, 155
Women's suffrage, 72
Wonder-Book, 39
Woods, George, 256, 260, 266
Woods, Louise, 256-58, 260-63, 266
Woolworth, Mrs., 117
World Bank, 256
World's Fair (1939), 236
World War I, 98, 196; Cyrus Sulzberger and, 111; Julius Adler and, 173-75; *New York Times* coverage of, 74-77, 90-91, 93-94, 205
World War II, 153, 162, 180, 183, 229-30, 285; Arthur Sulzberger's efforts during, 195-98; Churchill's account of, 254; effects of, 213-14, 216-19; Julius Adler and, 174-75, 215-16; *New York Times* coverage of, 204-205, 220-22; resettlement after, 223-24; Spanish Civil War and, 192
Worth, Blakie, 269
Worth, Robert, 269
WPA, 153, 160-61
WQXR, 88, 113, 203

Yaddo, 86-88
Yale University, 185
Yangso, 283

Yellowstone Park, 64
Yom Kippur, 62, 110
Yosemite National Park, 64
Youth Forum, 88

Zangwill, Mrs. Israel, 115
Zeek, Madame, 40
Zimbalist, Efrem, 84
Zinn, Louis, 192-93
Zionism, 111, 223-26